Federalism, Fiscal Authority, and Centralization in Latin America

This book explores the politics of fiscal authority, focusing on the centralization of taxation in Latin America during the 20th century. This issue is studied in great detail for the case of Mexico. The political (and fiscal) fragmentation associated with civil war at the beginning of the century was eventually transformed into a highly centralized regime. The analysis shows that fiscal centralization can best be studied as the consequence of a bargain struck between self-interested regional and national politicians. Fiscal centralization was more extreme in Mexico than in most other places in the world, but the challenges and problems tackled by Mexican politicians were not unique. The book thus analyzes fiscal centralization and the origins of intergovernmental financial transfers in the other Latin American federal regimes – Argentina, Brazil, and Venezuela. The analysis sheds light on the factors that explain the consolidation of tax authority in developing countries.

Alberto Diaz-Cayeros is an assistant professor of political science at Stanford University. He previously taught at the University of California, Los Angeles. He received his M.A. and Ph.D. in political science from Duke University. His dissertation won the award for best dissertation granted by the political economy section of the American Political Science Association. Diaz-Cayeros has published articles in the *Journal of Theoretical Politics*, *Comparative Political Studies*, *Política y Gobierno*, and several edited volumes.

Cambridge Studies in Comparative Politics

General Editor
Margaret Levi   *University of Washington, Seattle*

Assistant General Editor
Stephen Hanson   *University of Washington, Seattle*

Associate Editors
Robert H. Bates   *Harvard University*
Peter Lange   *Duke University*
Helen Milner   *Columbia University*
Frances Rosenbluth   *Yale University*
Susan Stokes   *University of Chicago*
Sidney Tarrow   *Cornell University*
Kathleen Thelen   *Northwestern University*
Erik Wibbels   *University of Washington, Seattle*

Other Books in the Series

Continued after the Index

Federalism, Fiscal Authority, and Centralization in Latin America

ALBERTO DIAZ-CAYEROS

Stanford University

CAMBRIDGE
UNIVERSITY PRESS

CAMBRIDGE UNIVERSITY PRESS
Cambridge, New York, Melbourne, Madrid, Cape Town, Singapore, São Paulo

Cambridge University Press
32 Avenue of the Americas, New York, NY 10013-2473, USA

www.cambridge.org
Information on this title: www.cambridge.org/9780521861632

First published 2006

Printed in the United States of America

A catalog record for this publication is available from the British Library.

Library of Congress Cataloging in Publication Data

Diaz-Cayeros, Alberto.
Federalism, fiscal authority, and centralization in Latin America / Alberto Diaz-Cayeros.
   p.   cm. – (Cambridge studies in comparative politics)
Includes bibliographical references (p.   ) and index.
ISBN-13:   978-0-521-86163-2 (hardback) – ISBN-10:   0-521-86163-2 (hardback)
1. Fiscal policy – Latin America.   2. Federal government – Latin America.
3. Decentralization in government – Latin America.   4. Fiscal policy – Mexico.
5. Federal government – Mexico   6. Decentralization in government – Mexico.
7. Latin America – Politics and government – 20th century.   8. Mexico – Politics
and government – 20th century.   I. Title.   II. Series.
HJ99.53.D53   2006
336.8–dc22   2005033365

ISBN-13   978-0-521-86163-2 hardback
ISBN-10   0-521-86163-2 hardback

To Beatriz, hospes comesque

An identifying feature of centralized federalism is the tendency, as time passes, for the rulers of the federation to overawe the rulers of the constituent governments.

William Riker, Federalism, 1964, p. 7

Contents

Figures

Tables

Preface

This book is the product of 15 years of thinking about and working on issues of fiscal authority, federalism, and centralization, and I have incurred numerous debts to many institutions and individuals. I first became interested in these topics in 1990 while a researcher at the Centro de Investigación para el Desarrollo (CIDAC), a think tank in Mexico City. At the time, it was hard to imagine the types of transformations that Mexico would go through in the coming years. The director of CIDAC, Luis Rubio, had the keen insight that the country was not going to be isolated from the globalization and democratization processes sweeping the world or from the radical transformations that were taking place in Eastern Europe and the former Soviet Union. He inspired me and a cohort of young social scientists to study those transformations from a political economy perspective. Over the years, I have learned so much from all my colleagues at CIDAC, but on the topics of this book in particular, especially from Roberto Blum, Edna Jaime, Claudio Jones, Jacqueline Martinez, Olivia Mogollon, and Luis Rubio.

At CIDAC, I worked for a team that prepared a book that assessed the implications for Mexico's future of a Free Trade Agreement with the United States, years before NAFTA came into effect in 1994. I wrote a chapter analyzing the patterns of intraindustrial and interindustrial trade in Mexico and assessed the risks of regional polarization and growth divergence that could result from such an agreement. From then on, I became convinced that the territorial dimension was essential for understanding the political economy of development. I went on to pursue a Ph.D. at Duke University, where I was fortunate to be introduced to the fascinating field of comparative politics. I thank my *maestro*, Robert Bates, who over the years has been a continuous source of inspiration, encouragement, and insight. I also thank my teachers John Aldrich, Herbert Kitschelt, and Peter Lange, whose input was essential for my dissertation, on which the first part of this book is based.

The fieldwork in Mexico involved traveling across the country interviewing state finance ministers and public officials, national and local politicians, and scholars and journalists, and gathering data from numerous institutions, libraries, and archives. For a comparativist, no text or secondary source can substitute for the sensibility that emerges from traveling and talking with the real citizens and politicians who are the subjects of the research. The social, economic, and political variations of regions become tangible as concrete expressions of a marvelous diversity but also the painful realization of how the levels of well-being varied among similarly situated persons just as a result of living in one territory rather than another. I thank many individuals for the countless number of hours and insights generously shared with me on those trips.

Thanks to an invitation from Bob Bates, I wrote up my dissertation in the stimulating environment of Harvard University in the 1996–1997 academic year. Much of the historical background for the book was researched with the help of librarians at the Iberoamerikanishes Institute in Berlin, Widener Library at Harvard, and Hoover Library at Stanford University. In Venezuela, Michael Penfold and Francisco Rodríguez supplied me with data and invaluable insights. Matías Iaryczower shared a dataset on Argentine revenue-sharing. In order to complete the manuscript, I have received generous financial support from UCLA's Faculty Senate Grants; the Stanford Social Science History Institute (SSHI); the Stanford Institute for the Quantitative Social Sciences (SIQSS); the Rule of Law Program at Stanford's Center for Democracy, Development and Rule of Law (CDDRL); and Stanford's Vice Provost for Undergraduate Research.

Since 1997, I have divided my time between Mexico and California. I have had the fortune of learning from, and discussing my work with, colleagues at Instituto Technológico Autónomo de México (ITAM), Centro de Investígación y Docencia Económicas (CIDE), the University of California, Los Angeles (UCLA), and Stanford, as well as in numerous conferences, workshops, and forums. I wish to thank, in particular, Federico Estévez, who taught me the most about Mexican politics over these years. At Stanford, I thank my colleagues Jim Fearon, David Laitin, Isabela Mares, and Barry Weingast. Many individuals have provided me with useful comments and criticisms on various sections and parts of the book manuscript. At the risk of failing to mention some of them, I acknowledge Barry

Ames, Juliana Bambaci, John Coatsworth, Linda Cook, Jorge Domínguez, Katherine Firmin, Barbara Geddes, Catherine Haffer, Stephen Haggard, Joy Langston, Dan Posner, Daniel Treisman, and Steve Webb. I also thank Ana Gardea, Steve Haber, Katherine Kelman, Alberto Simpser, Jessica Wallack, and two anonymous referees of Cambridge University Press who read and commented on the whole manuscript. For several years, the series editor, Margaret Levi, persevered in asking me for my book manuscript every year she saw me at professional conferences, and she was the one who suggested the shift of focus in my work that led me to write the second part of the book. I also thank Lew Bateman for his support in steering this process to completion.

Last, but not least, I want to thank my wife, Beatriz Magaloni, to whom this book is dedicated. She has not only been my sounding board, colleague, friend, and fiercest critic over the years, but as this book was written, we have discussed, laughed, and learned together, but most importantly, we have raised our three beautiful children, Emilia, Nicolas, and Mateo. Without the joy of my life with them, this book would not have been written.

Federalism, Fiscal Authority, and Centralization in Latin America

1

Federalism, Party Hegemony, and the Centralization of Fiscal Authority

1.1. The Fundamental Dilemma of Fiscal Centralization

The centralization of authority is essential to national politics. Acephalous societies are characterized by violence, warlords, and the constant threat to property and life. Some degree of central control over a territory is essential for the formation of a state. Although the threat of force can create a territorial unit, its consolidation only occurs when political authority becomes expressed in the capacity to tax. This book explores the politics of fiscal authority, focusing on the centralization of taxation in Latin America during the 20th century. The first half of the book explores this issue in great detail for the case of Mexico. The political (and fiscal) fragmentation associated with civil war at the beginning of the century was eventually transformed into the highly centralized regime we associate with Mexico today. Fiscal centralization was more extreme in Mexico than in most other places in the world, but the challenges and problems tackled by Mexican politicians were not unique. The second half of the book thus analyzes the other Latin American federal regimes – Argentina, Brazil, and Venezuela. My hope is that this book will shed light on the factors that explain the consolidation of tax authority in developing countries not only in Latin America but elsewhere. The basic premise of the theoretical framework of this book is that fiscal centralization can be best studied as the consequence of a bargain struck between self-interested regional and national politicians.

The book argues that fiscal centralization occurs when national politicians use the power of the central government to protect regional politicians from challengers and electoral threats in exchange for financial resources. In turn, regional politicians are willing to forgo fiscal authority. This exchange cannot easily be made: Local politicians are initially unwilling to give up

1

their capacity to tax absent guarantees by the national elites that a strong central government will not later exploit their financial dependence. This is the fundamental dilemma of fiscal centralization.

1.2. Fiscal Centralization around the World

Fiscal centralization is ubiquitous in the contemporary world. According to the International Monetary Fund (IMF) *Government Finance Statistics* (GFS), revenue centralization, measured as the share of tax and nontax revenue collected by the national level of government, averaged 81 percent at the close of the 20th century. Expenditures were less centralized, with national governments' share of total expenditures by all governments averaging 74 percent.[1] Although there are wide differences among countries in the level of centralization they exhibit, and both types of centralization (revenue and expenditure) usually go hand in hand, in all countries – regardless of their level of development and political organization – there is far less centralization in expenditures than in revenues. The gap between these two indicators is usually filled by various forms of financial transfers.

Why is tax collection so centralized? Even as expenditures have been decentralized the world over since the 1980s, why do countries seldom devolve revenue authority to subnational spheres of government? How did tax authority become centralized initially? In order to address these issues, this book explores the political process of tax authority concentration in the Latin American federations. An in-depth study of the Mexican case is contrasted and compared with the evolution of other Latin American federations. I show that in Mexico, as in Argentina and Venezuela, tax centralization was accompanied by the creation of overarching revenue-sharing and other expenditure transfer systems. State and provincial politicians in those three federations agreed to give up their power to tax in exchange for financial transfers and secure political careers protected by the power of the federal government. Brazilian states, in contrast, did not abdicate their tax

---

[1] The data correspond to 1997. According to the GFS, 13 federal countries averaged 70 percent in revenue centralization and 64 percent in expenditure centralization; the corresponding figures were 85 and 78 percent, respectively, for the 39 unitary countries for which information is available. In no country is revenue less centralized than expenditure, and only in small countries with little decentralization are those two indicators relatively similar. The GFS accounts for tax and revenue-sharing as subnational revenue, when strictly speaking they should be considered a transfer. This means that decentralization in taxation is, in fact, much lower than what these numbers suggest, particularly for federal countries where revenue-sharing is relatively common.

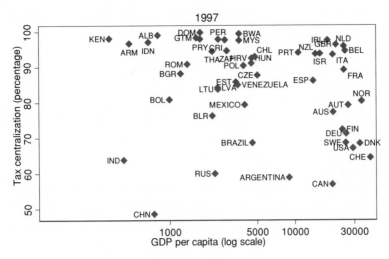

Figure 1.1. Revenue centralization and level of development (based on data from World Bank, 1999).

authority. This allowed Brazil to remain a highly decentralized federation. The circumstances under which the Latin American federations solved the dilemma of fiscal centralization or remained revenue-decentralized differed greatly. In all cases, political representation conditioned the construction of regional coalitions that determined the specific way in which fiscal bargains unfolded. Altogether, the experience of the four countries sheds light on the process of consolidation of central political and fiscal authority in federal developing countries.

Figure 1.1 shows the range of variation in revenue authority centralization prevailing around the world. The figure shows the amount of revenue from tax and nontax sources that was controlled by national governments as a percentage of total revenue collection (national plus local and intermediate governments).[2] Countries are ranked on the horizontal axis according to their level of development measured by their purchasing power parity per capita gross domestic product (GDP, logged) from the *Penn World Tables*. Latin American federations are placed on the graph at similar values in terms of their development, but they vary widely in their degree of revenue

---

[2] The data are for 1997. The source is a careful compilation done by the World Bank (1999) in which an effort was made to ensure that decentralization was well accounted for. The ranking of countries is similar to that in the data reported by the International Monetary Fund's *Government Finance Statistics* (GFS), although the coverage is more systematic.

3

centralization. Mexico and Venezuela show levels of centralization found in many unitary states, whereas Brazil and Argentina show low levels of centralization more in line with those found in other federal regimes.

These statistics consider revenue-sharing systems, which are one specific form of intergovernmental transfers, as revenue collected by the recipient government. This means that the graph exaggerates the level of revenue decentralization in Latin America, where revenue-sharing arrangements are an important source of subnational revenue. Taxes subject to revenue-sharing are collected and controlled by the central level of government, not the recipient units. The nature of fiscal authority and the scope for redistribution are radically transformed when revenue-sharing arrangements exist.

When fiscal bargains are struck between local and national politicians for the creation of revenue-sharing systems, the locus of authority over taxation is shifted away from state governments. In Argentina, Mexico, and Venezuela, local elites were willing to make such bargains and create encompassing revenue-sharing systems, abdicating their authority to collect taxes. In Brazil, revenue-sharing was created by the military governments. From the outset, that transfer system played a more limited role in Brazil than in the other Latin American federations because the most important revenue source for the rich states in Brazil was the value-added-tax, which states controlled. If revenue-sharing systems are accounted as transfers rather than subnational revenue, decentralization in Argentina, Mexico, and Venezuela is lower than 10 percent. Tax authority in those three federations then looks more similar to the patterns of relatively centralized countries such as Indonesia or Thailand, which are not federal. Of the Latin American federations, only in Brazil has tax authority remained decentralized in the sense that revenue decentralization is large, even subtracting revenue-sharing.

The Latin American federations were far less centralized at the beginning of the 20th century than they are today. State governments had substantial fiscal authority at the time. Figure 1.2 compares the level of tax centralization around the world observed in 1935 with the average centralization observed during the 1990s.[3] In this graph, revenue-sharing

[3] It is possible to calculate the change in fiscal centralization witnessed during the course of the 20th century only for some countries. Ideally one would like to have information for the 1920s. By then, many countries had implemented income taxation, which was a revolutionary innovation in tax technology, but most of them had not yet initiated revenue-sharing systems. However, cross-sectional information for that decade, and for a fuller sample, is not available (see Diaz-Cayeros, 2004).

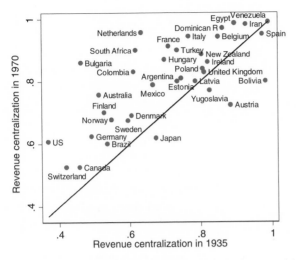

Figure 1.2. Revenue centralization in the 20th century. *Note*: 1990s data for Eastern Europe and former Soviet Union countries.

in the four Latin American federations is accounted as belonging to the government collecting the taxes, not the recipient government. In most countries, tax collection became more centralized at the end of the century than it was at the beginning. However, some countries resisted this trend toward centralization more vigorously than others. Specifically, of the Latin American federations, Brazil retained a high level of decentralization, Mexico and Argentina became highly centralized, and Venezuela retained the high level of centralization it has had since the end of the 19th century.

At the beginning of the 20th century, state (provincial) and local governments around the world maintained a large degree of fiscal authority. The authority to levy excise, sales (turnover), income, or inheritance taxes did not belong exclusively to national governments. But over the course of the century, most national governments centralized and obtained exclusive authority over these taxes while local and state governments instead got transfers from the central level. The fundamental problem of such fiscal centralization is that the credible construction of intergovernmental transfer systems, where state and local tax authority is substituted by financial transfers from the central (federal) government, is never easy to achieve. The Latin American federations illustrate that this is not a linear process of centralization. Tax centralization hinged on the ability of regional and

5

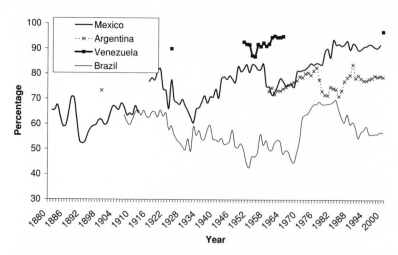

Figure 1.3. Fiscal centralization in the Latin American federations (own calculations from country-specific sources).

national politicians to face critical challenges and find specific solutions for them.

Figure 1.3 shows the evolution of the share of taxes collected by the central governments in the Latin American federations as a percentage of total revenue coming from all levels of government (central, state/provincial, and municipal).[4] The statistics for subnational revenue collection in Brazil and Mexico are rather complete. In Argentina and Venezuela, in contrast, there are long periods of time for which there is no reliable information on which to construct a good indicator of the share of subnational tax collection, because of the paucity of state- and provincial-level revenue-collection

---

[4] Budgeting and statistical practices differ among the Latin American federations, and a consistent methodology, such as that offered by the International Monetary Fund's *Government Finance Statistics*, is not available for a long enough time frame. Rather than attempting to engage in the daunting task of reconstructing all the series in a uniform method, I adopted the conventionally accepted indicators of the "size" of the different levels of government as used in each individual country. It is important to note that in these data revenue is accounted for according to the level of government collecting it and before any fiscal transfers take place. Virtually all comparative statistics count federal revenue-sharing to states/provinces and municipalities/localities as subnational revenue, blurring the important distinction of who has tax authority. Moreover, the data series corrects for double accounting of transfers made in two stages: from federal to state (provincial) governments and from the latter to municipal (local) ones. Details on data sources are provided in the chapters of this book.

data. The gaps in the graph are periods during which it was not possible to reconstruct the fiscal shares, although a detailed reading of country sources suggests that those shares probably remained more or less constant during the years without information.[5] It should be pointed out from the outset, particularly for the case of Argentina, that the relative shares of revenue collection do not mean that the fiscal relations between the federal governments and the provinces remained fixed: In fact, much of the story that this book tells is about the role of federal transfers to provinces (for which we have far more information), which witnessed radical transformations throughout those years. Hence, while fiscal authority became centralized, the amount of resources at the disposal of subnational governments varied widely through time.[6]

The federal government share provides, despite its deficiencies in Argentina and Venezuela, an indicator of the degree of centralization in fiscal authority. During the course of the 20th century, taxation became centralized in the hands of national governments in virtually all the countries, but the evolution and final levels of centralization varied widely. This book provides an explanation for the variation in the paths toward centralization followed by the Latin American federations. Venezuela was always a highly centralized country. Argentina, in contrast, remained a rather decentralized country, notwithstanding frequent changes in the financial relationship between the provinces and the federal government. Brazil has been highly decentralized, although the years of military rule saw an increase in fiscal centralization. Mexico has gone through waves of centralization: one that started in the 19th century, another one after the 1930s, and a third one after the 1970s.

There are common international shocks that explain the tendency of all countries to centralize revenue collection after 1929. However, the graph makes it patently clear that much of the variation depends on the individual

---

[5] In order to appreciate the range of variation in Latin America, it is useful to compare these figures with the long-term levels of centralization observed in federations in the advanced industrial world. The average share of revenue collected by the federal government in the United States between 1947 and 2000 was 68 percent; the corresponding share for Germany between 1881 and 1975 was 71.8 percent; for Canada, between 1933 and 1969, it was 62.4 percent; and for Switzerland, between 1856 and 2000, it was 39 percent. Hence, at some point in their history some of the Latin American federations have resembled Switzerland or Canada in their tax decentralization.

[6] I thank Margaret Levi for this clarification.

domestic processes that each country underwent. The relative importance of the federal government in revenue collection in Mexico hovered at around 65 percent until the 1940s and then increased after 1947. Centralization was reduced during the 1960s, only to increase steadily since the early 1980s. The federal government in Mexico today concentrates around 90 percent of fiscal authority.

The Brazilian path was quite different from the one exhibited by Mexico. In 1886, the central government in the Brazilian empire collected 76.8 percent of the national revenue (Murilo de Carvalho, 1993: 39–41). This was reduced to 65.8 percent in 1907, when the data in the graph for Brazil begins, after federalism was introduced. Brazilian states retained high levels of fiscal authority throughout the 20th century, as shown in the graph, notwithstanding the growth in the overall size of the federal government. Even when the military governments in the 1964–1988 period sought to centralize fiscal authority, Brazil remained far more decentralized than Mexico.

Venezuela did not experience any significant decentralization in revenue throughout the century. Once tax authority had become concentrated in the federal government in the 19th century, states could not wrest control of taxes away from the central jurisdiction. Argentina has often been regarded as a country experiencing ebbs and flows in fiscal centralization (Eaton, 2001). The evidence suggests, however, that once the centralization of tax authority was achieved in Argentina in the 1930s, the federal share of revenue collection never fell below 70 percent.[7]

Why were states and provinces willing to give up their relative weight in the federal pact, as reflected in their fiscal authority? This centralization of fiscal authority is puzzling on several grounds. In contrast to unitary regimes, in federations, state (or provincial) governments have the constitutional authority to collect taxes. The argument of this book is that from the point of view of the constituent members, there are gains to be reaped from a centralized system of revenue collection. However, federal governments face a commitment problem in order to credibly promise to substitute decentralized systems of tax collection with transfer arrangements. The credibility of transfer systems has been taken for granted in most research on federalism. I argue that credibility in transfers emerges

---

[7] Although the graph actually does not provide specific values, given the unreliability of the data discussed in Chapter 7.

from a political bargain articulated through both political institutions and the party system.

In Mexico, a hegemonic party provided an institutional solution to the dilemma of commitment encountered by regional politicians in the process of state-building. This institutional solution tempered the centrifugal forces unleashed by the Mexican Revolution and set the stage for a period of moderate growth with political stability. The hegemonic party structured a highly disciplined system of progressive ambition. Local politicians were willing to empower the federal government to pursue a centralized national "developmentalist" strategy.[8] The PRI system protected local politicians from electoral challenges and ensured them attractive political careers. Local politicians surrendered their fiscal authority because they were protected from competition in local electoral and economic markets.

An institutional solution to the federal commitment problem was attempted in Argentina through the delegation of enforcement of the fiscal bargain to a third party, namely the central bank. This solution turned out not to be self-enforcing given the shifts between democracy and authoritarianism that the country witnessed throughout the 20th century. The distrust between the provinces and the federal government was further enhanced whenever partisanship differed between levels of government. By the 1980s, the system of revenue-sharing collapsed altogether. In Venezuela, authoritarian federal governments during the first half of the century were able to impose a virtually unitary system of government, blurring federalism and often cheating states from their constitutionally mandated transfers. The fiscal arrangement only became binding when a stable two-party system and a transition to democracy were achieved after 1958. In Brazil, state governments instead kept fiscal authority, so the system remained highly decentralized. A credible threat by the most powerful states to challenge the federal government always remained in place. Not even the military rulers successfully centralized the system to the extent that they envisaged. Instead, in order to stay in office, they had to construct a ruling coalition through a crafty combination of respecting the fiscal authority and political autonomy of the powerful states while constructing a redistributive revenue-sharing transfer system.

---

[8] I use "developmentalism" in the sense of Sikkink (1991). I am not making a judgment as to whether the strategy successfully generated development.

1.3. Federalism, Political Parties, and Fiscal Authority

A federal system can be defined by two (necessary and sufficient) conditions. First, state (or provincial) executives must emerge from elections held within a state (provincial) jurisdiction independently from the national one. Second, states (provinces) must possess inherent fiscal authority.[9] Such an ideal-typical definition of federalism is not incompatible with other characterizations found in the literature. This definition highlights, however, the conditions of representation and taxation in federal systems.[10] To the extent that state executives are the product of state elections and, once in office, possess an independent tax base, one can say they reside in a federal regime.

According to the previous definition, so long as a candidate for office must face election at the state level independently from the national candidates (regardless of the level of threat imposed by the challengers), and if once in office can exercise tax authority and decide the allocation of financial resources, we should regard the institutional arrangement as federal.[11]

---

[9] In the case of so-called local governments, their capacity to tax is always derived from an authority granted by national political institutions. Those governments do not possess an inherent capacity to tax. It should be noted that the definition assumes the existence of an intermediate jurisdiction. States, provinces, or departments are at an intermediate level between a national authority and municipal governments. Throughout the book, I will use state, provincial, and local to refer to the intermediate level of government, whereas municipal is used to denote the smallest political units. Centralized regimes retain decentralization in small political units, where, for example, elected mayors have complete authority over the property tax; but those mayors are not an intermediate level. The definition of federalism allows for the "state" executive to be indirectly elected or emanate from an elected "state" parliament. In this case, the executive is responsible to representatives who were elected in the local jurisdiction.

[10] In contrast with mainstream theorists, I am not concerned with understanding where the federal arrangement originally comes from or how "authentic" it might be. Political theories of federalism usually stress the "covenant" nature of the federal pact (Elazar, 1984), the origin of cooperation among constituent members arising from an external threat (Riker, 1964), or the formal powers and attributes of each constituent level of government (Duchacek, 1970). Those are important questions, but they do not provide much insight into what happens in federal regimes once decades or centuries have passed since their "founding."

[11] This would also mean, notwithstanding fascinating parallelisms, that I do not consider China, where provincial leaders are appointed, to be a federal regime (see Montinola, Qian, and Weingast, 1995). Italy, although nominally unitary, would be considered federal since the reform of regional governments in 1976 (see Putnam, Leonardi, and Nanetti, 1993). A possible source of ambiguity could be the difficulty of determining how "democratic" subnational elections need to be in order for a state official to be considered elected.

This does not mean that the orientation of a politician is more likely to be national in unitary systems and local in federal systems. As much of this book will argue, such an orientation depends on the equilibrium reached in the complex interaction among fiscal authority, political ambition, and party systems.[12]

Riker believed that the characteristics of local political support and fiscal authority operated differently in each specific federal system, depending on the structure of the party system. In particular, "the structure of the system of political parties is what encourages or discourages the maintenance of the federal bargain" (Riker, 1964:51). Specifically, the peripheralizing tendencies of the party system were central to the maintenance of federalism. Moreover, Riker believed that decentralization in party nominations and multiparty competition determined the degree of decentralization characterizing each federal regime.

Filippov, Ordeshook, and Shvetsova (2004) have recast the Rikerian argument in more contemporary terms, explaining the stability in federal arrangements as the product of self-enforcement through political parties. The question of federal stability has received considerable attention in the last few years (see Bednar, 2000; Solnick, 2002). This body of work suggests that the success of federal systems depends on being able to strike a balance between states being strong enough to protect their rights and having a federal government that is strong enough to provide goods and services to the constituent jurisdictions.

According to Riker, countries where the federal government overawed the constituent governments were centralized because they shared a common trait: "that one and only one political party rules all levels of government" (Riker, 1964:131). However, recent work by Garman, Haggard, and Willis (2001) suggests that the crucial variable is not party competition but rather the degree to which nomination to local office is controlled centrally. When local politicians look toward their territorial constituencies, rather than the national party leadership, as the basis of support and nomination to office, they will be more responsive to state interests. Because the defense of state interests is what keeps a federal system peripheralized, when the local assertion of authority is not observed, the system becomes centralized.

Electoral processes can be noncompetitive, as in the southern United States during the first half of the 20th century, and the country can still be considered federal.

[12] I thank an anonymous reviewer for this point.

One of the most controversial issues in federal regimes concerns the distribution of tax authority and financial resources among members and levels of government. Most accounts of the distribution of tax authority and financial resources in federal arrangements overlook the fact that this trait is contingent on the party system. That is, state fiscal authority and the regional allocation of expenditures will depend on the incentives faced by local politicians according to the way in which political parties structure their political opportunities and careers.

The main theoretical argument for limiting the tax authority of state governments rests on the grounds of economic efficiency (see Inman and Rubinfeld, 1997). A federal government can presumably prevent the erection of state tariffs that would hinder the mobility of goods and services, and it can generate a uniform tax system that would reduce deadweight losses caused by regional allocative inefficiencies produced by multiple state tax systems. In short, centralized taxation provides the benefits of a common market. Of course, the problem is that too much centralization can also be inefficient in terms of foregoing a close match between government policies and citizens' preferences. State governments are reluctant to accept limits on their fiscal authority, and federal regimes vary widely in the degree of fiscal centralization they exhibit.

Tax authority is one of the primordial features of state power (see North, 1981; Levi, 1988; Steinmo, 1993). A state without the capacity to tax is subject to the power and abuse of the national government or of powerful private agents. Margaret Levi has argued that the process of central state-building must be explained by "a theory of how central governments can wrest power from other entities, whether they be individual actors, colonies, regions, or . . . states" (Levi, 1988:146). In her discussion of Australia, she argues that tax centralization was not simply a Hobbesian solution, where authority was taken over by the center in order to avert a "war of all against all." Levi instead provides an account where, in the context of collective-action problems, an incremental sequence of choices led to centralizing policies, where states were eventually co-opted to abide by a centralized tax arrangement. This solution involved an increase in the bargaining power of an expanded federal sphere and the selective use of fiscal inducements (Levi, 1988:147). My account is consonant with Levi's idea of co-optation, but it moves beyond her account by providing a rationale for fiscal centralization as a commitment problem within a fiscal bargain.

Ruling out the use of military force, local politicians can cede fiscal power if a bargain is struck between the members of the federal arrangement.[13] Such a bargain, I argue, can be based on two types of side payments: financial transfers from the federal to the state governments and assured political careers to local politicians. Financial transfers and assured careers are only viable if the national government can credibly commit to providing them, an issue that is explored in the next section. Whereas financial transfers can be understood in a relatively straightforward manner as side payments, careers as concessions require some further explanation.

A national government can secure political acquiescence to limiting local fiscal power by ensuring that local politicians can retain office, or at least offering attractive careers in which political threats are minimized. Security of tenure in office can be achieved, in general, through the use of national political organizations – parties – that provide local politicians with a ladder of political ambition they can climb from local to national political office. Moreover, the centralized control of electoral processes can help local politicians win their elections. In the extreme case, the establishment of a hegemonic party as in Mexico or dominant political machines such as the Peronist Party in the Argentine provinces offers long political careers while eliminating electoral threats.

The remainder of this chapter provides the theoretical building blocks for subsequent chapters. I discuss the nature of the federal bargain as a commitment dilemma and the limits of fiscal redistribution within federal systems. I then outline the organization of the chapters in the rest of the book.

1.4. The Federal Bargain: Delegation and Commitment

Under what conditions would regional politicians bestow power on a higher authority in order to achieve their common ends? Can the center be prevented from overawing, to use Riker's (1964) term, the constituent parts? In this section, I argue that a fiscally centralized federation is created when

---

[13] In my view, too much of the literature on federalism written after 1990 highlights the threat of secession, which in most developing countries would probably require the use of military force. In advanced industrial countries, that threat might not imply the use of force (i.e., Quebec probably would not use military force to enforce a separation from Canada), but the conventional models are inspired by a world of anarchic international relations, where the threat of the use of force is crucial for the viability of independent states. For some references to this type of model, see Alesina and Spolaore (2003) and Bolton and Roland (1997).

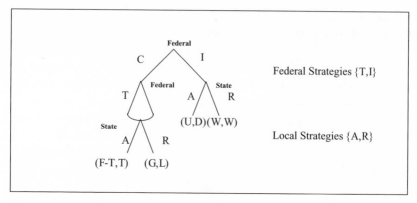

Figure 1.4. Federal bargain: Commitment game.

constituent units and the national government can solve problems of delegation, enforcement, and credibility of federal promises.[14]

Figure 1.4 provides a commitment game that represents the credibility problem a state or provincial government faces when taxation becomes centralized in a federation. For the sake of simplicity, the game assumes that the states and the federal government only care about collecting revenue (North, 1981; Levi, 1988). In this game, the tax rates are fixed by governments through a process that may or may not be democratic. I abstract from the issue of whether citizens have specific preferences over the outcome of the commitment game. Although this is clearly unrealistic, it reflects the fact that matters of federal design usually involve negotiations among politicians rather than direct appeals or consultations with citizens.

I refer to the creation of a centralized tax collection system as a "federal fiscal compromise." The national government moves first, either seeking a federal fiscal compromise (*C*), which is embodied in the promise to transfer financial resources in amount *T* to the subnational governments, or

---

[14] The discussion that follows is not intended to provide an understanding of the historical origin of federal arrangements. Riker (1964) observed that federal systems emerge wherever a large jurisdiction is constructed that faces an external military threat. Filippov, Ordeshook, and Shvetsova (2004) provide a nuanced discussion of whether this hypothesis stands up to close scrutiny. The question that I address refers to the maintenance of a federal bargain and the tendency toward centralization within it. To highlight the process, I will speak of federalism and centralism as opposites, but this is really a matter of the degree of decentralization or centralization within a nominally federal constitutional arrangement.

imposing a unitary mode of government $(I)^{15}$ and risking open conflict with the regions, even leading to a civil war. The local levels of government (the game only shows one) must either accept the deal offered by the federal government (A) or reject the arrangement (R).[16]

Accepting the federal fiscal compromise means obtaining a transfer from the federal government but giving up the capacity to tax at will.[17] Accepting the unitary model means losing independent local power (while perhaps retaining a dependent administrative position) and forfeiting the tax base. Rejecting the federal bargain means maintaining the system of local taxation in place, rejecting the transfer, and keeping a system of overlapping taxation between levels of government, even if that system is inefficient from an overall economic and revenue-maximization point of view. In the case of a unitary imposition, the rejection strategy means resisting a national army, leading perhaps to civil war.

The payoffs of the game are given by the value of F, which is the federal revenue collected under a centralized federal bargain; U, which is the revenue collected under a unitarian imposition; G, the federal revenue collected when a federal bargain is rejected; T, a federal transfer to the states or provinces, paid out from federal revenue collection; L, the revenue collected by states in a federal regime with no tax centralization; D, subnational tax collection under a unitary imposition (which in the limit could be $D = 0$); and W, the expected value of conflict that could lead into civil war.

The game as depicted in the figure allows for any set of values in the payoff structure. However, federalism only makes sense if there is something to gain out of a federal arrangement, so I assume that $F > U + D$ and $F > 2W$.[18] That is, I restrict payoffs so that the federal outcome is Pareto

---

[15] Notwithstanding that the latter strategy might mean less economic efficiency. On the economic benefits of federalism, see Tiebout (1956) and Weingast (1995). It is important to note that my argument is agnostic about the benefits to citizens: Federal systems probably strike a balance between being decentralized enough to force competition while not being so decentralized that "market preservation" might be imperiled.

[16] To simplify matters, I am only modeling one state, although a central issue might be the possibility for states to act collectively in order to extract more concessions from the federal government. For a model and an insightful discussion of this process in Russia, see Solnick (1998, 2002).

[17] This is not to say that no local taxation remains, but the idea is that it must be coordinated with the tax authority of the federal government. To simplify matters, the model assumes that the tax authority local governments keep is encompassed implicitly in the federal transfer.

[18] This means that the federal arrangement collects more revenue than the unitary imposition or the taxes exacted by warlords in conflict.

efficient.[19] This is not to say that the federal outcome is necessarily achievable or that the distribution resulting from it is attractive to all players; it only means that under federalism no player can be made better-off without making some other player worse-off. The Pareto efficiency of federalism also implies that, regardless of the size of D, $F > U$. If transfers are sufficiently low, the national government should prefer a federal setting to a unitary imposition.

It is useful also to restrict the payoffs so that a conflict outcome is so damaging to the national government that it would rather have a federal offer be rejected than risk a conflict (and perhaps civil war), so $W < G$. The idea is that the game depicts a moment when, although the threat of war exists, regional conflicts have been pacified. Such a restriction gives states or provinces a strategic advantage, the importance of which will become obvious in the discussion that follows.

With these restrictions in mind, the problem for the federal government is to find a minimum T that would be acceptable to the local government ($T > L$) but that is still rational to offer from the national government's point of view. If such a transfer does not exist, the federal government can attempt instead to impose a unitary solution. The state government, in turn, must decide whether to accept or reject the transfer T being offered in the federal compromise branch of the game or whether to accept or reject a unitary imposition.

In this game, which is solved through subgame perfection (i.e., solving the subgames at the end first, and working backward to the beginning of the game), a fiscal federal bargain is sought by the national government if threats of conflict are credible. If $W > D$, the local government is better-off fighting against the federal government than accepting a unitary system. Looking down the game tree (the structure of payoffs is common knowledge), the federal government can avoid such an outcome by providing a large T (as long as $T < F - W$). That is, the national government pays transfers to avert conflicts. Feasible transfers are thus bound by the value of conflict and, implicitly, the risk of civil war.[20]

---

[19] See Stiglitz (1994) and Scharpf (1988) for discussions of the plausibility of such an assumption.

[20] In the simultaneous game depicted in Table 1.1, the federal compromise is a (unique pure strategy) Nash equilibrium as long as $F - T > U$ and $T > L$. That is, the transfer needs to be smaller than the added benefit the national government obtains from having a federal instead of a unitary arrangement, but large enough so that states prefer to give up local tax authority in exchange for the transfer.

Table 1.1. *Federal Bargain in a Simultaneous Game*

	Federal Compromise (T)	Unitary Imposition (I)
Accept (A)	$F - T, T$	U, D
Reject (R)	G, L	W, W

$G > W$
$F > U + D, F > 2W$

To achieve the federal compromise, the transfer must be such that $T > L$. If the federal government is unable to provide such a transfer (because $L > F - W$), it could still avert the conflict to the extent that $G > W$. That is, the federal government can choose to offer a transfer of any size, knowing in advance that the local government will reject it, in order to prevent conflict. This strategy has a limit given by the value of G, the federal revenue when the fiscal bargain is rejected. It is crucial to note that these results all hinge on conflict (including the risk of civil war) not being an empty threat for state governments; that is, on $W > D$.

At the beginning of the 20th century, the status quo of federal tax arrangements in Latin America was analogous to a rejected federal bargain. Argentina and Mexico were characterized by overlapping taxation, whereas in Brazil the constitution explicitly granted authority over distinct tax bases to each level of government.[21] Federal governments did not find these arrangements optimal, but they would only seek change under very specific conditions that the game highlights: The federal government must be unwilling to risk open conflict, and the payoff structure "off the equilibrium path" for the local government must make civil war better than a unitary imposition. In other words, the state or provincial government's

Under such a simultaneous setting, the threat of going to war plays no role in the determination of equilibrium. This is because simultaneous games have no place for credibility. If no transfer exists within the range $L > T > F - U$, the fully functioning federal outcome is impossible. In that case, one possible outcome of the game is that states reject a federal offer of $T < L$, which is still made because the national government will not risk a civil war. A second (pure strategy) equilibrium might also exist where the unitary system is successfully imposed if $D > W$. Thus, when there is no prior information for local governments to decide their strategies on the basis of the national government's moves, the federal arrangement only depends on whether federalism is productive enough relative to a successful unitary imposition.

[21] In Venezuela, a federal fiscal compromise had been reached in the 19th century, although before that time the constitution provided for exclusive jurisdictions over tax bases by level of government.

threat must be credible. In this scenario, states or provinces would rather risk a civil war than lose their authority to tax under a unitary system.

This suggests that the emergence of centralized federal bargains is attributable to the preservation of state and provincial threats of open conflict and the expansion, through tax technologies, of potential revenue generated through centralized income or value-added federal tax arrangements. When states can no longer threaten conflict, a unitary imposition would be preferred by the federal government. The centralized fiscal federal bargain is contingent not only on how much revenue it can generate but on the power of states or provinces.

In this game, state or provincial governments acquiesce to a unitary imposition only if $D > W$, no transfer falls within the range $F - U < T < L$, and $U > G$. The last condition, $U > G$, can be interpreted as meaning that the national government cannot threaten to impose a unitary arrangement unless this threat is credible in the sense that it should be better for the federal government to have the unitary outcome accepted than to have a transfer rejected. Hence, two insights emerge: namely, that states can acquiesce to a unitary system, provided that they are not willing to risk conflict; and that national governments can impose a unitary system if the advantage of the federal organization is not too large. If there is no feasible federal transfer, this reflects that local bases of taxation generate much more revenue than federal transfers could.

The comparative statics of the model also suggest some additional insights. The more revenue states or provinces collect in their jurisdictions, the larger transfers must be if a centralized federal bargain is to remain in place. However, a larger value of conflict does not generate larger concessions from the national government. This is because the size of transfers depends on the opportunity cost of local tax collection, L, not on the threat of conflict. Centralized fiscal bargains that are produced on the left branch of the game can occur only if the value of conflict on the unitary path is sufficiently large for the states to be able to play it credibly, hence forcing the federal government to seek a compromise. This means that in this game, in contrast to models of threat of secession, transfers depend on the underlying economic base of the state, which becomes reflected in local taxation, not in the political or military might of states. Of course, it is possible that economic and political power are correlated, but the game highlights that they need not be. An off-the-equilibrium-path threat (i.e., a strategy that is not played) is what induces players to bargain over fiscal transfers, but the transfer is not larger when the political threat is greater.

Given this feature, the national government can offer a token transfer, fully aware that it will be rejected, only to avert conflict. The size of such a rejected transfer has no substantive meaning except for exhibiting the willingness of the federal government to avoid a conflict from a unitary imposition. In this outcome, what the federal government does is keep the country together by allowing tax authority to remain at the state level through overlapping tax jurisdictions.[22]

1.5. Time Inconsistency Exacerbating the Commitment Problem

This first game highlights credibility problems related to "off the path" threats. Credibility problems can also arise over time because promises are not always kept. Unfulfilled promises give rise to classic problems of time inconsistency.[23] Imagine that the game is long-lasting in the sense that once a state government accepts a federal transfer, there is one more round, but that in a subsequent stage, the provincial government has no choice but to accept whatever transfer it is given. Such a game is depicted in Figure 1.5. Payoffs now correspond to two periods, where δ is a time discount factor.

If the federal government is completely free to set whichever transfer it wishes and the local government has accepted the federal bargain, the optimal strategy at time $t+1$ is $T_2 = 0$ because there is no retaliation the local player can give in case $T_2 < L$. This condition gives rise to an intertemporal commitment problem. The only way the federal government can credibly commit to producing the federal outcome is by making a transfer in the first round that is large enough that $T_1 > (1 + \delta)L$.

If the discount factor is low – that is, local governments care little about their future – they will accept a federal arrangement in spite of the possibility that the federal government will renege on its promise to provide a transfer in subsequent rounds. If one were to interpret the discount factor not as a psychological temporal preference but as the probability that the incumbent will remain in office in the second period, this result suggests that the acceptability of a centralized fiscal bargain depends on the extent to which state or provincial powerholders are entrenched in office. If

---

[22] In addition, in contrast to the simultaneous game in Table 1.1, the game suggests that in environments with more information, states or provinces can decide on their actions once they have observed the national government's strategy, which gives them leverage to extract more transfers from the federal government than when the game is simultaneous.

[23] To my knowledge, the only contribution highlighting the credibility problem of transfers in a similar way is found in Alesina, et. al. (2001) and Alesina and Spolaore (2003).

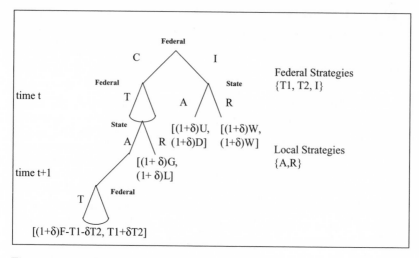

Figure 1.5. Federal bargain: Time inconsistency.

state or provincial incumbents are likely to remain in office and the federal government has no way to affect this probability, they are more likely to reject a transfer system. In contrast, if state authorities were appointed and removed at will by the federal government, they should have short temporal horizons, making the game more similar to a one-shot scenario. Term limits or the prohibition of reelection should have an effect analogous to reducing the discount factor.

Is there a way to mitigate this temptation for the national government to provide no transfer once the federal bargain has been accepted? One solution would consist of setting up an institutional rule that the national government will have no discretion at time $t + 1$. That is, a rule might establish that transfers must be the same in both periods, $T_1 = T_2$, which would make the game similar to the one-shot case. In that situation, the condition for local government to accept the federal deal would require that $T > L$, a far less stringent condition than the previous one. The problem, of course, is that such a rule is not necessarily self-enforcing unless one takes into account features of the overall political environment that make political actors respect their institutions.

A second possibility is that the local politicians discount the future very highly. At the extreme, if $\delta = 0$, the only transfer that matters is the one obtained in the current period and not the promises. If political careers are structured in such a way that local politicians do not expect to continue

20

in local office at time $t + 1$, they will be more willing to accept a smaller transfer as a side payment. The same would be true if they expect to have a political career that is detached from what happens with the local government at time $t + 1$.

The game of commitment over time thus highlights the role of institutions as credibility-enhancing mechanisms that might solve problems of temporal inconsistency. Institutional rules governing the size of federal transfers have often been placed in constitutions, or federal governments have opted for some third-party enforcement of the fiscal pact, placing the obligation to pay revenue shares on an independent central bank. Another possibility is that a malapportioned senate with significant budget authority can grant veto power to minority political actors who can find assurance in that decision body to the effect of generating compliance on the part of the federal government. These institutional devices can reduce the amount of resources the national government needs to transfer in order to make a federal bargain palatable to the states or provinces.

An additional mechanism, which might make commitment through time more credible, is to link the political fates of state or provincial politicians with those of the federal level of government. This can be achieved through national political parties. The notion here is that nationalized party systems might make advances in political careers less contingent on the processes taking place at the local level and more dependent on the national-level trends (Chhibber and Kollman, 2004). It is possible for the party system, in fact, to insulate state and provincial politicians from political threats at the local level so that their career advancement is seen as something occurring in the national arena. Specific political and institutional configurations that can remove political incentives from the state or provincial realms include features such as closed-list proportional representation for assemblies, concurrent elections, appointment of regional representatives, and national-level control of local nomination procedures.

1.6. Redistribution

Revenue centralization opens the gate to regional redistribution. When the federal level collects the most important sources of revenue, future increases in tax collection can be distributed among the partners to the fiscal federal bargain in many ways. All actors in the federal bargain benefit from additional resources that are brought in by centralized taxation, but they may disagree on how the extra revenue should be distributed. One possibility

21

would be for states to delegate to the federal government the decision over the allocation of additional resources, breaking any territorial connection in their use. Another possibility is that states could agree on rules that allocated transfers financed from federal tax collection "equally." Norms of equality might involve equal state shares or equal shares in per capita terms, for example. A third possibility is that states might agree on using any additional resources as a redistributive tool, allocating more funds to regions with larger needs, more poverty, or unfulfilled public services. Finally, it is conceivable that states will demand that resources be allocated according to what they perceive as their own effort or the local economic base that makes federal tax collection possible. What determines that a particular distributional outcome obtains rather than another?

Once the commitment problem is solved among the members of a federal arrangement, it seems plausible to propose that they can divide the benefits of their agreement in a cooperative manner. Individual rationality requires positive net benefits to each of the members in an agreement because otherwise it would not be individually rational to belong to the federal bargain; but having said this, there exist a virtually infinite number of possible distributions that would fulfill a condition of individual rationality.[24] This is a classic problem of distributive justice that involves the question of how to divide a "pie" among a fixed number of players. Dividing a pie can be a complicated issue, particularly when agents or shares are heterogeneous (see Young, 1994; Brams and Taylor, 1996; Moulin, 2003). All federal systems face the problem of how to allocate federal fiscal transfers in an acceptable manner. Redistribution can be pursued, but only to a limit, because members should not perceive that the system produces fiscal exploitation, which might lead them to exit the arrangement (see Inman and Rubinfeld, 1997:101).

The problem of sharing tax resources among states can hence be understood as a cooperative "divide the dollar" game in which a fund of fixed size must be allocated among $n + 1$ players (n states and the federal government). The model developed herein sheds some light on what determines the share that each state would be willing to accept in order to stay within a

---

[24] Of course, this notion rules out the possibility that a state might be forced to join a federation. The idea here is that there is unanimous agreement on the benefits of federation, but the problem is how to distribute those benefits. For a view in which those outcomes depend on the possibility of states acting collectively, see Solnick (2002).

revenue-sharing system.[25] Representing the game of fiscal distribution as a zero-sum noncooperative interaction is not an appropriate model.[26] A cooperative model highlights that an agreement can make everyone better off but that some allocation must be found that will make an agreement possible. In particular, a bargaining model, although neglecting the mechanisms through which states solve possible conflicts among themselves, stresses the distributive outcome one can expect – among the Pareto optimal ones – and the opportunity cost of negotiations breaking down (Osborne and Rubinstein, 1990).[27]

Following a wage negotiation model proposed by McDonald and Solow (1981), a revenue-sharing problem can be solved through a "contract" between state and federal governments that stipulates a share (P_i) given to each state and the effort (e_i) each state exerts as an agent of the federal government in the collection of federal taxes. State governments are treated as unitary actors, represented by their governor, who seeks to maximize revenue. The utility function of the governor is determined by the way in which total revenue-collection effort (E_i) is allocated among federal and local taxes according to

$$U_i = [p_i e_i + r_i(E_i - e_i)] \qquad \text{for states } i = 1, \ldots 32, \qquad (1.1)$$

[25] An important limitation of the framework is that it is completely silent on the procedural mechanisms involved in the cooperative outcome. A noncooperative model of counteroffers, in the spirit of Rubinstein (1982) could make the strategic interaction more explicit. The development of such a model entails important difficulties, however. On the technical side, there is a "folk theorem" type of problem when the Rubinstein model is extended to n players that yields a disappointing and impractical result: It can be shown that every partition (of revenue) constitutes a subgame perfect equilibrium, where agreement is immediately reached. On the substantive side, a game of counteroffers is counterintuitive in terms of the informal accounts that exist of the way in which governors in Latin America have bargained over fiscal issues with their federal governments.

[26] Such a setting would imply pure conflict, which does not make sense in a federal setting. When queried on how they understood the problem of revenue allocation, state finance ministers interviewed in Mexico often mentioned a zero-sum conflict, but their federal counterparts were also quick to point out that the size of the "pie" to be divided in revenue-sharing has been increasing in absolute and relative terms since 1980. (Evidence of this is provided in Díaz-Cayeros, 1995: Table 8.)

[27] Cooperative games solved through a minimal winning coalition (MWC) are not an appropriate way to study the problem. An MWC only makes sense if the size of the fund to be distributed is unaffected by leaving some players outside of the coalition. If a state is left out of the coalition, it would not contribute to the collection of federal revenue, probably even decreasing the tax base of the country as a whole.

where, dropping the subscripts, E are the total units of administrative effort available for revenue collection; e are the total administrative resources allocated to the collection of federal taxes so that $0 < e < E$; r is the yield of each unit of administrative effort in local revenue, so that total local revenue is $R = r(E - e)$ and the maximum local revenue is $R_{\max} = rE$; and p is the revenue share per unit of administrative effort, so that by definition $P = pe$.

The federal government is also a revenue maximizer, but it "owns" the federal tax system, behaving as a "residual claimant" of the revenue produced by federal taxes in each state minus the total share (P_i) it distributes. Hence, the federal utility function is given by

$$U_F = \sum_{i=1}^{n} [f_i(e_i) - p_i e_i] \qquad \text{for } i = 1, \ldots n, \tag{1.2}$$

where the function $f(e)$ is the federal tax-revenue "production function," which is well behaved and is always more productive than state tax-revenue production, so it is assumed that $f(e) > re$. It should be stressed that the local revenue collection actually observed is not equivalent to what a state could theoretically collect if it devoted all its administrative resources to collecting its own taxes; that is, $R = re$. The restriction of the federal tax-revenue production function is crucial because it provides a rationale for the federation in this model: Federal taxes are more efficient than local taxes.[28]

A compact and convex bargaining set S can then be defined by

$$S = (U_F, U_i, \ldots U_i, \ldots U_n) \in \Re^{n+1} : r_i \leq p_i \leq f_i(e_i); 0 \leq e_i \leq E_i. \tag{1.3}$$

This bargaining set S includes a disagreement outcome, d, in which the federation does not exist because it does not collect any revenue and where all taxation is local because the full tax effort is devoted to local taxes, giving a smaller yield:

$$d = (0, r_1 E_1, \ldots r_i E_i, \ldots r_n E_n). \tag{1.4}$$

Hence, $<S, d>$ constitutes a bargaining game (Osborne and Rubinstein, 1990, Definition 2.1) that can be solved uniquely through the Nash

---

[28] In order to simplify matters and to abstract from issues of side payments between states, I restrict attention to the case where the residual that the federation obtains from *each* state is positive so that $r < p < f(e)/e$.

solution. The Nash solution is the only cooperative solution that satisfies simultaneously the axioms of invariance to equivalent utility representations (INV), symmetry (SYM), independence of irrelevant alternatives (IIA), and Pareto efficiency (PAR). The unique Nash solution to the bargaining game described by (1.1–1.4) for all i is given by the optimal share

$$P_i^* = \left[\sum_{j \neq i}^{n-1} f_j(e_j^*) - P_j + f_i(e_i^*) + R_i \right] \Big/ 2,$$

which means that a state will obtain a larger share of revenue the larger the opportunity cost of collecting federal taxes instead of local ones ($R_i = R_{max} - R_i^*$), the more productive it is in collecting federal taxes ($f(e)$), and the more important the state is in contributing to the federal residual (the term with the j subindex). (See the proof in the Appendix to the chapter.)

The predictions of this proposition are threefold. First, as long as taxation is territorially based, the contract involved in revenue-sharing must consider revenue collection efforts in order to induce performance. Second, the size of the shares is highly dependent on the economic base of each state, reflecting the revenue that would be collected if the state does not enter the bargain, as the opportunity cost. This is because the Nash solution concept selects that outcome that, on the Pareto frontier, maximizes the difference with respect to the disagreement point, and the disagreement point is precisely that each state would collect its own revenue. Third, the more "productive" a state is in collecting federal taxes and the more important its share of total federal revenue, the more resources it can bargain for. This is a consequence of the fact that in this game the pool of resources to be shared is variable, depending on how much the players are contributing. To the extent that Pareto optimality is assumed in the solution concept, states will make a maximum effort, but the federal government must reward that effort because otherwise the pool of resources will be smaller for everyone and the gains of cooperation would not be reaped.

The implication of these predictions is therefore that the system of revenue-sharing (and in general any system of resource allocation where states can threaten to go on their own) will not be particularly redistributive because states will only accept a share that is highly correlated with their economic capacity. This means that a systematic redistribution of resources in favor of the poorer states is not to be expected, at least with regard to tax sources, and that if a government wishes to carry out regionally redistributive policies, it will have to do them through some items on the expenditure side that rich states cannot control, not through taxation.[29]

What happens when the game is played repeatedly? State governors would discount the future flow of resources, being more interested in the resources they can get today than those they will obtain tomorrow. If they are at the end of their careers, governors should disregard transfers promised after the end of their term. They would also discount the future to the extent that they perceive more or less insecurity in their tenure in office. One can formulate discount rates for the governors that take into account the institutional calendar of state and federal politicians together with two distinct sources of discounting: a pure time preference and risk of insecurity in tenure. From a straightforward application of a theorem provided by Osborne and Rubinstein (1990), one knows that, for any bargaining game, if there is a transformation v of utility functions u according to a risk parameter h, $v_i = h \circ u_i$, the player that discounts her payoff, more will accept a smaller share. (For proof, see Osborne and Rubinstein, 1990:18). This is true as long as h is an increasing concave function and hence does not imply a linear transformation of the utility functions.[30] The result extends easily to n players because the proof involves the ratio of risk-neutral and risk-averse utilities being equalized among individuals.

Therefore, the h variable indicates that governors who are more risk averse, or alternatively heavily discount the future, will get a smaller share of total revenue, whereas the federation, with a lower risk aversion because

---

[29] The Nash solution fulfills an independence of irrelevant alternatives axiom, which – leaving aside the technical issues – implies that when dividing the fund, the players do not care about the maximum potential revenue each state could produce if all the shares were distributed exclusively to it, a condition that presumably would give more bargaining power to the richer states. If this bargaining power is taken into account (even if the allocations that yield individual maxima are, strictly speaking, irrelevant alternatives), in the Kaläi-Smorodinski solution of the bargaining game the revenue-sharing system should be more biased in favor of the richer states, hence giving a rather regressive distribution to the system because otherwise the richer states would not participate in it. In the Kaläi-Smorodinski solution, the term $R_{max} - R$ drops out, so it does not matter if a state is relatively efficient at local tax collection as an opportunity cost of joining the system: All that matters is the potential revenue that can be generated in each state by federal taxation. If debates on the correct distribution of revenue shares disregard local tax-collection efforts, the most vocal critics of any effort at redistribution through the revenue-sharing system should be the richer states.

[30] If h were linear, due to the INV property of the Nash solution, h would just be dropped out.

of its security of tenure, will gain a larger share than would be the case if there were atemporal horizons and certainty about the future. Governors who feel safer in their posts or who are just starting their terms will have a longer-term perspective and will hence be able to bargain for larger revenue shares.

Hence, states would accept a revenue-sharing system that validates their differing bargaining strengths vis-à-vis the federal government and each other, as reflected in their local tax bases. But this model holds only to the extent that tax collection is linked to territorial jurisdictions. If the tax base is predominantly one that is not controlled by the states, such as, for example, oil revenue, transfer systems can become highly redistributive. Thus, federal expenditures can be redistributive when there is no connection to the revenue side.

1.7. *The Latin American Federations and Fiscal Centralization*

I use the insights from the fiscal bargain models to understand how fiscal centralization was achieved in Mexico and the Latin American federations. To anticipate some of the discussion, the game of commitment highlights two dimensions that determine what kind of fiscal bargain is struck between states and the federal government. On one hand, state politicians can exercise threats to the extent that they believe their careers and political future depend on their defense of local interests. Off-the-path threats by local politicians are binding when politicians are more locally oriented but may become noncredible when politicians are nationally oriented. Hence, one can think of outcomes of centralization as being divided according to whether local politicians are nationally or locally oriented. This is the political dimension of the centralized fiscal bargain.

On the other hand, the advantages of federation determine how much additional revenue might be available to provide as transfers. If a large amount of revenue can be extracted by a coordinated federal system of taxation, the fiscal federal bargain becomes more palatable. One can think of this as a dimension that divides outcomes depending on whether the amount of revenue that is controlled directly by the federal government is high or low. This is the financial dimension of the centralized fiscal bargain. The more revenue directly controlled by the federal government, the easier it is to buy off the states or provinces. When states control taxation, much larger transfers and concessions are needed to coax them into agreeing to a centralized fiscal arrangement.

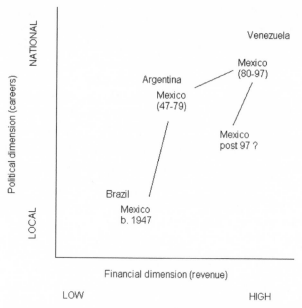

Figure 1.6. Political and financial dimensions.

Figure 1.6 depicts the possible outcomes of the combinations of variables and where the Latin American federations fit in this categorization. There are two dimensions, one political and the other financial, that can order countries from the most centralized to the most decentralized according to the sources of revenue and the structure of political ambition. In Brazil, a combination of local political entrenchment, a credible military threat on the part of the rich regions of Sao Paulo and Minas Gerais, and local control of economic resources and the fiscal base in each state led to an outcome where political careers have remained local and there are not many resources at the national level. Venezuela is an extreme opposite outcome. The lack of elected governors (until 1989), coupled with the enormous availability of revenue through oil and the strong role of the federal government, has meant that the country has been characterized by high revenue levels at the national level and national-level political careers. Finally, Argentina represents a case where local politicians, while advancing their careers in the provincial arena, enjoy significant coattails from national races, but the federal government has never had the windfalls of large revenue collection that oil can provide. Mexico has transited through all of these outcomes. Figure 1.6 suggests that no Latin American case falls in the high national revenue and local careers region, although Mexico might be moving in that direction.[31]

The account developed in this book draws on an in-depth analysis of the historical experience of Mexico throughout the 20th century. The ultimate purpose is to illustrate the logic of the dilemmas faced by federal systems in developing countries in the consolidation of national fiscal authority. I provide the rationale for the peculiar institutional solution created in Mexico, the hegemonic party, which in that particular case solved the dilemma of fiscal centralization but in the process degenerated into an extremely centralized federation. The detailed Mexican "analytic narrative" (Bates et al. 1998) is contrasted with the different paths followed by the other Latin American federations.

In Venezuela, federalism was also annulled, although the process involved a virtual transformation of the regime into a unitary one during the era of autocratic rule. The wealth of oil resources created incredible leverage for the federal government. When democracy was reestablished in 1958, local elites agreed on a power-sharing agreement that was not dissimilar from Mexico's *Partido Revolucionario Institucional* (Institutional Revolutionary Party, PRI): Long political careers were assured through the alternation of two parties in national office. As noted by Collier and Collier (1991), the AD–COPEI (Acción Democrática – Comité de Organización Política Electoral Independiente) arrangement in Venezuela was analogous in many ways to the PRI elite accommodation in Mexico.

In Argentina, the process was more complex, given that the country alternated between authoritarian and democratic regimes, while the Peronist Party constituted an "anchor" of the political arrangement. In many ways, the *Peronistas* were similar to the PRI (Gibson, 1996), but they also confronted greater threats, both from a strong democratic alternative (the *Radicales*) and a nondemocratic menace, the military. The regime's instability was reflected in the complexity of the revenue-sharing system and the frequency with which the federal government failed to keep its commitment.

In Brazil, the party system was never articulated at the national level. Local politicians continued the long tradition of politics being driven

---

[31] Nigeria can be conceived as being characterized by a rather disarticulated locally oriented system of careers, while most revenue comes from the national level through the rents from oil. Other cases that might fall in that region are decentralized regimes during wartime, which take extraordinary measures to boost federal revenues.

primarily by state governors, and notwithstanding efforts by President Getúlio Dornelles Vargas (1930–1945, 1951–1954) and the military administrations between 1964 and the 1970s, the system of revenue collection remained highly decentralized. This was a reflection of the highly fragmented and localistic features of the Brazilian political system.

In terms of the distributive features of the fiscal arrangement, the systems of federal tax transfers established in Argentina since 1934 and in Mexico since 1980 were regressive in that they were not used (and according to the logic of the Nash bargaining solution could not be used) as a compensation mechanism for poor states. On the other hand, when tax effort was no longer necessary in order to increase the size of the pie to be distributed because the federation had access to other sources of revenue, coming for example from oil, transfer systems became highly redistributive. As authoritarian regimes tinkered with the revenue-sharing system in Argentina, it became increasingly redistributive.

The outcome obtained in Venezuela was that from the outset resources were allocated among states according to population, with some degree of redistribution, because the backbone of federal finances was made up of oil revenue. In Brazil, the military governments introduced redistributive revenue-sharing formulas in the 1960s, but the most notable trait of that system was the fact that state governments never lost authority over the most important source of revenue: the sales tax. When the sales tax is considered in the calculation of Brazilian regional redistribution, it turns out that Brazil is *not* more redistributive overall than Mexico.

1.8. Plan of the Book

The various moments in Mexico's fiscal evolution structure the organization of the first part of the book. The first period, going from the aftermath of the Mexican Revolution until 1948, is marked by fiscal fragmentation. The process of what I call a "failed federal commitment" constitutes the focus of Chapter 2. I argue that during the 1920s and 1930s state and national elites in Mexico were unable to strike a regional fiscal bargain because they could not solve a commitment problem: If states gave up their capacity to tax and in exchange were promised fiscal transfers from the federal government, they had no mechanism to enforce federal compliance with its promises. After emerging from the armed conflict of the Revolution, regional strongmen could credibly threaten the federal government if it attempted to impose centralization by force. The federal government did not have enough resources to entice states into the federal bargain, so when transfers were offered in the form of the national tax conventions of 1925 and 1933, they were rejected by the states, as witnessed by the failure of those meetings.

I argue that only with the consolidation of a hegemonic party in the 1940s was the commitment problem solved, which led to the fiscal bargain of 1948 when the federal sales tax came into effect through the Third National Tax Convention. This moment marks the beginning of the end of state tax authority. Chapter 3 provides an explanation of the hegemonic party as a commitment-solving mechanism, analyzing its effects in the realm of fiscal authority. The second period, from 1948 to the early 1970s, comes with the establishment of a federal sales tax and the gradual incorporation of states into an arrangement of shared tax rates and revenue-sharing on federal excises. The sales tax proved to be a dynamic source of revenue, easy to collect and steadily increasing with industrialization and economic growth. States' finances were also booming because the fiscal bargain allowed states to collect revenue efficiently, together with federal taxes.

Political equilibrium was achieved during this period through a sophisticated system of local progressive ambition. Local politicians could follow long careers that often culminated in a governor's post. Presidents allowed local politics to flourish, influencing gubernatorial successions but by no means imposing viceroys as the conventional wisdom incorrectly suggests. The local political equilibrium enforced by the hegemonic party is analyzed in Chapter 4.

The developmental effects of the fiscal arrangement are studied through the prism of federal transfers to the states in Mexico in Chapter 5. The chapter analyzes both the revenue-sharing system and the discretionary federal investment in the states. In the second half of the 20th century, all federal governments in Latin America made massive investments in the states or provinces, consonant with an import substitution industrialization (ISI) strategy geared toward industrialization through protectionism.

The second part of the book opens up the discussion to a comparative perspective. Chapters 6, 7, and 8 contrast the development of fiscal authority in Mexico with that of the other Latin American federations, namely Venezuela, Argentina, and Brazil. In contrast to Mexico, Brazilian states never gave up their tax authority. Venezuela, on the other hand, witnessed a process of tax abdication much earlier than any of the other Latin American federations. Argentina's fiscal federalism reflected the instability of its political regimes. As I will argue, each fiscal arrangement was reflected in the

31

nature of the regime, the party systems, and the configuration of regional interests. The chapters also deal with the redistributive consequences and the political determinants of the allocation of transfers among states and provinces in each country. The final chapter concludes with some reflections about the significance of the findings of this book for the study of nation-building, fiscal politics, federalism, and regional compensation and redistribution.

Appendix to Chapter 1

Proof of proposition: First one must find the optimal level of effort. I take advantage of the fact that the Nash solution implies Pareto optimality. Hence, administrative effort (e) will be maximized in each state and is given by the first-order condition of optimal effort:

$$f_i'(e_i) = p_i.$$

Effort will thus be allocated to federal tax administration in each state up to the point where the marginal revenue generated by that effort is equal to the marginal value of the revenue shares received. That condition uniquely determines the optimal level of e and hence the total revenue collected by federal taxation.

The crucial question then is to determine, given an optimal e^*, what will be the level of revenue shares assigned by the federal government.

The Nash solution entails

$$\arg\max_{d \leq s \in S} \prod_{i=1}^{n+1} (s_i - d_i).$$

It is convenient to explicitly show the difference between any agreement and the disagreement point, for each state, as

$$e_i p_i + r_i [E_i - e_i] - E_i r_i = e_i [p_i - r_i].$$

Therefore, the Nash solution is the maximum value solved for every p of the multiplication of each difference times the residual claim of the federal government when there is an agreement:

$$\arg\max_{p_i \leq r_i} \prod_{i=1}^{n} e_i^* (p_i - r_i) \sum_{i=1}^{n} [f_i(e_i) - p_i e_i^*].$$

In order to maximize this expression, I single out one state i and separate it from the rest of the states so that the maximization involves finding the first-order conditions, with respect to p_i, of the expression

$$\varphi = \left(\sum_{j \neq i}^{n-1} [f_j(e_j^*) - p_j e_j^*] + [f_i(e_i^*) - p_i e_i^*] \right) \prod_{j \neq i}^{n-1} e_j^*(p_j - r_j) e_i^*(p_i - r_i),$$

where the j terms are constant for each maximization. The constraint of $r < p < f(e)/e$ ensures that the federal government's budget constraint is satisfied so that there are enough funds to pay every optimal revenue share.

The first-order conditions yield

$$P_i^* = \left. \frac{\sum_{j \neq i}^{n-1} [f_j(e_j^*) - p_j e_j^*] + f_i(e_i^*)}{e_i^*} + r_i \middle/ 2, \right.$$

which after using the definitions of P_i and R_i yields the expression in the theorem. QED.

PART I

Fiscal Centralization in Mexico

This book argues that the commitment problem in the dilemma of fiscal centralization was solved in the case of Mexico through a hegemonic party system. I show that the *Partido Revolucionario Institucional* (PRI), which ruled Mexico for seven decades, created a regional compromise: Local elites could maintain relative autonomy, being protected with the power and money of the federal government, while national elites could exercise discretion in the use of national financial resources in order to pursue a "developmentalist" strategy through import substituting industrialization (ISI).[1] Moreover, local elites were willing to go along with this arrangement because the center ensured a flow of financial transfers and respected their local political careers as long as they did not run into conflict with the federal ambition ladder.[2]

The consequences of this regional pact were perverse. On the one hand, Mexican federalism was diminished and political practices were far from any democratic ideal; on the other, regional development suffered because resources were concentrated in the regions that benefited from the centralized model of development. The arrangement was sustained for a long time because it was a strategic political equilibrium. Neither regional nor national elites would benefit from redrawing the federal pact. This arrangement was no longer feasible after the 1990s, once the center ceased to be

---

[1] Although, as noted by Steve Haber (personal communication), incipient efforts at industrialization can be traced back to the 19th century, the idea of developmentalism is usually associated with the 20th century in Latin America (Sikkink, 1991).

[2] Chhibber and Kollman (2004) have argued that the nationalization of party systems in the United States, Canada, Britain, and India was the consequence of the centralization of fiscal resources. I argue that in Mexico these processes occurred simultaneously.

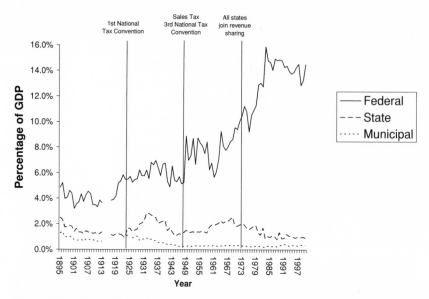

Figure I.1. Size of federal, state, and municipal governments in Mexico.

able to provide resources for patronage and protection from local electoral threats.

The process of fiscal centralization is reflected in the national public finances throughout the century. At the turn of the 19th century, during the so-called *Porfiriato*, the stable autocratic administrations of Porfirio Diaz (1877–1880, 1884–1911), federal government revenues amounted to around 4 percent of GDP. Since the 1950s, the size of the federal government (excluding public sector agencies) grew, coming to represent around 13 percent of GDP since the 1980s. The increase in federal tax authority was not just an expansion of the federal sphere but was inextricably connected to the erosion of tax authority at the state and municipal levels. Figure I.1 shows the relative sizes of the federal, state (including the Federal District), and municipal governments in Mexico, measured through tax collection, as a percentage of GDP.[3]

Relative to the size of the economy, state and municipal governments in Mexico became less important as the 20th century progressed. The graph

[3] Because this is measured through tax authority, the graph differs both in its levels and composition from what would be observed if measuring expenditures, which would include debt financing.

reveals that municipal tax collection was well above 1 percentage point of GDP since the late 1880s and then abruptly declined in the 1930s and 1940s to a level of less than half a percentage point of GDP, where it is today.[4] This is a rather low share, particularly considering that since 1983 municipal governments have controlled collections from the property tax. The size of state governments goes through various shifts. At different peaks – during the *Porfiriato*, in the 1930s, and in the late 1960s – state tax collection amounted to around 3 percent of GDP. Since the 1970s, however, a steady decline in revenue collection by state governments to levels below one and a half percentage points of GDP is observed.[5]

This process of fiscal centralization was not steady. A great deal of centralization occurred during the 1940s and 1950s, but it was reversed in the 1960s, only to steadily grow again during the 1970s and 1980s. A reversal in the process of centralization, which is seen in the steady increase in state revenue during the 1960s, suggests that subnational governments retained a larger degree of autonomy than what most of the literature on Mexican politics has suggested. The conventional account claims that after the Mexican Revolution, when regional strongmen were prevalent, the emergence of the hegemonic party in 1929 steadily decreased the importance of governors, states, and local politicians: All politics became national.

In a similar vein, Riker dismissed Mexico as a "unitary [system], while maintaining the trappings of a bygone federalism" (Riker, 1964:86–88). According to Riker, "federalisms in which the central government is invariably able to overawe the constituent governments, vis. Mexico, the Soviet Union and Yugoslavia" (Riker, 1964:130) should not really be considered federal. Riker's treatment of the Latin American federations was superficial at best. As my account of the process of fiscal centralization in Mexico suggests, although the PRI ended up muting federalism and overawing the states, fiscal centralization was not completely achieved until the 1980s. States in Mexico were far more powerful than what conventional accounts suggest. During much of the 20th century, the federal government's attempts to centralize revenue repeatedly failed, and it was not until the windfall of oil revenue into federal finances that states became fully dependent on federal transfers and finally ceded their authority to tax.

[4] Municipalities or localities in a typical OECD (Organization For Economic Cooperation and Development) country collect revenue of around 1 percent of GDP.
[5] These figures would be even lower if one excluded the Federal District, which strictly speaking is not a state but accounts for one-third of the state-level revenue collection.

Figure I.1 highlights three moments in the formation of fiscal authority in Mexico that structure the coming chapters. The first moment starts with the First National Tax Convention, in which the federal government failed to provide a credible commitment for a centralized fiscal arrangement. The failures at fiscal centralization are the main focus of the next chapter. The second moment starts with the creation of the federal sales tax and the Third National Tax Convention in 1947. During that period, the federal government and the states were able to strike a balance in which the former pursued a centralized fiscal arrangement while the states retained fiscal authority. This second moment is the focus of Chapters 3 and 4, which study the Mexican official party as a regional compromise and local power and governor stability in the Mexican states. The last moment indicated in the graph starts when all states join the revenue-sharing agreement, leading to the ultimate fiscal centralization scholars often associate with Mexico. The bargaining over the allocation of resources and the distributive consequences of fiscal centralization are the primary focus of Chapter 5, which concludes Part I of the book.

2

Regional Fragmentation and Failed Commitment

2.1. Taxation, Federalism, and the Dilemma of Regional Development

Taxation lies at the boundary where politics meets economics. In the classical political economy of Adam Smith and David Ricardo, the structure of the tax system (including tariffs restricting trade) determined the development prospects of a country. Fiscal institutions are shaped by the struggle between political organizations and private interests, the former seeking revenue and the latter protecting their assets. In order to collect revenue, rulers must overcome complex issues of measurement, compliance, and monitoring (North, 1981; Levi, 1988). Once tax authorities establish mechanisms to measure the tax base as well as detect and punish tax evasion, such institutions are difficult to change. Adding to the stability of the fiscal system, powerful economic interest groups will lobby to prevent the loss of tax exemptions. Even when not efficient, tax institutions are often stable, changing only when they experience shocks, such as a war, or unexpected windfall revenues (Steinmo, 1993).

Studying the institutional arrangements of tax systems provides a particularly clear view of politics (Schumpeter, 1991[1918]; Steinmo, 1993). Powerful economic and political actors are usually shielded from expropriation or excessive taxation, as reflected in tax institutions, under both democratic and nondemocratic systems. In democracies, representative organizations, court systems, or specific arrangements that divide power – such as the division of federal power into state jurisdictions – provide for effective vetoes to avoid radically redistributive decisions (see North and

Weingast, 1989; Acemoglu and Robinson, 2001).[1] Under nondemocratic regimes, powerful economic interests often capture state bureaucracies to shield their activities from taxation and sometimes even obtain favorable expenditure allocations.[2]

Mexico provides an example of the difficulty faced by a large country seeking to lay the foundations for political order and prosperity in the aftermath of a social revolution. Local governments taxed in the most expedient way, notwithstanding the consequences that their revenue collection activities had on interstate trade or the level of economic activity in the country as a whole.[3] From the point of view of each local government, such behavior was fully rational: Why limit opportunities for taxation if every other state was also taxing? State politicians were aware, however, that an alternative arrangement was possible and even desirable. Such an arrangement involved the delegation of authority to a federal regime in which revenue could be collected in a centralized manner and states compensated for curbing their tax authority through transfers.

The prospect of improved fiscal arrangements led state executives to accept the invitation by the federal government to national tax conventions in 1925 and 1933. The conventions proposed a simple solution to the problem of tax fragmentation: States would retain authority over property (land) taxes, but the federal government would possess the exclusive authority to levy taxes on industry and trade, providing states with transfers to compensate them for their foregone revenue. The proposals from those conventions were never approved by the Chamber of Deputies. Consonant with the commitment model in the last chapter, I argue that the centralized fiscal arrangement failed because it was not self-enforcing. It required

---

[1] Adam Przeworski (1990) discusses why the extension of the franchise in advanced industrial democracies did not lead to a radical redistributive strategy by social democratic governments as the conservatives of the turn of the century believed would be the case. For a more general theoretical statement of the problem, see Przeworski (1985), and for the development of a formal model in the median voter framework, see Acemoglu and Robinson (2001).

[2] The review by Hettich and Winer (1997) on the political economy of taxation shows how little research actually exists that provides a link between the presence of democratic or nondemocratic institutions and the tax structure or explains the variance of tax systems within democratic systems as a reflection of underlying institutional or political differences. (For a study in OECD countries, see Swank and Steinmo, 2002.)

[3] This view of interjurisdictional competition as harmful is at odds with much of the literature on local government in the United States, which views local taxation as a virtuous arrangement that leads to competition and greater government efficiency (see Inman and Rubinfeld, 1997).

states to trust the federal government to provide fiscal transfers, regardless of the federal government's own revenue needs. The federal government possessed no commitment mechanism to make a transfer system credible. The status quo remained, with overlapping taxation and fragmentation that limited the opportunities for the expansion of markets, trade and specialization, or the emergence of redistributive transfers.

The discussion of the failed Mexican tax conventions provides an opportunity to show that federalism is not, by itself, self-enforcing. When the mobility of resources is limited, federal systems can multiply potential state predation because they increase the number of constituent jurisdictions. Federalism in this case will not promote economic performance unless a way is found to constrain local governments. When factor mobility is limited at relatively low levels of development, such restraint is only possible when states can trust the federal government. In terms of the model presented in Chapter 1, the discussion in this chapter suggests that a centralized fiscal bargain that might have made every government better off was unachievable because of the lack of a regional compromise.

This chapter is organized as follows. The next section provides a brief historical overview of the Mexican tax system at the beginning of the 20th century, discussing the perverse incentives that political fragmentation generated for economic growth. Section 2.3 analyzes the debates in the First National Tax Convention (1925), calculating state "ideal points" in an issue dimension of conflict and explaining the factors that polarized states' positions. That section provides an understanding of why the richer and larger states could not trust the federal government, and it distinguishes structural and coalitional factors explaining such distrust. Section 2.4 discusses the Second National Tax Convention (1933), also calculating state issue positions and addressing the social choice problems that made the agreement in that meeting very fragile. The Second Convention ultimately failed because it left too much discretion to the federal government. Finally, Section 2.5 introduces the role of political parties as commitment-generating devices, a discussion that is then developed in Chapter 3.

2.2. The Mexican Fiscal System after the Revolution

The Mexican Revolution (1911–1917) provoked a loss of regional integration in the country. Production was disrupted, and trade was reduced by the destruction of the means of transportation and by the partition of markets. Although political arrangements might have allowed for growth in specific sectors, as demonstrated by Haber, Razo, and Maurer (2003), the protection provided by warlords and their claim to political authority were tenuous at best. When national reconstruction started in the 1920s, local politicians sought to create a national market. The local factions emerging from the Revolution did not agree, however, on how to do so; nor, in particular, could they agree on how powerful the national government should be.

In the aftermath of the Mexican Revolution, the most pressing problem was the establishment of clear property rights, especially in agriculture. Land reform was carried out in the early phases of the armed conflict, particularly in the central highlands, but it slowed during the 1920s when the central government attempted to base economic development on small private plots. Moving in the opposite direction, "radical" state governments (among others, those of Lázaro Cárdenas in Michoacán or Adalberto Tejeda in Veracruz) pursued land distribution on the basis of communal landholdings (*ejidos*). The coexistence of these two models of agricultural production created insecurity in land tenure because producers did not know what type of organization would prevail in the end. This also led to a legacy of governors who could either be considered to be more to the right or to the left of the political spectrum in the coming decades.

The second major problem was that Mexico in the 1920s did not have the institutional conditions that could produce limited government (both in the federal and the local spheres). In a way, Mexico during the 1920s resembled an institutional system almost opposite to that observed in England after the Glorious Revolution by North and Weingast, where "increasing the number of veto players implied that a larger set of constituencies could protect themselves against political assault, thus markedly reducing the circumstances under which opportunistic behavior by the government could take place" (North and Weingast, 1989:829). In Mexico, federalism multiplied the opportunities for predatory behavior by state elites rather than creating more veto players or limited government. To be sure, federalism allowed regional strongmen to place constraints on the federal government, but predatory behavior trumped any beneficial effect veto players might have had on the system. This problem was illustrated most clearly in revenue collection.

Economic growth required an expansion of markets, but the revenue requirements of state governments generated tax systems that hindered the free mobility of goods and services, hence restricting markets within local jurisdictions. The federal government adopted a more prominent role in the economy after the 1940s, which was made possible by the centralization

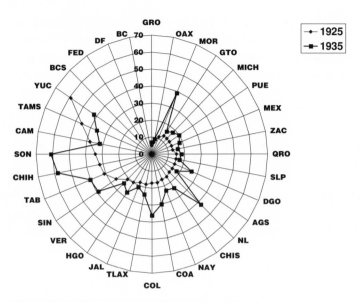

Figure 2.1.   State revenue collection per capita.

of the party system. This led to a state-led strategy of development that produced moderate economic growth. Coordination in taxation among regions and a greater role for federal financial transfers were orchestrated once the party could make credible fiscal promises. The hegemonic party led to the relinquishment of federalism. But the abdication of tax authority by the states was a protracted process that could not have been anticipated from studying the first decades of hegemonic party rule.

Before the 1940s, states exercised fiscal authority freely. Figure 2.1 shows tax collection by state governments in per capita terms in 1925 and 1935. The way to read the graph is by noting the clockwise ordering of states according to their per capita revenue collection in 1925. The axis in the graph represents an index where federal per capita revenue collection is 100. Hence, to the extent that a state is far from the center, it is collecting more revenue. States closest to the center of the graph have the weakest tax authority. Poor states in the south, such as Guerrero or Oaxaca, collected very little revenue compared with the federal government (around 6 percent of the federal per capita amount). Some states, however, were collecting revenue equivalents, in per capita terms, of around 60 percent of the federal collection (Yucatán in 1925, while the international price of its main export crop, sisal, was high, and the agriculturally prosperous states of Sonora and

Chihuahua in 1935).[4] The two years roughly correspond to the dates of the first and second national tax conventions. It is clear from the graph that most states had higher revenue collection in 1935 than 10 years earlier relative to that of the federal government. Some states, however, suffered some setbacks in their tax collection, mostly attributable to the use of tax bases that fluctuated according to the international prices of the commodities the states exported.

The graph represents the degree to which states varied in their fiscal authority as compared with that of the federal government. If tax authority and revenue collection can be translated into power, the ordering of states can be interpreted as an indicator of the power of individual states compared with the national government. Of course, this measure of "power" needs to be qualified by the relative size of a state among other things, because a very small state, even with high revenue collection in per capita terms, would probably pose little threat to the federal government. Nonetheless, it is safe to say that the capacity to tax citizens, and therefore state power, was very limited in some states.[5] Moreover, because the index of per capita revenue collection for 1935 is above that for 1925 for almost all states, it is likely that state power increased in that time interval.

According to the Mexican Constitution of 1917, states were free and sovereign with regard to their internal regime (art. 40), and citizens had to contribute to cover federal, state, and municipal expenses (art. 31-IV). Hence state governments were free to determine their own tax laws and collect revenue within their jurisdictions. All taxes were concurrent except when explicitly granted to the federal sphere as exclusive taxes not to be levied by local governments. The constitution included a limitation of state fiscal authority in article 117, forbidding state taxes from hindering inter-state trade through the taxation of the movement of goods or anything resembling local tariffs. But in the aftermath of the Mexican Revolution, states did not abide by the constitutional rules and simply imposed any taxes they saw fit.

---

[4] The graph does not provide per capita revenue collection for the two federal territories (Baja California Norte and Baja California Sur), the Federal District, and the federal government, only their ranking. Per capita revenue collection in Mexico City and the sparsely populated federal territories was much larger than in the states.

[5] Rich agricultural states (Sonora and Chihuahua), states where incipient industrialization was taking place (Nuevo León), or states enjoying windfall revenue from high prices for their exports (sisal in Yucatán or oil in Tamaulipas) could pose a real challenge to the federal government, which would presumably be reflected in their bargaining power.

Beneath the overall levels of state revenue collection depicted in Figure 2.1, the structure of local taxes was often chaotic and inefficient. Given the financial disarray of both local and federal governments, public expenditures were usually financed by debt or by printing money, and taxes were levied by local governments on whatever was most expedient. The federal government primarily relied on customs duties for its revenue. The phantom of the *alcabala* – the colonial tax on the movement of goods across jurisdictions, which inhibited the extension of markets well into the late 19th century – haunted the regional economies of Mexico during the first three postrevolutionary decades.[6] Local governments relied on taxes on immobile assets or transactions that could be easily measured and superintended. Immobile property taxes, although they produced high yields, were hard to measure and collect. Therefore, the preferred tax base was market transactions or internal tariffs disguised through specific taxes on commodities at the stages of production or sale. Mexico did not have an integrated national market, even as some producers might have been benefiting from the opportunities afforded by international trade in specific commodities. Given the destruction and inadequacy of the physical infrastructure and the collapse of the financial system, producers focusing on the domestic market had few exit options to protect their assets from local taxation.[7]

Figure 2.2 shows the composition of state revenue around 1928 in a barycentric (ternary) plot. The graph suggests that the variation in state extractive capacity was accompanied by wide differences in the choice of instruments of taxation. The way to read the figure is to note that each corner of the triangle corresponds to 100 percent of state revenue being collected from land (property), industry, or excise taxes. Combinations of revenue collection move away from those vertices into the center, which would represent a state where each type of tax contributes equally to revenue. States falling along the lines of the triangle represent combinations of only two types of taxes. For example, in many states excise taxes collected very little or did not exist, so there are many states aligned along the

---

[6] For an in-depth study of the *alcabala* in colonial times, see Caravaglia and Grosso (1987); for the 19th-century discussions attempting to get rid of this tax on the movement of goods across regions, see Carmagnani (1993).

[7] There was little tax competition among states because productive activities that would have been highly mobile across regions, such as industrial activity, were overwhelmingly attracted to Mexico City and Monterrey because of favorable conditions in transport, mass demand, skill of the labor force, and even subsidies on crucial inputs such as electricity (See Romero Kolbeck and Urquidi, 1952; Yates, 1961).

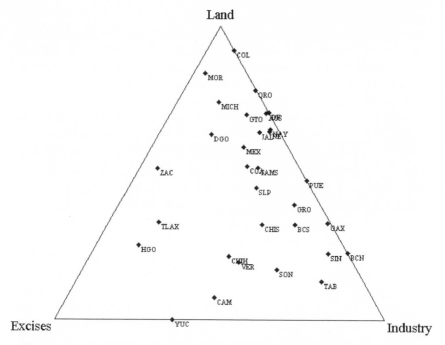

Figure 2.2. Revenue composition of state governments in 1928.

right-hand side of the triangle. However, a state such as Yucatán, with one of the strongest tax collection systems in the 1920s, did not collect any revenue from property taxes and instead relied heavily on taxing its sisal exports. Tamaulipas, the state with the strongest tax collection in 1925, had a relatively modern, balanced tax base that relied relatively more on property taxes and less on excises than most other states. The graph in Figure 2.2 makes it clear that most states relied on a combination of taxes on land and industry.

Taxes on industry were levied in such a way that they limited the mobility of merchandise across jurisdictions, and in this sense they were internal tariffs. If excises and taxes on industry were to become an exclusive prerogative of the federal government, states that relied more heavily on them were more likely to oppose tax centralization. Taxes on industry were considered to be the most distortional on economic activity because they often constituted implicit tariffs. Excises were most often criticized on the grounds of their transaction costs and the effect of differential rates, suggesting that collection and enforcement would be improved with a single rate in a centralized administrative system. In line with the current tax-design policy prescriptions, property taxes were considered the least distortional of local levies.

Alberto J. Pani, the charismatic federal finance minister who convoked governors to the tax conventions, diagnosed the fiscal situation of the states in 1925 in a way that became the standard diagnosis of Mexican fiscal federalism for the next 30 years:

> Each state establishes its own revenue system, the Federal Government maintains its own, and since the objects taxed happen to be the same, since there is no concrete and defined plan for the limitation between the federal capacity and the local capacities to create taxes, since states often rival each other, leading into true economic wars and creating, in the name of a sales tax, true local import duties in order to sustain internal production taxes that are incorrectly established, the tax becomes increasingly burdensome due to the multiplicity of rates, fines and penalties, increasing the complexity of the system and increasing in a disproportionate and unjustifiable manner the deadweight expenses for revenue collection, surveillance and administration. (My translation, "Primera Convención Nacional Fiscal," [CNF1]: 6)[8]

The conclusion, repeated again and again during the first half of the century, was that the prevailing tax system fragmented the economic unity of the country, that this "fiscal anarchy" hindered economic growth, and that it imposed a disproportionate share of the tax burden on just a few contributors.[9] Despite the fact that this conclusion was shared by both federal and local politicians, they were unable to solve the collective dilemma of providing themselves with a unified – or at least more coherent – system of taxation across regions.

The First National Tax Convention (*Primera Convención Nacional Fiscal*, CNF1) was convened by the federal government as an explicit attempt to eliminate the multiplicity of what at the time were called the "anti-economic" (i.e., inefficient) taxes levied by state governments, and sought

---

[8] It is worth noting that this is perhaps the most often quoted observation about the problem of fiscal coordination in Mexico, as witnessed by the reference made to it in the Second Convention in 1933 (CNF2, Vol. 1:3–4), the articles by Vázquez Santaella (1938) and Silva (1941), the Third Convention in 1947 (CNF3, Vol. 1:27), and the National Investment Program of 1953–1958 (*Antología de la Planeación en México* 1985:835).

[9] It might be noted that Pani was not just a disinterested third party but a player representing his political and economic interests. (I thank Steve Haber for this insight.) However, Pani was first and foremost an institutional creator, and within his somewhat technocratic mold, it is clear from reading his writings that he believed this diagnosis was grounded in economic theory and best practice around the world.

to substitute them with general income and sales taxes exclusively in the federal jurisdiction. States would not be able to tax industry or trade but would instead be compensated with a share of the revenue collected in each of their jurisdictions through unconditional transfers (at the time called *arbitrios*, known today as *participaciones*) granted by the federal government. Property taxes would remain exclusively local revenue sources. This design would complement the newly created income tax, which would remain in the federal jurisdiction and would presumably become, together with some excises, the most important source of revenue, gradually replacing customs duties.

The convention had a paradoxical result: Although state delegations approved a bill for constitutional reform creating a new tax system, their recommendations were not accepted by the federal congress. An explanation of this outcome hinges on exploring the configuration of state interests, the decision processes of the assembly, and the political coalitions of the time. In a nutshell, I argue that the convention recommendations failed largely because they did not create a credible mechanism through which the federal government would promise to respect the interests of rich and large states. A majority of state delegations had approved the recommendations, but this majority did not include the states most affected by the arrangement.

The Second National Tax Convention (*Segunda Convención Nacional Fiscal*, CNF2) revisited the conclusions of the first meeting, attempting to generate a coherent system of fiscal coordination. In addition to the unsolved problems that the First Convention had identified, by 1933 there was a new source of fiscal tension: States were being treated unevenly by the federal government. The most important transfer between states and the federation at the time was the *contribución federal*, a transfer of around 25 percent of state taxation *to* the federal government. After the failure of the First Convention, the federal government made individual deals with the states, exempting them from the *contribución federal* if they were willing to eliminate their taxes on industry and excises. Around half of the states accepted this deal. The differential fiscal treatment was regarded by many as another example of the arbitrariness and scope for abuse by the federal government.

The Second Convention met the same fate as the first, although the sources of failure were somewhat different. In addition to the incapacity of the federal government to create a credible commitment to a transfer system, states were caught in a social choice dilemma: The sources of conflict among states no longer reflected a unique dimension that pitted large and rich states against the federal government, but they now involved additional dimensions of conflict that were related to the differential tax structures that had made states willing to make individual deals with the federal government rather than coordinate and agree on a comprehensive fiscal arrangement for all. I now turn to a discussion of the First National Tax Convention.

2.3. Explaining the National–Local Cleavage in the First National Tax Convention

The First National Tax Convention met in an effort to create a coherent national tax system. The invitation was made by the federal secretary of the treasury to all the state governors to discuss a system of tax "settlement" that would eliminate the overlapping local taxes and substitute them with a national sales tax. In the proposal, states would retain the exclusive authority over the land tax and receive a transfer from the federal government. Specifically, the federal government offered the state governments a tax system that involved eliminating local taxes on industry and trade, converting an exclusively local property tax into the backbone of state public finances. In exchange for the abolition of those state taxes that were to become exclusively federal, the national government would provide financial transfers according to a revenue distribution system, the *Plan Nacional de Arbitrios*. The agreement promised to make everyone better off by expanding economic opportunities and increasing revenue through higher tax yields. The alternative was to retain the status quo, a system of overlapping taxation and fragmented markets.

The federal government sought centralization. Where did this preference come from? It is important to note that the federal government was not just some form of aggregation of the regional interests as expressed by the states. In the aftermath of the Revolution, politicians from the various regions in Mexico had different motivations, interests, and priorities. The federal politicians had interests of their own, even when they had some regional strongholds in the regions they came from (Calles in Sonora and Cárdenas in Michoacán, for example). The heterogeneous nature of their territories and the specific social structures of each state shaped their policy preferences regarding a national tax system. Except for anecdotal evidence, no systematic mapping of state interests or governor preferences over a policy space has ever been made to distinguish state positions from those of the federal government. The national tax conventions, however, provide a unique opportunity to infer exactly these political preferences using the voting behavior of state delegations.

In contrast with the federal Chamber of Deputies or the Senate, where individual roll call votes have rarely been recorded in postrevolutionary Mexican history, the proceedings of the national tax conventions include information on individual voting patterns on different issues that reflect the fiscal debates of the time.[10] Executive dominance and parliamentary discipline were not imposed by the PRI until the second half of the century. During the 1920s and 1930s, contentious debates took place in the federal congress, whereby local politicians often defended state interests in the legislative arena. Most accounts agree that legislators at the time were primarily agents of their state governors (Garrido, 1982:51–55; Weldon, 1996).[11] Unfortunately, because the parliamentary records registered only final vote tallies, studying the federal legislature does not provide information on the policy positions of states or individual legislators.

The records of the first and second national tax conventions, on the other hand, contain roll call votes by the state delegations on proposals reported by committees. Most votes were taken under a closed rule, which in this case meant that when a committee recommendation was discussed and rejected on the floor, it was returned to the committee rather than allowing amendments to be proposed on the floor. Delegates had no power over the voting agenda because agenda-setting power was given to the federal delegation presiding over the deliberations, so opportunities for strategic voting were limited, and hence voting patterns can be regarded as sincere statements of preferences. Moreover, copious information is available about the delegates, the committee structure, the ordering of agendas, and the issues under debate, as well as the circumstances of each state during the time of the conventions. The analysis of the voting behavior of state delegations

[10] To my knowledge, the only roll call analysis of the Mexican Senate during the *Porfiriato* is that of Razo (2003). After the defeat of the PRI in the 1997 congressional elections, Jeffrey Weldon (personal communication) analyzed roll call votes in the Chamber of Deputies and calculated "nominate" scores.

[11] In fact, at that time, one often observed that presidential initiatives were defeated in the Chamber of Deputies because they were not congenial with governors interests. Perhaps the only systematic analysis of Congress during this time is by Weldon (1996). In this groundbreaking study, he finds that much of the conventional story of excessive presidential power during the period, namely the 1920s and 1930s, is simply wrong.

in the conventions provides a unique insight into the political cleavages among Mexican states at the time.[12]

Voting choices can be used to infer the ideal points or policy positions of each state delegation. Ideal points provide indicators of how close or how far each state delegate stood from other state delegates and from the federal delegation. If one state delegation frequently voted with another, their positions can be considered "closer" in a policy space. Although there are several techniques that can be used to infer ideal points in a legislature, two methodological problems call for a careful choice of technique for the case of the Mexican conventions. First, a small number of votes were cast from which to draw inferences. Second, there are many missing values in the roll calls either because of abstentions or absences of individual delegates. Techniques that can map voting positions, such as multidimensional scaling or factor analysis, have been used extensively to analyze the dynamics of choice in assemblies with roll call votes (Poole and Rosenthal, 1987; Jillson and Wilson, 1994). However, a Bayesian simulation approach is most appropriate to deal with the small n and missing value problems just noted.[13]

Clinton, Jackman, and Rivers (2004) offer such a Bayesian estimation method. Using Markov chain Monte Carlo methods, the Bayesian method finds a joint posterior density function for n legislators, m roll calls, and a d-dimensional policy space. The technique can be easily implemented through IDEAL, a program developed by Simon Jackman.[14] An advantage of a Bayesian method is that informative priors can be used to gain

---

[12] In the discussion throughout this chapter, I refer to states, governors, local executives, and state delegates in a loose fashion, meaning in all cases the local politician or politicians who make decisions in each state. Within a rational-choice perspective, states as institutions do not have preferences or interest; it is the politicians and officeholders who head the organizations that embody the states who do. For a defense of this position, see, among others, Ostrom (1991) and Elster (1989a, 1989b). For a thoughtful critique of methodological individualism, provided from a functionalist perspective in anthropology, see Douglas (1986).

[13] In Diaz–Cayeros (1997), I used multidimensional scaling to estimate ideal points of the national tax conventions. Although the results are not too different, the Bayesian method is more robust.

[14] I thank Simon Jackman for clarifying some issues of estimation and for his help with running the IDEAL software in two dimensions. Londregan (2000b) offers an alternative for estimation of ideal points with small n in a maximum likelihood approach where agendas are used to constrain the parameter space. A substantive application of this alternative approach is found in Londregan's (2000a) analysis of committees in the Chilean Senate.

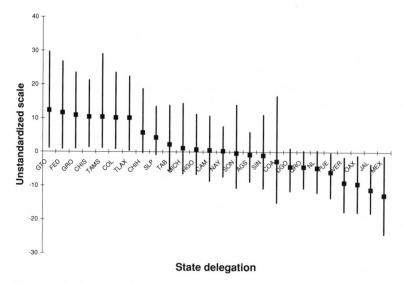

Figure 2.3. Latent national–local dimension in First National Tax Convention.

better insight into the substantive meaning of the dimensions emerging from the analysis. Moreover, the Bayesian method can impute abstentions and absences by treating them as missing at random values.

Figure 2.3 provides estimates of the ideal positions of each state and the federal delegation along a one-dimensional issue space obtained from the IDEAL procedure applied to the votes in the First National Tax Convention.[15] The vertical axis provides a scale that denotes the position of each individual state and the federal government in a policy dimension that can be thought of as a national–local cleavage. This means that the policy position and distance between states must be read on that scale, although states are ordered on the horizontal axis according to their ideal points. The bands around each point estimate provide a 95 percent confidence interval of each state position. Given only 10 recorded roll call votes, the error bands in the state positions are relatively large.

Nonetheless, it is safe to say that states on the negative end of the scale are those that most opposed the concentration of tax authority in the national government. The policy dimension shows the willingness of state governments to abide by the federal proposal of a national system of federal

[15] The simulation was run 5,000 times, sampling observations every 10th time, with a burnout period of 250.

52

transfers (the so-called *Plan Nacional de Arbitrios*) and to accept the elimination of local taxes restricting trade or overlapping with federal ones, restricting their tax authority only to collecting a local property tax. Hence I call the scale the national–local dimension.

Note that the six delegations with the highest scores are at virtually the same position as the federal government (the national end of the scale). These states voted, in each roll call, in the same direction as the federal government. The IDEAL procedure exaggerates the level of uncertainty regarding the estimates for those states: From a statistical standpoint, the standard errors are wide because of the random process of simulation. However, there is really little uncertainty concerning these positions because we know after the fact that those states always voted with the federal government. This "unconditional" block of states probably would have accepted the federal proposals that were reflected in the committee referrals even without calling for a convention because roll calls suggest their preferences were akin to those of the federal delegation.

For a proposal to be adopted as a recommendation, the rules of the convention required that the federal delegation and at least 15 states support it; that is, they required an absolute and distributed majority. The federal government had veto power over the recommendations, but it needed to garner the support of enough states to get any proposal passed. Hence, to get any recommendation approved, the federal delegation always needed nine states, beyond the "unconditional" block, for a majority. Eleven states in the midrange of the national–local dimension therefore became decisive: They were most likely to shift a vote in favor of the federal delegation.[16] The states at the negative end of the scale remained distant from the federation, hardly ever voting along with the federal delegation. This is clear from the fact that, even considering the wide error bands, one can be quite confident that the eight states to the extreme left were not in the same issue position as the federal delegation.

In this analysis, I conceive of the federal government as being primarily motivated by the desire of a group of ambitious politicians, who had successfully consolidated their hold onto power, to collect revenue and remain in office. In this sense, I want to be clear that my conception assumes that even though politicians might have ideological leanings and preferences

---

[16] This is the same as saying that, assuming only connected winning coalitions form (Tsebelis and Garrett, 1996), these states were pivotal most of the time because a winning coalition, given the accepted rules, always included the federal vote.

for some policies, their overriding concern was to pursue their political ambitions to remain in control of the federal government and to obtain revenue in a predatory manner. This does not mean that political ambition at the federal level could be pursued with no constraints: State politicians were the main restriction and their most powerful potential challengers. Nor does this mean that federal revenue extraction could be obtained easily: Other political actors in the states competed for the same sources of revenue, and citizens resisted the extraction of revenue to the extent they could.

What I have called the unconditional block (all the states to the left of Chihuahua, which always voted with the federal delegation) was mainly the result of political alliances. The unconditional block includes Tamaulipas, probably reflecting the political alliances of presidents Alvaro Obregón (1920–1924) and Plutarco E. Calles (1924–1928) with the powerful politicians who dominated the politics of that state. Emilio Portes Gil (governor of Tamaulipas from 1925 to 1928 and provisional president from 1928 to 1930) was crucial in the power-sharing arrangement between regional and local bosses (*caudillos*) achieved by Calles after 1929. Some states belonged to the unconditional group because they lacked independent military power. Tlaxcala is perhaps the clearest case, although its closeness to the federal position could be the outcome of what Buve (1990) has argued was a mutually beneficial and highly pragmatic alliance between one of the local factions seeking power in that state and the victors of the Revolution. A similar explanation could account for Chiapas, where the governor took office only because he enjoyed federal military support.[17]

States in the midrange of the scale, from Chihuahua to Coahuila, can be thought of as the "pivotal" states making a pragmatic alliance with the federal government. They include Chihuahua, where the powerful Northern Division of Francisco Villa (and his brother Hipólito, who had supported a rebellion by Adolfo de la Huerta in 1924) had only recently been defeated by the federal army. Michoacán, San Luis Potosí, Hidalgo, and Tabasco were all characterized by extremely powerful local bosses (*caciques*), some of whom survived well into the latter part of the 20th century. Saturnino Cedillo in San Luis Potosí has often been characterized as the archetypical example of a powerful regional boss in this period (see Falcón, 1984;

---

[17] Paradoxically, when Chiapas governor Carlos Vidal opposed Obregón's reelection in 1928, his rebellion was crushed and he was summarily executed, being substituted by still another federally imposed governor (Benjamin, 1990:79).

Martínez Assad, 1990b).[18] Michoacán was governed by Lázaro Cárdenas (military governor in 1920, who would become the constitutional governor in 1928 and president in 1934). Another pivotal state, Coahuila, was then governed by General Manuel Pérez Treviño, who became a crucial ally of President Calles and the first secretary general of the official party, the Partido Nacional Revolutionario (National Revolutionary Party, PNR), which was founded in 1929. The previous strongman of Coahuila, Venustiano Carranza (president 1917–1920), had been overthrown in a coup led by the Sonora faction of the revolution in 1920.[19] Sonora was the home state of the triumphant revolutionaries, although it had just gone through the upheaval of the de la Huerta rebellion.[20] Interestingly, all of these states appear to have shared a structural characteristic, namely that the base of support of their governors was mainly rural.

Finally, there is an "adamant" group of states that usually voted against the federal delegation: the states of Mexico, Jalisco, Oaxaca, Veracruz, Puebla, Nuevo León, Querétaro, and Durango. Veracruz was dominated by twice-governor Adalberto Tejeda, a powerful *cacique* who had pursued radical land reform and enjoyed the support of an armed peasant militia. That state was endowed with a very productive agricultural sector, possessed the nation's most important port, and had shared in the oil boom, all of which made its governor somewhat independent from the rest of the country.[21]

---

[18] Member of the revolutionary "inner circle" during the time of Calles, according to Brandenburg (1964), together with generals Amaro, Cárdenas, and Almazán (the group Brandenburg labels CACA). Cedillo had an alliance with Calles, but he rebelled against President Cárdenas in 1938. His uprising was defeated, the same fate that awaited all the generals in the CACA group except for Cárdenas.

[19] Governor Carranza originally rebelled against the encroachment on the federal pact by Victoriano Huerta, who deposed and murdered the first (and some claim the only) democratically elected president in the 20th century, Francisco I. Madero, during the initial years of revolutionary turmoil. Carranza put an end to the civil war, pursued a vigorous land reform plan influenced by Luis Cabrera, and initiated the reforms that led to the drafting of the 1917 Constitution. He was, however, toppled by an insurrection in 1920 by the Sonora group headed by Alvaro Obregón (president 1920–1924) and Plutarco Elías Calles (president 1924–1928).

[20] The factional division among Sonora politicians between *Obregonistas* and *Callistas* had not yet surfaced in the mid-1920s. Adolfo de la Huerta was defeated and forced into exile in the United States.

[21] Veracruz was involved in the two rebellions against the federal government, one led by de la Huerta, who installed his provisional government in that state, and the other one in 1929 by the *Obregonista* faction opposing the PNR candidate Pascual Ortiz Rubio (Brandenburg, 1955:58). Governor Tejeda, however, was extremely skillful in backing the federal government in both instances, using his armed peasant militias against the rebels. The

Puebla was a relatively rich state where incipient industrialization was taking place and profiting from the strategic location of its capital and other major cities between the main port of Veracruz and Mexico City. Jalisco had one of the longest traditions of state autonomy, being the first state to be constituted as such in the federal republic during the 19th century. Jalisco was also to witness an important armed rebellion against Calles, the *Cristero* movement, during the 10 years following the Convention. Oaxaca was the cradle of liberal executives who had dominated the political scene during the 19th century, including dictator Porfirio Diaz. These liberal states shared the commonality that they were all large. Thus they could more credibly threaten to go it alone than other states if the deals offered by the fiscal convention were not attractive enough.

The positions states took toward the proposals for tax centralization during the 1920s can be accounted for both by structural factors and strategic choices. State executives varied in their willingness to accept the federal proposals in the convention, depending on the fiscal interests of their states, their relative and absolute bargaining power, and the political coalitions to which they belonged, all of which impinged on the credibility of federal transfer promises.

In terms of the theoretical framework developed in Chapter 1, the fiscal interests of each state determined the amount of funds that states could have collected had there not been any centralized fiscal bargain; their bargaining power depended on the threat of conflict and the potential outcome of a continuation of the civil war, and the political coalitions to which different governors belonged determined the extent to which a transfer promise could be taken as credible. When politicians belonged to the same coalition, they might expect to get fair treatment, in terms of the distribution of resources from transfers, as compared with an expectation of being exploited if they were outside the political coalition.

Local governments had vested interests in retaining authority over taxation. To a large extent, this is because politicians prefer fiscal discretion. Authority over taxation provides flexibility to adjust taxes. It also reduces the risk that the federal government might make adjustments at the expense of particular states.[22] As discussed in Chapter 1, lacking a

---

peasant militias backed Tejeda to a large extent because of his radical land reform; see Falcón (1977).

[22] This is because, even with a promise of compensatory federal financial transfers, no contract between federation and state governments can completely specify all unforeseen

credibility-enhancing mechanism, governors would rather retain control over taxation than receive compensatory transfers from the federal government.

States were not characterized by the same ability to bargain with the federal government. Differences in absolute and relative power among states should account for a greater unwillingness by politicians to accept federal initiatives in the tax realm. Some states could make higher demands on the federal government. To the extent that governors could issue credible threats or possessed outside options, as discussed in the credibility model, they would take a more confrontational stance toward the federal government.

I give four different econometric estimates to explain the positions states took in the national–local dimension. The first estimate is a conventional ordinary least squares (OLS) estimate with robust standard errors; the second one is a variance-weighted least squares estimate that takes the uncertainty of the IDEAL procedure into account when calculating the errors; the third is a tobit model (i.e., a combination of OLS and probit) where unconditional states are truncated in the local–federal dimension to highlight their perfect agreement in voting choices; and the fourth is an ordered probit model of the frequency with which states voted in the same way as the federal government, where there are three groups: unconditional, pivotal, and adamant. The reason for estimating using different models is that, given the small number of recorded roll call votes, the dimension is estimated with very large errors. Because all the models yield basically the same results, one can be more confident about the findings.

The independent variables are operationalized as follows.

> Composition of Local Revenue. Characteristics of local tax collection should provide a measure of differences in state interests.[23] States should be more likely to support the federal proposals in the convention to the extent that the new arrangements do not impinge upon their own revenue. Other things being equal, states prefer to retain tax sovereignty. The federal government proposed that taxes on industry and trade were to become exclusively federal. States that relied more heavily on those taxes should therefore be less willing to go along with

---

contingencies, so in signing such a contract state executives are actually granting residual authority to the federation.

[23] States should care about retaining the revenue sources they already rely on for themselves. This is consonant with the notion that rulers maximize revenue (North, 1981; Levi, 1988).

the federal delegation.[24] Hence, I expect the percentage of revenue generated by taxes on industry (*industry*), as reported in Figure 2.2, to have a negative effect on the probability of voting with the federal delegation.

State Size. The interests of a state would also be determined by its bargaining power. The simplest indicator of size is population. During the 1920s, there was no estimate of state GDP. Hence, the analysis uses population according to the 1921 census as a measure of size to reflect the power of each state. The larger a state's population, the more reluctant it will be to accept a proposal the federal government supports.[25]

Level of Development. Population size is not the only determinant of bargaining power. Governors from the less "modernized" states (i.e., urbanized, industrialized, literate, in contact with means of communication, etc.) are less likely to face a politically active local population, so they would be less likely to have an independent position.[26] I expect illiteracy, taken from the 1910 census (*analf10*), to show a positive sign, reflecting that less developed states would be likely to vote with the federal government. The more powerful a state in terms of its development, the more likely it might be to threaten to reject a federal bargain in terms of the commitment game from Chapter 1.

Revenue Collection "Yield." Illiteracy might be a proxy for development, but an alternative monetary indicator would be the revenue collected in each state. Total revenue collection is highly correlated

[24] According to Burgess and Stern (1993), countries evolve from taxing primarily foreign trade, to relying on indirect taxes, and finally, at high levels of development, to relying most heavily on income taxes. At the local level, the evolution probably would go from taxes restricting trade, to indirect taxation, to property taxes. Hence the level of development could be reflected in the capacity of states to collect revenue from an exclusive property tax.

[25] In his widely accepted hierarchy of Mexican offices, Brandenburg (1964) places governors of large states at a high level just under the level of Secretarios heading federal ministries and members of what he calls the "inner circle" – the powerful players that dominated, in his account, the revolutionary "family." On the other hand, he placed governors of small- and medium-sized states, together with directors and managers of medium-sized state-owned enterprises and ambassadors, at a lower level than Supreme Court justices or senators but above federal deputies and judges (Brandenburg, 1964:158–159).

[26] Rich micro history analyses of Nuevo León, for example, suggest that many of the tensions between that state and the federal government at the beginning of Nuevo León's industrialization were related to the fact that this region was richer, more literate, and more industrialized than the rest of the country; see, for example, Cerruti (1993).

with population ($r = 0.741$), reflecting the size of each state's economy. The tax yield of each state is, however, a "noisy" indicator of development because states vary in their tax structures, bases, rates, and levels of evasion and elusion. The lower the yield of local tax collection (measured as a low per capita tax collection), the more willing states might be to participate in a transfer system. But states with higher-yielding taxes often hindered trade and local markets, so it might not be the case that greater tax collections corresponded with more development.[27] Controlling for other factors, I expect states with high per capita tax yields, as reflected in per capita revenue in 1925 (*revpc*) from Figure 2.1, to be more likely to vote with the federal government for a change in the status quo.

Core–Periphery Cleavage. Regional alliances should also determine policy positions. One might think that the closer they are to Mexico City, the more states should support the federal government. However, in the aftermath of the Mexican Revolution, the triumphant Sonorense faction that held national power had come from the periphery, in the north, defeating forces in the center of the country. The southern states were in fact more likely to support the Sonorense faction than the states in the center. Hence, somewhat paradoxically, peripheral states were the ones most likely to support federal government proposals. To measure these regional alliances, one could use the distance to Mexico City in kilometers. However, this would not account for the real cost of moving from one state to another. Tabasco and Campeche, for example, are geographically closer to Mexico City than, say, Durango and Sonora, respectively, but whereas the former had no railroad connection with the center, the latter did.[28] I therefore constructed an ordered categorical variable for distance (*dist*) with a 6-point scale (0 being closest to Mexico City and 5 farthest) that takes into account not only geographic distance but also the quality of the

---

[27] The problem with most tax efficiency indicators, including measures of tax burden and effective rates, is that, as the principal–agent literature suggests, what one really wants to measure is tax effort, which is unobservable. Lacking information on the characteristics of the tax base, evasion, elusion, and tax rates, what might resemble a greater effort on the part of the tax collector might in fact reflect very high rates or government predation on local resources. Because per capita revenue only measures effort imperfectly, its interpretation should be very cautious.

[28] When de la Huerta was named provisional president in 1920, it took him nine days in a special train to travel from the well-connected state of Sonora to Mexico City! Getting to Tabasco or Yucatán took weeks.

infrastructure available.[29] The hypothesis is that membership in the alliance of the peripheral states affected the willingness of political leaders to go along with federal proposals, so *dist* should have a positive sign.

Committee Membership. The structure in the assembly provided differential power to members according to their membership in committees. Because the federal government decided the allocation of committee seats, these assignments can be viewed as indicators of how much the federal government trusted a state to go along with its proposals. States that were excluded from committee assignments represented nonmembers of the ruling coalition and hence would be expected to be positioned far from the federal delegation on the national–local dimension. An exclusion from committee membership (*Nocom*) would indicate a state where federal promises were not credible.

Table 2.1 shows the results. All signs except for tax yield are as expected, although not all are statistically significant. The composition of local revenue is not very robust as an explanation of the position states took on the national–local dimension. The share of taxes from industry does show a negative sign, suggesting that states that were more reliant on the taxes they were to give up were more reluctant to vote with the federal government. The results suggest that the tax base per se was not the main source of contention between states and the federal government. States were aware that a fiscal pact would make both the federal government and the states better-off, assuming it was possible to enforce it. Thus, even though states differed in the extent to which they would be affected by a proposal that granted exclusive jurisdiction to the federal government over their most important taxes, presumably a transfer system could be crafted to make them better-off.

I believe the principal source of contention was the lack of a mechanism to create federal credibility and the real threats states posed to the federal government. This is reflected in the fact that any state that was excluded

---

[29] The scale divides the states as follows: 0 for Tlaxcala, México, Puebla, Hidalgo, and Querétaro, all bordering Mexico City; 1 for Aguascalientes, Guanajuato, Jalisco, Michoacán, San Luis Potosí, and Veracruz, all well connected with the center; 2 for Tamaulipas, Durango, and Colima in the north and Oaxaca and Guerrero in the south; 3 to Nayarit and Tabasco; 4 to the northern border states of Nuevo León, Coahuila, Chihuahua, and Sonora; and 5 to isolated Campeche and Chiapas.

Table 2.1. *Determinants of State Issue Positions in the First Fiscal Convention*
Dependent Variable: State Position on the Local–National Dimension

Independent Variable	OLS	VWLS	Tobit	Ordered Probit
Porind	−0.020**	−0.007	−0.024**	−0.030
	(0.009)	(0.008)	(0.011)	(0.023)
Pop (1,000s)	−0.895***	−0.014***	−1.007***	−0.392**
	(0.262)	(0.037)	(0.353)	(0.169)
Analf10	0.030***	0.014	0.034**	0.058*
	(0.010)	(0.009)	(0.013)	(0.032)
Revpc	0.074***	0.054	0.094	0.130
	(0.052)	(0.062)	(0.073)	(0.167)
Dist	0.157*	0.259	0.172*	0.345
	(0.084)	(0.0278)	(0.101)	(0.702)
Nocom	−0.594***	−0.519***	−0.674***	−0.776
	(0.185)	(0.166)	(0.218)	(0.598)
Cons	−1.405*	−0.368	−1.551	
	(0.769)	(0.753)	(1.021)	
Adj R2	0.4914			
F (6,18)	10.78***			
Lchi2(6)		27.84***	18.4***	11.44*
Pseudo R2			0.3244	0.2177

* Statistically significant at 90% level.
** Statistically significant at 95% level.
*** Statistically significant at 99% level.

from committee assignments is predicted by all the estimations to be far from the federal government. That distance is even greater to the extent that a state had greater bargaining power as measured by its size. The level of development of a state as measured by illiteracy, and its peripheral status in the coalition, seem to increase the likelihood that it will vote with the federal delegation. The variance-weighted least squares estimation shows the size and committee variables reaching significance, which suggests that, even considering the great uncertainty surrounding the ideal points, we can be quite confident that these two variables are crucial to the disagreement between states and the federal government. The only estimate under which the committee variable is not significant is the ordered probit, which suggests that this variable is particularly important in distinguishing voting patterns among states rather than between them and the federal government. The exclusion from committee membership created a divide between those that believed and those that did not believe the federal promises.[30]

Of course, it is possible to argue that committee membership is endogenous to the position states adopted in the convention because the federal government could have known beforehand which states opposed it and therefore could manipulate committee assignments accordingly. However, a reading of the debates in the convention suggests that committee assignments were considered to be relatively reasonable by the participants. Committee assignments were made in a low-information environment prior to the debates in the meeting, where state positions on the national–local position were defined and made public. I do not believe delegations got a committee seat because of the position they held on the issues of federalism because such positions were rather unknown before the meeting. In contrast to the voting rules and the procedural discussions of agenda control, which were thoroughly debated, the committee membership was quickly accepted by all the states after a very brief discussion that allowed any state delegate to attend committee meetings. The results hold even when the committee membership variable is not entered in the estimations.

In terms of the theoretical model in Chapter 1, the significance and direction of the effect of the population size and the illiteracy variables suggest the structural features that can signal the threats of a powerful state. The committee exclusion variable instead represents the credibility of a commitment offered by the federal government.

To get a better sense of the size of the effect of exclusion from committee membership, one can simulate the importance of this variable together with its range of error, as reflected in 95 percent confidence intervals.[31] Figure 2.4 performs a simulation for the case of the OLS estimation. The simulation graphs the predicted position of a given state, according to its size, and whether it was granted a committee assignment.

The effect of size implies that for every additional 100,000 inhabitants in a state, its position would be shifted by 0.16 points in the scale. The effect

---

[30] Diaz-Cayeros (1997) explored alternative explanations. The variables used were patronage in the form of federal jobs in the states, *ejido* land distributed, and electoral support to the president. The basic results always hold because competing explanations do not account for the national–local dimension.

[31] Using CLARIFY (Tomz, Wittenberg, and King, 2001).

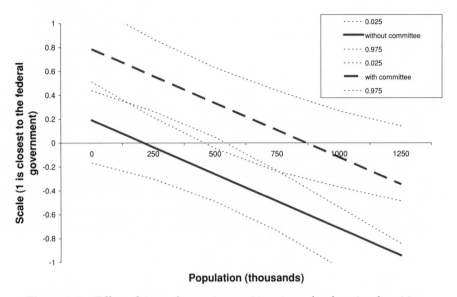

Figure 2.4. Effect of size and committee assignment on local–national position.

of committee membership involves a clear differentiation of delegations, even taking into account the very large error bands: At any size level, one can be confident that a state with a committee seat is located to the left (i.e., closer to the federal delegation) of one without it.

Hence, votes in the convention divided states along a dimension that reflected their bargaining power. Larger states were less willing to agree with the federal government. The level of development also provided states with more bargaining power against the federal government. Political distrust as reflected in committee assignments implied that many states did not believe the federal government's promises. Although the structure of local taxation and the types of taxes that states would eliminate explain some of the positions taken by the states, they were not the main sources of contention. A tax agreement promised to make states fiscally better-off, but the most reticent states were those that perceived that because of their size they could go it alone, or those that did not believe in the federal promises.

The convention drafted a proposal for constitutional reforms that were meant to set the stage for a system of tax coordination between states and the federal government. Each level of government would have exclusive jurisdiction over some taxes, and states would receive revenue shares from federal taxes.[32] Revenue-sharing was "undoubtedly inspired in the purpose of not diminishing the revenue of the states" (Gómez, 1947[1933] in CNF2), but the way in which the provision was established would undermine its success. The federal government was granted exclusive authority to tax income, natural resources (including mining and oil), internal trade, industry, and any agricultural products found in two or more states. States and municipalities would receive a share of revenue according to a proportion to be determined by the federal congress.

The indeterminacy of the share posed a serious problem for state representatives in Congress, considering that, after peaking in 1925, federal revenue was falling. The fall was related to the decline in oil production, which contributed largely to federal revenue, and to the global depression after 1929. How could governors know that the federal government would not adjust its revenue shortfalls by reducing the states' proportion of shared revenue? By leaving an indeterminate percentage for revenue-sharing and no institution to create a federal commitment, the convention failed.

2.4. Collective Action and Social Choice in a Federal Bargain

The recommendations of the First National Tax Convention were shelved in the federal congress, never to be approved. In contrast to the convention, where each state had one vote, in the federal Chamber of Deputies the group of states farthest from the federal government controlled enough deputies to block any constitutional reform requiring a two-thirds majority. This resulted from both the special majority and the particular apportionment of those states in the federal legislature. This adamant group of states had by itself 63 deputies out of a total of 147, which made 43 percent of the votes.

In subsequent years, the status quo remained in place, although international and domestic circumstances exerted greater pressures on the finances of local governments. In the early 1930s, state governments were eager to find ways to enhance their revenue without increasing the tax burden paid by their citizens. In their view, the two most pressing fiscal issues were:

---

[32] The proposal also included the institutionalization of convention meetings every four years and a provision for their recommendations to become obligatory for state and federal powers unless they were explicitly rejected. Such a provision was in fact equivalent to making the convention the decision-making body (although not the exclusive one) on matters related to fiscal federalism.

(1) to reserve the land tax exclusively for the local levels of government; and (2) to reduce the burden of the so-called *contribución federal*, a transfer that states provided to the federal government. Both issues involved asserting state fiscal jurisdiction in their own territories, an issue that had not been dealt with by the First Convention. Although the convention had failed, the federal government expected property taxes to become the backbone of local finance in the hope that states would improve their collection of property taxation. To coax them, they were granted an exemption from the *contribución federal*.

During the 1930s, there was an increasingly widespread perception of unfairness in the taxation of land, particularly the land that had been distributed by the federal and state governments. The 1926 *ejido* law stated that federal, state, and municipal governments were prohibited from imposing more than one property tax (*predial*) on *ejido* properties and that such a tax would not exceed 5 percent of annual production (Simpson, 1937:329). A federal decree in 1922 had previously determined that no property taxes should be levied on *ejidos* at all and directed governors to prohibit the imposition of such taxes (Simpson, 1937:340). In 1923, another federal disposition was enacted, stating that *ejidos* would pay a federal tax of 0.1 percent on the value of land (Vázquez Santaella, 1938). State-level fiscal legislation varied widely in its treatment of *ejido* property. Hence, implementation of property taxes in rural areas was often chaotic. In the end, peasants on *ejido* land refused to pay any tax at all.

Simpson notes that the federal government had failed to solve the most essential matter of fiscal responsibility for *ejido* communities. In his words, "for the first seventeen years of the agrarian reform the whole question of *ejido* taxes was either ignored or muddled by vague and conflicting legislation" (Simpson, 1937:341). The real effect of what Simpson calls this "indecision in theory and law" was a real injustice emerging in the realm of taxation: Some agricultural producers paid no taxes whatsoever, whereas other communities paid even more than private plantations (*haciendas*). The issues at stake reflected more than revenue questions: They lay at the core of alternative strategies for economic development in the countryside, either making *ejidos* the backbone of rural social, political, and economic organizations or relying on a more "liberal" view of agricultural production based on private farmers.

The main contentious issue regarding the *contribución federal* that developed during the 1930s was provoked by the federal finance ministry's efforts at tax coordination. Having failed to pass a constitutional reform

65

establishing exclusive tax jurisdictions, the federal government exempted states from the obligation to pay this transfer if they would voluntarily adopt the recommendations of the First Convention. By 1933, 19 states were paying the *contribución federal*, whereas the rest were either partially or fully exempted. State governments found this situation highly objectionable. Instead of making the tax system a public good that would bring benefits to all states, the federal government had granted selective exemptions from the *contribución federal*. This improved regional integration and eliminated some harmful taxes in those specific states, but it generated a sense of inequality, which made coordination in taxation even more difficult. As in Levi's (1988) theory, quasi-voluntary compliance in federal tax collection was rendered less effective by a perception of fiscal unfairness.[33]

A new national tax convention met in 1933, to a large extent in order to eliminate the inequitable treatment given to different states. The Second Convention was in many ways a repetition of the previous meeting, especially with regard to its recommendations. However, this time the federal government did not seek to exclude powerful states through the rules of committee assignments. Learning from the previous experience, the convention established special majorities for proposals to be approved and did not attempt to reform the constitution, rather proposing legislation requiring an ordinary majority in Congress. This Second Convention, however, failed to provide effective mechanisms for federal commitment.

Regional politicians in Mexico did not possess a coordination device that would allow a national coalition to enact a coherent tax program. The analysis of the state cleavages emerging from the roll call votes of delegates to the Second National Tax Convention in 1933 provides evidence of this. Lacking structured political parties, the potential divisions between states in Mexico during the 1920s and 1930s were multidimensional, making coalitions shift according to each decision.[34] Unstable majorities made "legislative" action ineffective.

As with the First Convention, I infer the position of state delegates according to their voting patterns by using IDEAL. In the case of the Second Convention, there are 28 roll call votes, which allows for a more precise estimation of ideal points. Figure 2.5 provides the results of the scaling. As

[33] The differential treatment of states did generate divisions among the states, which strengthened the federal government. For a theoretical account of the obstacles to overcoming collective-action problems by members of a federation, see Solnick (1998, 2002).

[34] For an argument on how political parties can solve social choice problems in multidimensional issue spaces, see Aldrich (1995).

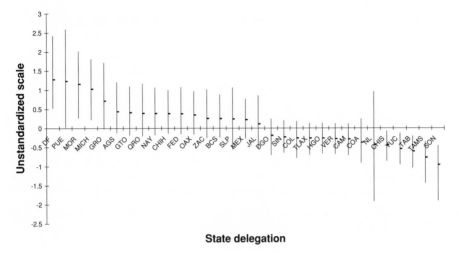

Figure 2.5. Latent dimension of disagreement in Second National Tax Convention.

with the dimensional representation of the First National Tax Convention, states that were farther from the federal government were more unlikely to vote with it; states clustering close to the federal delegation voted similarly not only to the delegation but also to each other. The error bands are large, given both the small number of votes involved and, more importantly, the highly unstable voting patterns observed in this convention. The dimension reflects fiscal interests different from the local–national dimension of the First Convention. In what follows, I am mainly concerned with the way state delegations were divided, the stability of cleavages, and how far the positions of state delegations drifted from those of the federal delegation.

In this estimation, the federal government is centrally located. This should have made a compromise solution more likely than in the First Convention. The federal government seems to no longer represent an extreme position in a national–local cleavage. Nonetheless, states differed along the lines of their fiscal interests over changes to the status quo. The states farthest away from the federal government were Sonora, Tamaulipas, Tabasco, Yucatán, the Federal District, Puebla, Chiapas, and Nuevo León. Although distant from the federal delegation, these states did not share common interests because they are on opposite extremes of the scale. The cluster of states with voting patterns similar to the federal one are: Chihuahua, Nayarit, Querétaro, Guanajuato, Oaxaca, and Aguascalientes. In this fiscal dimension, there is no single pivotal group of states because that depends on whether in each specific vote the federal government is receiving support from states to its right or to its left.

The analysis of each specific vote can provide an understanding of the voting alignment that arose during this convention. I seek to highlight the dynamics of social choice taking place in this assembly rather than the specific explanation for why the votes turned out the way they did. The most noteworthy aspect of the Second Convention was not so much the relative position of the states in the fiscal dimension but rather the shifting coalitions observed in it. There was no stable coalition solving problems of social choice in the tax realm. Absent a partisan organization, the dimensionality of political conflict was high and decision making along single cleavages was ineffective.[35]

A way to show the shifting nature of coalitions is to estimate the dividing point between states in each of the votes. This can be done by drawing in the issue space the dividing threshold of the coalitions that supported or opposed each voted proposal (see Jillson and Wilson, 1994:322–329). This involves calculating the slope and constant term of a probit. Each vote is the dependent variable and the latent dimension calculated with IDEAL is the independent variable. Table 2.2 shows the coefficients of each vote together with their statistical significance. It also reports the dividing point predicted by the dimension. The last column shows the percentage of correctly predicted votes.[36]

The dividing point can be understood in the following way. Take, for example, votes 1 through 5, which cut the issue space in different ways: Votes 2 and 3 generate a dividing line where the states in the extreme right of the dimension in Figure 2.2 (Yucatán, Tabasco, Tamaulipas, and Sonora) are excluded; votes 1 and 4 place a dividing point at the extreme left of the dimension, suggesting that all states agree unanimously; and vote 5 places the dividing point at the extreme right but still generating unanimity. The differences between those dividing points reflect the nature of the votes taken. Votes 2 and 3 were taken on two closely related federal initiatives: a proposal that the inheritance tax should be uniform across states and that

---

[35] The best way to show the high dimensionality of the issue space would be to estimate ideal points on several dimensions. However, the very small number of votes precludes doing a reliable analysis this way. For a two-dimensional depiction of the decisions involved in these data using multidimensional scaling techniques, however, see Diaz-Cayeros (1997).

[36] The dividing point is calculated by dividing the slope coefficient by the coefficient of the constant term.

Table 2.2. *Vote Patterns Predicted by Latent Variable in Second Convention*

Vote	Beta	Significance	Alpha	Significance	Dividing Point	Percentage Correct
V1	0.24		1.14	***	4.82	55%
V2	−0.96	***	0.53	**	−0.56	68%
V3	1.15	**	−0.78	**	−0.68	77%
V4	0.31		1.57	***	4.99	84%
V5	−0.34		1.37	***	−3.99	55%
V6	1.04		11.32	***	10.90	61%
V7	0.39		−0.46	**	−1.17	65%
V8	−8.94	***	7.46	***	−0.83	90%
V9	0.07		0.48	**	6.62	68%
V10	−10.92	***	−8.38	***	0.77	32%
V11	10.77	***	7.60	***	0.71	26%
V14	2.11		2.66	***	1.26	29%
V15	0.29		12.80	***	43.61	61%
V16	0.12		−1.05	***	−8.74	65%
V17	11.62	***	5.79	***	0.50	36%
V18	6.55	***	4.05	***	0.62	39%
V19	1.05		1.54	***	1.47	68%
V20	1.31		1.30	***	0.99	48%
V21	−0.84		0.87	***	−1.03	84%
V22	2.91	***	1.09	***	0.38	39%
V23	13.80	***	0.56		0.04	55%
V24	1.52		1.86	***	1.22	39%
V25	−0.36		1.59	***	−4.35	71%
V26	−11.22	***	−4.80	***	0.43	32%
V27	1.37		2.27	***	1.66	45%
V29	−0.89		−1.28	**	1.45	65%
V30	−0.77		−0.72	***	0.93	39%
V31	−0.30		1.35	***	−4.51	84%

* Statistically significant at 90% level.
** Statistically significant at 95% level.
*** Statistically significant at 99% level.

the federal congress would be in charge of proposing the characteristics of that tax. Clearly, the states that were against this proposal were interested in keeping the inheritance tax to themselves.

Votes 1, 4, and 5 refer to contentious issues with strong "antifederal" content but in which the states ended up agreeing to abide by the federal proposals. Vote 1 was a procedural issue, debated for two days at the beginning of the convention, that related to voting rules. The vote, if approved, would strip the federal delegation of its veto power over the recommendations because it proposed that the federal delegation's vote would count just the same as that of any state delegate. When that proposal was approved by all the states, the federal government announced it was withdrawing from the meeting. Confronted with such an extreme threat, state delegates declared a recess, held an unrecorded debate, and when they reconvened they decided to backtrack on their decision, accepting the federal veto. They realized that without federal participation the convention would be useless.

Votes 4 and 5 concerned an amendment, proposed by some state delegates, to leave authority over the inheritance tax within the states. The amendment was possible because, in the first days of the convention, committee referrals were discussed under an open rule. Under general discussion on the floor, the federal government's recommendation, which had just been approved in vote 2, was rejected and the amended one accepted. The assembly was generating chaotic outcomes in its voting patterns. The presidency (which was controlled by the federal delegation), realizing how troublesome this vote had been, decided from then on to debate committee referrals under a closed rule.

Subsequent votes concerned various specific discussions, including whether states were capable of administering and collecting taxes and if it were possible for the federal government to transfer more resources to the states, for example by paying for a national land registry. The most interesting aspect of the votes during the early debates of the convention was that no clear voting alignment emerged because votes cut the issue space at various points. This can be seen by both the great variability in the beta coefficients and the way in which the dividing line shifts from vote to vote. The debates of the convention provide an explicit articulation of the social choice dilemma facing the assembly, in Marte Gómez's surprise that the assembly opposed the passage of a proposal that had previously been agreed among what he called the "majoritarian group" (CNF2, Vol.2:306). A delegate from San Luis Potosí complained that the convention was becoming dominated by the formation of "blocks of states," which left those outside the blocks at a clear disadvantage (CNF2, Vol.2:322). His state was rather isolated, but in fact the problem of the convention was the opposite: No stable voting block had been generated. As suggested by the percentage of votes correctly predicted, the issue space of debate was probably multidimensional because the latent variable dimension accounts for only a small fraction of the variance in the voting patterns.

Frustrated by the difficulty at passing proposals, after vote 17 the federal government proposed a change in the voting rules. Controversial votes 18 and 19, just like vote 1, involved procedural changes. The issue under debate was whether to change the oversized majority rule. The requirement of a two-thirds supermajority was becoming too difficult to fulfill. The proposal was that a recommendation would not require the oversized majority made up of 21 states but instead only two-thirds of those present. Given the quorum rules, this in fact meant that recommendations could be passed with as little as 14 delegates, which is one less than in the simple majority rule of the First Convention. The procedural change was approved. Subsequent proposals were approved with small majorities. The change of rule had the effect of generating easier approval of recommendations, but, as suggested by the dividing points in Table 2.2, it did not reduce the previously observed instability.

To sum up, the internal structure of the assembly did not produce stable majorities, and the external structure of partisan affiliations did not help. Thus, the assembly proved ineffective as an institution for structuring choice. When the federal government realized it was immersed in a social choice dilemma, it tinkered with the rules of procedure of the convention. In particular, it changed the voting rule so that an absolute majority was no longer required to pass any recommendation. Such a change made it easier to create majorities but made them even more fleeting, and in this sense it undermined the aim of creating an oversized coalition for reform. The recommendations of the Second Convention were never implemented.

2.5. *Commitment and Failed Fiscal Coordination*

The conventional view of why the national tax conventions in Mexico did not produce tangible results has been that states were reluctant to coordinate because they did not possess "efficient" local tax systems and were unwilling to make an effort to improve their tax yields (Martínez Almazán, 1980; Martínez Cabañas, 1985). In this view, opponents of change seek to retain their inefficiency in tax collection. That argument resonates in debates on Mexican federalism after the 1990s that identify the problem of local governments as a question of poor administrative structures and a purported failure by local politicians to see the benefit of collecting taxes. The federal Ministry of Finance (*Secretaría de Hacienda y Crédito Público* – SHCP) has argued throughout the years that local government taxation in Mexico was not only inefficient in the economic sense but also yielded little revenue. In

71

this view, because the federation was presumably more effective at collecting taxes, the history of the Mexican tax system and the national tax conventions is imagined as a progressive movement toward a more rational, modern – and in this view clearly better – fiscal arrangement. I disagree with this Whig view. The sources of opposition to tax centralization were political.

Neither the first nor the second national tax conventions achieved their aims because federal commitments were not credible. Although the delegates agreed on a set of recommendations, mostly centering on the elimination of local taxes that duplicated those of the federal government and the unification of other taxes and tax rates, those recommendations were never implemented. The most concrete results of the Second Convention were that the Tax Act of 1934 eliminated the federal property tax (Vázquez Santaella, 1938) and that the burden of the federal contribution was reduced and made less unequal (the general rate was set to 15 percent but for those states that had previously been granted an exemption it was increased to 5 percent [Servín, 1956:43]). The elimination of the federal property tax gave states the exclusive authority over revenue from land. However, given the acceleration of land reform during the late 1930s, this was an empty concession. The tax base of land was to become increasingly small as more agricultural production was organized under the *ejidos*, which would not be paying taxes.

The analysis in this chapter provides two general lessons about the problems of commitment in federal regimes. First, fiscal interests provide meaningful insights into initial conditions under which national integration or the consolidation of central authority can be achieved. Even if in theory they could be better off with a centralized collection and transfer system, politicians in local jurisdictions prefer to have discretion over taxation and control over the resources they extract to sustain government activities. Local jurisdictions would rather remain sovereign on matters of financial resources than attempt to have the federal government write a one-sided contract of revenue transfers. Because contracts are always incomplete, unforeseen contingencies entail that the party that retains residual authority would decide to solve those contingencies to its advantage.

Second, a federal bargain entails striking a balance between providing enough enticements to the most powerful players, in order to prevent them from making the threat of playing on their own, and the federal government retaining enough resources in its realm. If a region is endowed with advantages over other regions, this will be reflected in the feasible set of federal bargains. Asymmetric arrangements are more likely to generate agreement by powerful parties than systems that treat all partners equally just because the bargaining power of each regional politician is different. However, treating each member of a federal system differently can reduce the incentives for cooperation because of perceptions of unfairness in the treatment of constituent members. In Mexico, an effort to treat states unequally through selective exemptions from the *contribución federal* led to the failure of efforts at centralization.

3

The Official Party as a Regional Compromise

3.1. Party Politics and Regional Fragmentation

The previous chapter has shown that the debates surrounding the efforts toward centralization of the tax system during the 1920s and 1930s reflected underlying political differences between national and regional leaders. A fragmented fiscal system remained the status quo, imposing economic losses on both the state and federal governments. The origins of this economic failure were *political*. A successful resolution came only in subsequent decades as Mexican politicians crafted an institutional innovation, namely a hegemonic corporatist political party, that provided means to solve the problems that had bedeviled the fiscal regime. The party brought about political stability and limited taxation through fiscal integration, but ultimately at the cost of undermining democracy and federalism. In terms of the logic spelled out by the theoretical account in Chapter 1, the party created a commitment mechanism that made transfers credible.

During the early postrevolutionary years, thousands of regional political "parties," mere personal organizations centered around revolutionary leaders, competed for local and national offices. Local elections were characterized by postelectoral conflict in which contenders declared victory regardless of the vote count, resorting to arms in order to settle their disputes.[1] The lack of national political integration was reflected in the federal legislature, which, providing veto power to regional politicians, often proved ineffective in national policymaking.

---

[1] Although the national government attempted to disarm revolutionary factions and restructure the federal army, this proved to be a difficult and protracted process. The most comprehensive reorganization was made in the 1920s by General Amaro under Calles, but rebellions subsisted and civilian control over the army was not achieved until 1946.

The Official Party as a Regional Compromise

The establishment of the PRI's predecessor, the *Partido Nacional Revolucionario* (PNR), in 1929 represented an explicit attempt to address the problems of regional fragmentation. The prime objective of the party was to provide an institutional mechanism to structure political ambition. In 1938, the PNR was reorganized along corporatist lines with the establishment of the *Partido de la Revolución Mexicana* (Party of the Mexican Revolution, PRM). The party was now made up of four functional sectors: peasant, worker, the military, and the so-called popular sector encompassing all other groups. Through the PRM, the president appealed directly to special interests at the national level. Consolidation of hegemony was finally achieved with the centralized control of the federal electoral processes by the federal authorities and the interior ministry (*Secretaría de Gobernación*) in 1946, the elimination of the military sector in the party, and the party's final transformation into the *Partido Revolucionario Institucional* (PRI). Hegemony meant that a party nomination was equivalent to the attainment of office. Whoever was not nominated by the party could not be elected. The president gradually came to control most nomination processes, although, as discussed in the next chapter, governors and corporatist organizations remained important veto players in the nomination process.

Regional politicians accepted the new political arrangement embodied in the PRI because they were offered attractive careers to pursue their political ambitions and because the party, through the power of the federal government, mustered vast electoral and financial resources. Moreover, regional economies had been hit hard by the global depression of 1929. In the midst of the crisis, governors were willing to let the federal government play a larger compensatory role. The need for economic assistance was especially acute among once-powerful export-oriented states whose local producers, because of their links with world markets, were now in serious distress. By mid-century, the regional cleavage of the 1920s and 1930s became increasingly muted.

This chapter is organized as follows. The next section briefly discusses political parties as institutional devices that solve problems of progressive ambition, collective action, and social choice. Section 3.3 provides an account of the establishment of the PNR as a territorially based organization, stressing its role in channeling political ambition. Section 3.4 studies the transformation of the PNR into a corporatist party, underscoring the role that reorganization played in reducing policy disagreements, even though regional politicians remained key political players. Section 3.5 discusses the assertion of federal control over electoral processes and the final centralization of nomination procedures that took place after 1946, when the party assumed its final shape as the PRI. Finally, Section 3.6 returns to the question of fiscal authority, arguing that the compromise reached by Mexican regional and national politicians through the party involved reducing local electoral and career risks in exchange for gradually losing control over financial resources and tax authority.

3.2. Parties as Institutional Solutions to Ambition, Collective Action, and Social Choice

During the second half of the 20th century, Mexican politicians constructed a regional compromise that centralized political authority. The central institutional innovation was the creation of a hegemonic political party. The Mexican PRI provided a durable solution to what Aldrich (1995) has shown are the three critical problems that parties solve: political ambition, collective action, and social choice. Most accounts of Mexican political development have stressed the role of the party as a mechanism for solving questions of political ambition (Brandenburg, 1964:64; Smith, 1979:133, 250; Nacif, 1996). Political parties indeed enhance the prospects of a long-term political career, and the PRI in Mexico was an especially effective mechanism.

Viewed from the perspective of an office-seeker, a party primarily solves problems of progressive ambition (Schlesinger, 1966; Rohde, 1979) because it provides structure to behavior that could become violent in the pursuit of power. Because politicians are self-interested actors who are driven by the hope of attaining office, according to Schlesinger, "ambition is the heart of politics" (Schlesinger, 1991:34). This claim does not rule out a role for ideology or principle in political action, but the underlying motivation of political leaders is ambition as channeled by the existing institutional provisions.

Nonetheless, political parties are not only about ambition. Parties also solve problems of collective action and social choice (Aldrich, 1995). Politicians often face problems of collective action when it comes to the provision of public goods. The nature of public goods is such that even if everyone would be better-off cooperating to provide them, nobody wants to spend his own resources for their provision.[2] Third-party enforcement sometimes

---

[2] This situation is often characterized as a "prisoner's dilemma," where individual rationality dictates that players choose dominant strategies that yield the worst outcome. Many public goods are not prisoner's dilemmas, however, but are characterized by problems of coordination of outcomes with different distributive implications.

provides a solution to such problems.[3] This can be brought about through specific "selective incentives" that make unilateral cooperation profitable or through the enactment of rules of cooperation that comprise punishments (and a third party capable of inflicting them) in case of noncooperation. Compliance and coordination are more difficult if players do not feel they are being treated fairly (Levi, 1988:53). Political parties can provide institutional rules, rewards for cooperation, and rules of fairness in order to solve politicians' collective-action problems.

Parties also provide a means by which coalitions can address problems of social choice. Social choice problems emerge when issues are multidimensional and majorities unstable. As Aldrich argues, when equilibrium exists, as for example when individuals have single-peaked preferences over a one-dimensional issue space, there are no incentives for party formation (Aldrich, 1995:44). Without further structure, individual incentives yield a unique result – the median – so players need not incur the transaction costs of forming a party in order to produce a specific outcome. When issue spaces are not one-dimensional, however, assemblies require institutional mechanisms, including legislative procedures (Shepsle, 1979) and political parties (Aldrich, 1995), to govern the passage of bills. When political debates are organized by political parties around some underlying cleavage, the potential for cyclicity is significantly reduced. Political parties can become an attractive device for providing stability over time. A coalition may commit to a joint course of action over future choices so that whenever a cycle arises among the coalition partners, they agree on a procedure to produce a unique outcome, and in all other cases they act according to their individual interests. Such a long-term arrangement would make members of the coalition better-off.

Once established, parties determine the way in which federalism works. If party nominations are highly centralized, the Rikerian hypothesis suggests that centralization in public policy will also be high.[4] There is an intrinsic

---

[3] Another solution is found in repeated interaction. If players are confronted with the same strategic situation over and over again, they can come to realize, as long as they care about the future, that they are better-off seeking a strategy of conditional cooperation than one of defection. The problem with the repeated game solution, however, is that repetition only makes cooperation possible; it does not ensure that it happens.

[4] See Filippov, Ordeshook, and Shvetsova (2004) for a general statement of the argument and Garman, Haggard, and Willis (2001) for a discussion of party nominations and decentralization in Latin America. However, see Chhibber and Kollman (2004) for an argument where fiscal centralization is the cause of party system nationalization.

link, as discussed in Chapter 1, between taxation and representation in the conformation of federal fiscal systems: When party nominations are centralized and the party system is dominated by a hegemonic player, territorial representation in the regions becomes attenuated, so one can expect a large degree of fiscal centralization and even the abdication of tax authority. In the opposite case, when nominations are decentralized, representation is more territorial and regions will fight to retain their tax authority.

Mexico's PRI provided an extreme case of the centralization process. The party generated a highly structured ladder of progressive ambition, a solution to social choice dilemmas, and laid the foundation for collective action. In terms of the workings of the federal pact, what this meant was that the party blurred regional differences. Regional politicians in the federal congress approved virtually all the legislation proposed by the president; they enjoyed the benefits of the expansion of the federal sphere of government in an ISI development strategy while being protected from electoral challenges to their political careers in their home states. The next section studies this process of political innovation.

3.3. Political Ambition and the Founding of the Regional Party

Governing Mexico during the late 1920s and early 1930s was not an easy task. After the murder of President-elect Alvaro Obregón in 1928, President Plutarco Elías Calles assembled a group of regional politicians to found the *Partido Nacional Revolucionario* (PNR) in an attempt to solve the recurrent succession crises that had plagued the fragmented political system. The party could not immediately create compliance in the sense that all politicians would accept its nominations. Nomination losers would rebel against the party during its first decades. A widespread armed rebellion headed by General Juan Escobar took place in 1929, precisely when the party was holding its founding convention. In 1938, the powerful strongman of San Luis Potosí, General Saturnino Cedillo, rebelled as the party changed its organization along a corporatist structure, and in 1940 Juan Andreu Almazán claimed electoral victory against the official party, only to be forced into exile.[5]

At the founding moment of the party in 1928, a political crisis was produced by the murder of Obregón. Calles remained the only strong

---

[5] Another disagreement within the party took place in the 1946 presidential nomination, but it posed no threat to PRI hegemony.

Sonorense leader. Calles forfeited his own reelection and instead became the Maximum Chief (*Jefe Máximo*; thus the period between 1929 and 1934 is referred to as the *Maximato*) of the Revolution.[6] The original intent of the party was, in the much quoted words of President Calles, to "transit from a more or less disguised system of 'government by *caudillos*' to a more forthright 'regime of institutions' " (*Partido Revolucionario Institucional*, 1981 [1928]: 30).[7]

Calles preserved a delicate balance between competing regional interests, playing one against another and constructing coalitions according to the requirements of his own political survival. First Obregón and then Calles had brokered pragmatic alliances and accords between the Sonora victors and the strongest political groups in each state (Womack, 1984, quoted in Hernández Chávez, 1993:279). Governors and agrarian leaders representing masses of landless peasants, such as Adalberto Tejeda in Veracruz or Lázaro Cárdenas in Michoacán, became powerful allies of Calles during the *Maximato*, even though they had important disagreements over policy. In return for their support, they demanded state autonomy and a decentralized political system. The major exception to the pacification of the country was the religious conflict of the Cristero War, which although regionally circumscribed mostly to the states of Jalisco, Michoacán, and Guanajuato

[6] The implications of such a title have been extended so as to consider Calles capable of controlling all the political events in the country in a fashion similar to the presidents during the years after the 1950s, when the PRI witnessed its strongest hegemony. The conditions of the country in the early years of the PNR were, however, very different from those that prevailed in the second half of the century. The main difference consisted in the regional fragmentation of state and local bosses that the new party meant to put an end to but could only achieve gradually.

[7] The party meant to unify politicians who shared "revolutionary" beliefs. At that moment, this did not mean turning the PNR into a single party because Calles, in his famous 1928 speech, did allow for the possibility that "reactionaries" would organize and compete in their own parties. Calles allowed a role for "conservative" or "reactionary" forces so they would remain represented in the legislature. After all, in the 1924 election, he had faced and defeated the candidate of the "landlord oligarchy and the Mexican catholic clergy" (Valenzuela, 1988:222), Angel Flores was deemed by the revolutionary leaders as a very "convenient" opposition candidate because he provided a clear enemy of the Revolution who could be defeated at the polls, not on the battlefield. Calles officially obtained 83 percent of the vote while Flores lost with 17 percent. Flores officially won in his native state of Sinaloa and in the two territories of Baja California, and he only lost by a small margin in Zacatecas and Nayarit. His candidacy was also strong (around 30 percent of the vote) in Coahuila, Chihuahua, Durango, and Guanajuato (Valenzuela, 1988:241). Additional evidence that Calles did not have a single party in mind is provided by Garrido (1982:73). The PRI, in contrast, officially was always declared victorious in all states, receiving huge margins.

had important effects on national politics. At the time, armed rebellions still had some chance of success, and threats of conflict by the states were credible.

It was a regional politician, the governor of the northern state of Tamaulipas, Emilio Portes Gil, who probably convinced Calles of the strategy of seeking a regional compromise through the PNR rather than trying to impose a strong hand. Portes Gil became the provisional president, succeeding Calles for the next 14 months, and he twice came to head the new party, in 1930 and 1935. The PNR's purpose was to unify regional parties around single candidates and provide a framework where conflicts and nominations could be resolved peacefully.

The prime tension in the early years of the PNR was the requirement of "discipline" toward the party, which was often at odds with the explicit promise of local political autonomy. Most accounts agree that the most pressing problem Calles faced upon the death of Obregón was "how to keep the army intact and the state governors and local *caciques* pacified" (Brandenburg, 1964:63). After all, it was in the provinces, headed by regional leaders, that uprisings usually started.[8] According to an appraisal published in the PNR's official party newspaper, "the general principle of [the party's] organization is the federalization of activities and the centralization of direction; a distribution of geographic zones in states, municipalities and municipal units" (*El Nacional Revolucionario* [1929], quoted in Lajous, 1992).

During the period from 1929 to roughly 1938, the party remained territorial in nature. The system was "clientelistic," dominated by the political machines of the constituent regional parties. Governors and the political groups to which they belonged constituted the crucial players. In those states where landed elites had been dislodged by the Revolution, land distribution became a powerful mechanism for buying political support. Senators and deputies in the federal congress were agents of their governors. *Caciques* controlled, initially through military force and later through clientelistic exchanges, regions that usually coincided with state boundaries. Many governors were so powerful that Alicia Hernández Chávez (1993) has even suggested the country was organized as a confederation of states rather than as a federal system.

The central advantage of the party over alternative political mechanisms was that it provided an internal channel to structure political ambition. At the presidential level, the solution was not easily achieved because the

---

[8] The de la Huerta rebellion in 1924 was national in its scope, however.

official party nomination kept being challenged by members of the "revolutionary family" until the 1940s. At the regional level, however, the party proved more effective. The key to its success was the 1933 constitutional reforms, when the party proposed and approved in Congress the reintroduction of an absolute prohibition of reelection for executives (governors and president) and for legislators in subsequent terms. Because the incentives to cultivate territorial constituencies for the purpose of reelection were subdued, the party became a powerful centralizing force in the political system.

Understanding why local leaders were willing to vote on limiting their own tenures is not trivial. An analysis of the motivations behind the 1933 reforms exceeds the scope of this work. However, it is worth mentioning that in reading the party debates, the general impression one gets is that circulating elites through successive posts was considered by most local politicians as more convenient than allowing individuals to become entrenched in specific posts. This became clear in a discussion surrounding a proposal by the delegation of Nuevo León, that would have forbidden circulation between the Senate and the Chamber of Deputies. That proposal was rejected by an overwhelming majority of the other delegates.

Once established, the rule of no reelection gave the party the opportunity to provide a ladder of progressive ambition. Regional leaders could follow careers that could reach their pinnacle either in the governor's seat or the federal cabinet. In order to reach such peaks, however, local politicians had to constantly move between offices: from a municipal presidency to local deputy, to federal deputy, to senator, then maybe back to deputy again, and finally to governor.[9] Those offices could only be reached, however, if one secured the backing of the party through a nomination.

The prohibition of reelection hence meant that regional leaders took turns in party nominations because they could not remain in their posts. More importantly, the reform entailed that the "best" political careers would not necessarily be advanced by making appeals to regional bases of support. National (i.e., federal) careers became more attractive, and as nominations were increasingly controlled by the president, ambition was channeled through the strict discipline of the national party. Affiliation with the party increased the probability of election. In fact, as the party became more hegemonic, this probability reached its upper bound: The nomination was

---

[9] For classic analyses of career paths in Mexican politics, see Smith (1979) and Camp (1984).

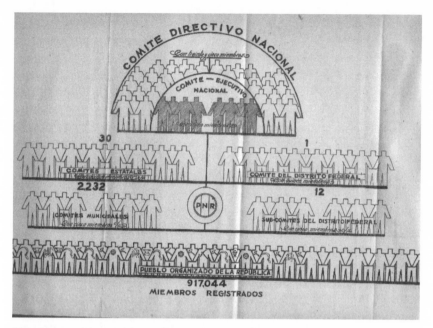

Figure 3.1. Territorial organization of the PNR.

equivalent to election. The party provided the structure for attaining higher office in the future. Hegemony meant that political ambition and the attainment of office were not viable outside the party. The party hence solved the issue of leadership succession and political turnover. A by-product of this process was the reduction of regionalism.

One must stress again that the PNR did not become the path to office from the very day it was founded. During its first years, party nominations were challenged by the same members of the "revolutionary family," and although we know after the fact that politicians who did not follow the rules of the party did not advance their careers, regional politicians did not know beforehand that this outcome would obtain. Events could have developed differently. In general, political institutions that structure ambition do not become sticky upon foundation but must prove through time that alternative routes (in the Mexican case, for example, a military coup, a rebellion, or a nomination by a different party) are no longer viable.

From the organizational point of view, the PNR was initially a regional-ist establishment. Figure 3.1 reproduces the organizational chart presented by the party in its 1931 report to members (PNR, 1931). As the chart indicates, the party had almost a million registered members, who were organized according to their class interests as signaled by sickles, hammers, smokestacks, and gears. The party did include, however, members with no specific functional organization, as reflected by individuals with no symbol in Figure 3.1. Yet, the life of the party was in the municipal and state committees. The pyramidal structure encompassed the 2,232 municipal councils plus 12 councils in the Mexico City wards; these in turn were organized into state committees. The 35 members in the national directorate at its peak reflected the regional organization. This territorial organization would change dramatically only after 1938.

3.4. The Corporatist Party and the Survival of Local Bosses

The consolidation of presidential power in Mexico involved the transformation of the PNR from a confederation of regional political organizations into the *Partido de la Revolución Mexicana* (PRM), a party representing peak corporatist organizations, namely peasant, worker, popular, and military groupings. This rather well-understood transformation was preceded by the drafting of a national labor law in 1931 that shifted the locus of decision making on labor disputes and matters of unionization to the federal sphere. A parallel precedent involved the activation of peasant organizations in the demand for land distribution as the president became the final arbiter in the processes of land distribution.

3.4.1. Corporatism Triumphant

The regime of Lázaro Cárdenas (president 1934–1940) constructed a ruling coalition through a combination of shrewd political maneuvering and the occasional use of force.[10] Cárdenas realized that his hold on national power depended on having the federal government play a more active role in labor issues, land reform, and the development of physical infrastructure. He therefore played the national corporatist structures against the regional loci of power. The *Maximato* would end in 1935 with a purge. Cárdenas expelled Calles from the country, removed more than half of the governors,

---

[10] For the best analysis of nation building during the Cárdenas period, see Cornelius 1973.

and reshuffled hundreds of military commanders around the country so that they would not cultivate regional bases of popular support (Hernández Chávez, 1979).[11]

During his first two years in office, Cárdenas removed 16 governors sympathetic to Calles. He had the Senate declare dissolution of power in 12 states and forced the resignation of four more governors during his first two years in office (Hernández Chávez, 1979: Appendix 2). Resorting to the dissolution of powers authority, rather than using military threats or political pressure through the interior secretary (*Secretario de Gobernación*) suggests that a political realignment was taking place within the political elite. Dissolution of powers in a state is not a presidential prerogative but depends on senatorial cooperation. Why did senators cooperate with Cárdenas? The PNR had created a clear mechanism of queuing for office in which senators knew they were quite likely to become the next governors in their home states once *Callista* governors were removed. This incentive was an important source of presidential power to threaten governors, but it only worked because the system of progressive ambition made relatively secure senatorial careers dependent on the president and corporatist organizations.

Thus, paradoxically, Cárdenas undermined the clientelistic system that allowed him to attain office, consolidating instead a corporatist system that allowed him, with the support of labor and peasant organizations, to end the grip on power of former president Calles.[12] Political bargaining was shifted from territorial to functional arenas. The worker and peasant confederations – the *Confederación de Trabajadores de México* (CTM) and the *Confederación Nacional Campesina* (CNC) – became the powerful players often cited as responsible for the stability of the regime.

---

[11] Even though Cárdenas was able to nominate governors more to his liking during his presidential term, by getting rid of those loyal to Calles, his power was not absolute. Perhaps the most obvious expression of this is that he was not able to impose his own preference to succeed him, Francisco Mújica. Mújica was regarded as too radical, so Cárdenas bowed to the nomination of the brother of the powerful *cacique* of Puebla, Maximino Avila Camacho, who commanded the support of the majority of the governors (Contreras, 1977). It would not be until the presidential succession of 1946 that the mechanisms of presidential power to nominate the successor (the so-called *dedazo*, or "finger tapping") became fully operational.

[12] The channel of ascent of Cárdenas was typical of this period in that a politician who seriously aspired to the presidency required regional backing in addition to previous experience as governor.

3.4.2. Developmentalism

The tension between Calles and Cárdenas reflected more than a power struggle between charismatic personalities. The incipient recovery from the 1929 global depression pitted two different models of development against each other. Radical land reformers, such as the leaders of Michoacán or Veracruz, were advocates of greater centralized state activism, whereas the Calles faction had a more liberal and decentralized outlook for the role of governments (federal and state) in economic development. Moreover, the liberal *Callistas* were pursuing a model of development based on the private sector and export-oriented agricultural production. The tension between the two views on the role of the federal government in the economy became increasingly difficult to handle.

Regional economic conditions were rather diverse across the country because the crisis of 1929 impacted each state in idiosyncratic ways. Regions that were most exposed to international trade and more dependent on the traditional exports subject to fluctuations in international prices (such as mining, oil, sisal, and some agricultural products) were more harmed by the economic decline of the early 1930s (Hernández Chávez, 1993:282). Thus, states such as Veracruz, Sonora, or Hidalgo were in greater need of federal help than those that could quickly shift into import substitution, such as Nuevo León and Jalisco. However, internal markets were not obvious sources of economic dynamism because physical barriers across regions were quite considerable. In 1933, the capital cities in 7 states did not have a railroad connection to Mexico City, and only 12 states could be reached by highway.[13] Hence, relatively rich states, such as Tabasco, Campeche, or Yucatán, lacking a connection with the rest of the country, could not easily exploit internal markets.

The first Six Year Plan of the PNR (1934–1940) clearly established a developmentalist strategy according to a so-called nationalist economic policy. The plan mentioned the need to "limit free competition, seeking an understanding between producers, so that prices can be regulated, so that they are not to be reduced to the disadvantage of wages, nor increased at the consumer's expense" (*Partido Revolucionario Institucional*, 1981 [1934]: 356) and that "the State must eliminate imports competing with national

---

[13] These data come from PNR (1931), which provides details on travel difficulties to each state, including information on states that could only be reached by airplane.

industries giving a satisfactory performance, or not constituting a burden for the country" (1981:357). That is, from the end of 1933, the federal government explicitly conceived a strategy of limited competition, price controls, and protection of national industries. However, the conditions for creating a powerful enough central government, rather than a decentralized regime led by state governments, were established in the political realm.

3.4.3. *The Reorganized Corporatist Party*

The political conditions for ISI were laid by the change of the party from the PNR to the PRM, which represented – beyond the defeat of the Calles heritage – a transformed logic of political representation. The PNR was organized along territorial lines, with a national convention responsive to state conventions and a national directorate selected by the state directorates. The PRM instead was organized as a hierarchical three-tiered institution, with national, state, and municipal levels organized along corporatist principles. The reorganization of the party meant that lower levels depended on the upper ones instead of the other way around. The national assembly was organized according to the four corporatist sectors: peasant, worker, military, and popular. The national executive committee was made up not of members drawn from the territorial units but from the national corporatist sectors. Garrido (1982) contrasts the organizational charts of the PNR and the PRM to show how the party became functionally organized along corporatist, instead of territorial, lines. Although the PRM retained a territorial hierarchy, a parallel structure had been created, based on national interests as represented by the executive committees, running side by side with the territorial grassroots organizations of the party. By 1938, the executive committees had become the most important bodies in the party, conformed through corporatist sectors.

The military sector had a rather ambiguous position within the party. The realignment of political forces that marked the end of the *Maximato* involved a certain degree of militarization in state politics. The importance of the military in the postrevolutionary regime had decreased steadily as generals became owners of construction companies or tourism development firms, for example. The share of military expenditures as a percentage of federal government expenditures was reduced to almost 20 percent by the late 1930s (my own calculation using data from Lieuwen, 1968). Calles had been quite successful at making governors predominantly civilian (by 1934, less than half of the governors were military) and reducing military expenditures. The share of military expenditures in the budget was further reduced to less than 10 percent after the 1950s.

However, after the Cárdenas purge, military officers governed in 23 states. Cárdenas had to tread along a difficult equilibrium, providing military officials with a sense of belonging to the party while reducing their importance in national politics. One of the most important debates during the convention that transformed the PNR into the PRM involved finding a way to provide the largest weight in nominations to the corporatist organizations while retaining a limited role for the military sector. The system agreed upon was structured so that nominations would henceforth be controlled by corporatist organizations and not regional strongmen. Military members, although constituting a sector, would vote together with the popular sector (the *Confederación Nacional de Organizaciones Populares* – CNOP) for the nomination of their candidates. This prevented competition between military candidates and the candidates of the peasant, labor, and popular sectors.

3.5. Nominations and Control of Electoral Processes

In contrast with the system of primaries, which the PNR used until 1938, the new corporatist conventions offered a solution to the conflicts that usually emerged after those contests. The party's solution was to call for assemblies that would nominate candidates from each of the corporatist sectors. Once those assemblies had nominated a candidate, the party would decide among the three sector nominees, depending on the strength of the sector in a given state or district. These assemblies would be carried out in each district. Hence, in rural districts the candidate of the CNC would become the party nominee and, given the hegemony of the party, would win office, whereas in urban settings the candidate could come either from the worker or the popular sectors.

An additional blow to the territorial organization of politics in Mexico came from the 1946 electoral reform, which gave the federal government total control over the organization and surveillance of national elections and allowed only national parties, registered through rather restrictive processes, to contest any national election (Molinar Horcasitas, 1991). This, in fact, was equivalent to letting the PRI in its local cells control elections and prevented entry by would-be challengers who did not belong to the party. In some states, this guideline was even extended to the local elections so that only national parties could compete for local office, effectively banning the entry of any non-PRI candidate.

According to Scott (1959), the combination of single-party rule and presidential control of nominations meant solving a tension between winning elections and governing. In his view, the president selected candidates for the party with a logic of governance, not of electoral victory. Thus, Scott argues that: "Control of the electoral process by a single effective political party and manipulation of that party, in turn, by the president, offers one real advantage. In selecting the next national leader, the incumbent must take into account all of the varied interests throughout the country; but having done so he chooses a man to govern rather than simply to win an election" (Scott, 1959:216–217).

The federal executive accepted some limits on its authority vis-à-vis regional interests. Meddling with the staggered timing that characterized state elections or resorting to the removal or appointment of governors were only used as exceptional governance strategies. This was a price the president had to pay for the concentration of authority in so many other realms, and as I discuss in the next chapter, it was key for the stability of the system.

3.5.1. Staggered Electoral Calendar

Arguably, the president possessed an enormous amount of authority in terms of setting the agenda within the party, subject to the acceptance of veto players, over the nomination of future governors. However, this authority was only gradually exerted because it was not until the fourth year of his term that the incumbent president would have nominated more than half of the sitting governors. The staggered electoral calendar of Mexican gubernatorial elections was first noted by González Casanova (1965), but it has not received the attention that it deserves. Brandenburg (1956) noted that there would be no governor nominations during the first years of presidential terms but did not give special significance to the fact.

The staggered calendar was generated through incremental decisions, not by a purposeful plan. It was not until 1947 that all states had six-year gubernatorial terms because the reform that gave state governors six-year terms was not implemented until 1943. On the other hand, the presidential six-year term had existed since 1928, although Cárdenas was the first to actually benefit from it because President-elect Obregón was assassinated and three provisional presidents governed during the *Maximato*. The fact that governors were not granted six-year terms as part of the reforms of 1927 or 1933 suggests that the Sonorense faction, which was the victorious political group after the Revolution, desired to keep a more powerful president and federal legislature. This centralization of authority at the national level was not really achieved until the corporatization of the party structure in the 1938 reforms became reflected in the tax realm in the 1940s.

The change to six-year gubernatorial terms in 1942 suggests that local politicians were not willing, after all, to abide by a temporal asymmetry that presumably would be reflected in the relative power between the president and governors. That they had their terms extended precisely when financial authority was being concentrated in the federal government seems to confirm the basic insight of the commitment model in Chapter 1. This was an exchange: Local politicians were assured attractive national and local political careers, which could peak in a long six-year gubernatorial post, and in exchange they gave up their authority to tax at the local level.

If the presidential term were concurrent with local terms, the political coalition attaining office at the national level and supporting the presidential candidate of the PRI would also nominate offices at the local level. But this is not the case: Incoming presidents inherited governors who still had long stretches of their terms to finish.

The complex staggered calendar of gubernatorial elections in Mexico ensured that the president in office could nominate the majority of the governors only into the fourth year of his *sexenio*. An incoming president would inherit all governors from the previous presidential term, except for some that were elected at the same time as he was. During the first three years in office, only a few gubernatorial races took place, so that it was not until the fourth year of government that a majority of the governors were nominees of the current president.

By the time he nominated a successor for the federal executive, the president would have nominated around 90 percent of the current governors. However, the Mexican system has been characterized by making presidents "lame ducks" in their last year of office. Once a presidential successor was nominated, the power of the sitting president tended to erode very quickly.

3.5.2. State Politics

The corporatist shift in the party was translated into a strong representation of the peasant and labor confederations (CNC and CTM, respectively) in the Chamber of Deputies. According to Smith (1979), 15 percent of the

PRI deputies in the 1940–1943 legislature belonged to labor corporations, primarily the CTM, while 30 percent belonged to the CNC. The combined share of corporatist deputies remained at around 50 percent until the 1970s.[14] The percentage was even higher if one considers that some other deputies were also part of the corporatist quota system, although they were officially affiliated with the popular sector of the party, such as representatives in the teacher's union *Sindicato Nacional de Trabajadores de la Educación*, (SNTE) or federal employee labor organizations that do not fall clearly into the peasant or worker sectors.[15]

Conventional accounts of Mexican politics suggest that corporativism should be observed in gubernatorial nominations, too. The evidence contradicts this view: Very few governors emerged from the corporate organizations of the party.[16] Only 12 percent of the governors from 1935 to 1995 belonged to the prominent peak organizations such as the CTM, CNC, or SNTE, a much smaller percentage than studies have found in the Chamber of Deputies. The study of Brandenburg (1954) already suggested that the corporatist element was much weaker in the Senate than in the Chamber of Deputies, but it is even less important among governors.[17]

---

[14] In the 1980s, the share of corporatist deputies was around 30 percent (Nacif, 1996).

[15] Even into the 1980s, some labor representatives, for example, had quotas allocated in nominations that included completely rural districts. Not surprisingly, these representatives were among the most unsuccessful PRI candidates once the system became more competitive. A marked decrease in the importance of corporatist quotas is observed over time (de Remes, 1998) from constituting around 60 percent of the legislature in the 1980s to 30 percent in the 1990s. To some extent, this is because of the failure of corporatist candidates to win their districts at a time of high electoral competitiveness.

[16] There are few studies based on systematic empirical material that study governors in Mexico. Anderson (1971) studies 367 governors between 1946 and 1964. Hernández Rodriguez (1992) provides a study of governors nominated in the period 1983–1988. Smith (1979) includes governors within his study of political recruitment in Mexico, although he does not devote special attention to them. Camp (1974) provides evidence of the educational profiles and cliques (*camarillas*) of governors from 1935 to the 1970s, and in another paper (Camp, 1977) studies winners and losers competing for gubernatorial nominations between 1970 and 1974. Nacif (1996) compares governors nominated between 1976 and 1995 with federal senators and deputies within a framework of progressive ambition. Finally, Diaz-Cayeros and Langston (typescript) study governor career profiles during the era of PRI hegemony (1935–2000) and nominations at the time of increased electoral competition. Details on my analysis of governor profiles are provided in Diaz-Cayeros (1997).

[17] It is important to note that in coding governors as corporatist, I am not including most members of the CNOP as corporate members. The reason not to consider all CNOP leaders as corporatist is that such an organization is a catch-all residual area of the PRI, where anyone who did not fall into the main peasant and worker organizations was affiliated. I do

These "corporatist" governors, if they can be classified as such, have been concentrated in just a few states: Zacatecas, Tlaxcala, Quintana Roo, Querétaro, Oaxaca, Nayarit, Hidalgo, and Aguascalientes. Thus, most states have never been governed by politicians who could be considered members of a peak interest organization.[18]

3.5.3. Local Politics and Bossism

If governors were not members of peak corporatist organizations, did they retain a local base of political support in spite of the centralization of nominations in the party? The empirical evidence shows that *cacique* governors remained crucial players in the PRI hegemonic system. Around 21 percent of the governors from 1936 to 1994 can be considered to have been local bosses.[19] The share of *caciques* was just 12 percent during the Cárdenas term, but it reached 34 and 38 percent, respectively, during the periods of Adolfo Ruiz Cortines (1952–1958) and José López Portillo (1976–1982).

consider leaders of the teachers' or the government workers unions (SNTE and *Federación Sindical de Trabajadores del Estado*, or FSTE) as corporatist governors. There is no reason to consider a businessman affiliated with the CNOP a representative of corporatism.

[18] Hernández Rodriguez (1992) suggests that corporatist elements should be inversely related to the level of political office. Hence, whereas representatives from corporatist organizations might be characteristic of the Chamber of Deputies, they are less important in the Senate, the governorships, or the cabinet.

[19] I established a *cacique* coding in the following way. First, some governors were considered *caciques* when they were explicitly reported as such by Brandenburg (1964), González Casanova (1965), Hansen (1971), or Camp (1995). Second, when a family has a *cacique* member, all the relatives of that family, when they attained the governor's office, were coded as *caciques*. Third, in some instances, when detailed histories of state politics could be relied on, governors who were reported to owe their nominations to a *cacique* governor were also coded as such. The indirect coding was used in particular for well-known political processes in the states of Hidalgo (Gutierrez, 1990), Nayarit (Pacheco Ladrón de Guevara, 1990), Puebla (Pansters, 1992), San Luis Potosí (Falcón, 1984), and Tamaulipas (Alvarado Mendoza, 1992). According to Brandenburg (1964), the states that remained subject to strongmen were Michoacán (Lázaro Cárdenas), Puebla (the Avila Camacho family), Nayarit (Gilberto Flores Muñoz), and Baja California (Abelardo Rodríguez). In those states, Brandenburg believed, nominations were made according to the desires of regional strongmen (Brandenburg, 1964:151). To this he adds the commanding role played by influential politicians from Hidalgo (Javier Rojo Gómez), the state of Mexico (Adolfo López Mateos and Gustavo Baz), Sinaloa (Gabriel Leyva Velázquez), Tamaulipas (Emilio Portes Gil and Marte R. Gómez), Tlaxcala (Alfonso Corona del Rosal), Veracruz (Adolfo Ruiz Cortines), and Zacatecas (Leobardo Reynoso). González Casanova believes the remnants of the *cacique* states are those dominated by Mexican ex-presidents (Michoacán, Puebla, Veracruz, and Baja California), to which he adds Nayarit, Hidalgo, and perhaps Zacatecas (González Casanova, 1965:47).

Thus, local bosses, as discussed in the next chapter, were an integral part of the hegemonic equilibrium achieved by the PRI system.[20]

Caciques have not tended to disappear over time. Figure 3.2 provides some patterns of *cacique* survival in the states of Hidalgo and Tabasco among a few families (the Rojo and Lugo in Hidalgo and the Gurría, Trujillo, and Madrazo in Tabasco) that dominated politics in those states for decades.

Through the PRI hegemony, local politicians were guaranteed long and attractive political careers that could culminate in a governor's seat. But in order for this to occur, they had to move out of office every three or six years. The incentives of the system were so powerful that ambitious local politicians complied with gubernatorial nominations, even when they did not favor them. Governors stepped down because they knew this was the end of their career. A few continued to hold some other office, and some even reached the federal cabinet and eventually received the party's presidential nomination. Many former governors anchored important cliques (*camarillas*) that sought to achieve national power. But, for the most part, governors retired from politics, usually becoming involved in business in their home states. Their enterprises were profitable, to a great extent thanks to privileged access to credit, suppliers, government contracts, and sometimes outright corruption during and after their terms. Such enterprises were characteristic of a time of heavy state involvement in the economy through ISI. Outgoing governors were rarely prosecuted after abusing their power in office. An informal rule was established in which former governors were protected by their successors, rendering them virtually untouchable.

3.6. The Hegemonic Party and Fiscal Authority

When the *Partido Nacional Revolucionario* (PNR) held its first convention at the end of 1933, in order to nominate Lázaro Cárdenas, the assembly included the following programmatic statement in its Six Year Plan:

For the proper organization of a national tax system that would strengthen the economic unity of the country within the norms that the Revolution must press in

---

[20] *Cacique* governors differ statistically from other state executives. They have, on average, three more posts of political experience than non-*cacique* governors. They are likely to belong to corporatist organizations seven percent more often. *Caciques* in the governor's office have been federal deputies nine percent more often and have just held a party post five percent more often than non-*caciques*. In contrast, they are seven percent less likely to arrive in the governor's seat from a federal subcabinet post. For explicit tests of means, see Diaz-Cayeros (1997).

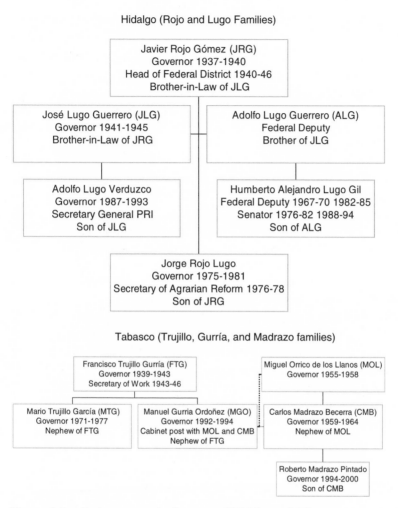

Hidalgo (Rojo and Lugo Families)

Javier Rojo Gómez (JRG)
Governor 1937-1940
Head of Federal District 1940-46
Brother-in-Law of JLG

José Lugo Guerrero (JLG)
Governor 1941-1945
Brother-in-Law of JRG

Adolfo Lugo Guerrero (ALG)
Federal Deputy
Brother of JLG

Adolfo Lugo Verduzco
Governor 1987-1993
Secretary General PRI
Son of JLG

Humberto Alejandro Lugo Gil
Federal Deputy 1967-70 1982-85
Senator 1976-82 1988-94
Son of ALG

Jorge Rojo Lugo
Governor 1975-1981
Secretary of Agrarian Reform 1976-78
Son of JRG

Tabasco (Trujillo, Gurría, and Madrazo families)

Francisco Trujillo Gurría (FTG)
Governor 1939-1943
Secretary of Work 1943-46

Miguel Orrico de los Llanos (MOL)
Governor 1955-1958

Mario Trujillo García (MTG)
Governor 1971-1977
Nephew of FTG

Manuel Gurria Ordoñez (MGO)
Governor 1992-1994
Cabinet post with MOL and CMB
Nephew of FTG

Carlos Madrazo Becerra (CMB)
Governor 1959-1964
Nephew of MOL

Roberto Madrazo Pintado
Governor 1994-2000
Son of CMB

Figure 3.2. *Cacique* pattern in the states of Hidalgo and Tabasco.

public finance, it is urgent to incorporate into the Federal Constitution the basis that will delimit the tax realms of the federation, states and municipalities, so that the cooperation of the diverse authorities may be assured, within a unitary regime in such cases when the tax concurrence be necessary, and eliminate fiscal barriers, interior taxes that hinder or block internal trade, since they create situations of inequality not derived from the peculiar economic and social conditions of our land ... The tax on trade and industry shall be simplified through the establishment of a uniform tax administered by the states, with the federation sharing part of its yield. At the same time, alcabalatory taxes should definitely disappear. (My translation, Six Year

Plan for the Presidential Period 1934–1940, in *Partido Revolucionario Institucional*, 1981, Vol. 2:370–371).

This was almost, word by word, the conclusion of the First National Tax Convention in 1925 and ratified by the Second Convention in 1933. The party had included a similar statement in its Declaration of Principles in 1929, but the fact that the party included it in the Six Year Plan is evidence that the recommendations were far from being adopted. The PNR–PRM–PRI would finally provide a mechanism for reducing the dimensionality of choice through the reorganization of the party, with the credible enforcement of the rule of no reelection and the corporatization of interest groups.

The transformation of the party was reflected in the fiscal realm. In the mid-1930s, Cárdenas tried to reform the constitution, defining exclusive taxes for each level of government. Notwithstanding his prestige and power, his initiative was blocked in Congress (Sentíes, 1942).[21] But in the years after 1938, the president used the party in order to obtain exclusive authority over most excise taxes and to provide for a law of federal revenue-sharing. By 1942, Octavio Sentíes, who was to become the head of the Mexico City government some years later, argued that the revenue-sharing system, at that time limited only to the realm of federal excise taxes, already foreshadowed the abdication of state authority over taxation: "The so called federalization of taxes is, rather, a concrete process of fiscal centralization" (Sentíes, 1942:67). Sentíes concluded that overlapping taxation had been resolved in favor of the federal government. According to him, the solution

---

[21] This reticence to accept a presidential bill is significant given that Congress in the 1930s started to tend toward rubber-stamping executive bills. In an interesting controversy in 1935 between Ramón Beteta (who had represented Aguascalientes in the Second National Tax Convention) and W. W. Cumberland concerning the Mexican Six Year Plan, Cumberland criticized the lack of checks and balances in Mexico: "A writer naively cites as evidence of 'the spirit of cooperation between the President and the national and state legislatures' the fact that an amendment to the Mexican Constitution which deals with the agrarian program was approved by twenty-nine State legislatures within three days after the amendment was introduced into the Mexican Congress. Of course what was really proved is that responsible legislatures do not exist, either for the federal government or for the several States. Agriculture, industry, education and general welfare alike fare badly under conditions such as these" (Cumberland, 1935:62). Beteta defended the Mexican system by arguing that this was not irresponsibility but that "when one party controls both the Executive and the Legislative and also the various local governments, an amendment of the constitution can be passed without difficulty, and without making Legislatures irresponsible" (Beteta, 1935:88–90).

involved a unilateral decision that yielded unequal revenue shares to states that never fully compensated the fiscal losses. In the end, Sentíes predicted that "if the centralization of taxes continues, the fiscal-legislative activity of the states will come to be reduced to zero. So will the authority to tax, a characteristic of local sovereignty.... The centralization of taxes, the way it is proceeding, denies the economic autonomy of States and Municipalities, destroying the political autonomy granted by the federal system" (Sentíes, 1942:68).

A centralized fiscal system was proposed during the Third National Tax Convention (1947). The system envisaged that: first, local governments would rely on the property tax and some other minor taxes as their exclusive sources of revenue, eliminating their taxes on trade and industry; second, states would receive revenue shares from federal excises on natural resources, alcoholic beverages, matches, and other items, and they would be guaranteed 25 percent of any additional revenue collected through those federal taxes; third, a national sales tax would be introduced, where the rate would be shared between states and the federal government, but it would be administered as a centralized federal tax; fourth, the income tax would become exclusively federal, although states would retain some authority over (very low yield) taxes on agriculture and livestock; and fifth, the *contribución federal* would be finally reduced to 5 percent in all states in order to gradually phase it out in the coming years. These proposals were fully accepted by the assembly, which was very different from its predecessors. In the Third Convention, no roll call votes were taken. Agreements were already in place through the hierarchy of the party.

The increase in the size of the federal government in the economy after 1940, and the fact that federal revenue exhibited the most dynamic pattern, keeping pace with the increase in national product (i.e., it had the largest elasticity) while state and municipal taxes did not (aside from those in the Federal District), accounted for a gradual increase in the federal share in overall revenue. The share of the states shrank, even with the granting of federal transfers. During the second half of the century, the proportion of federal, state, and municipal taxes would remain more or less fixed, although the composition would be transformed so that local governments would increasingly rely primarily on federal transfers and less on their own sources of tax revenue.

The federal government consolidated fiscal centralization by becoming the only level of government allowed to levy taxes on foreign trade, natural resources (including all oil and mining rights), banks, and insurance institutions, as well as excises on electricity, tobacco, gas, matches, alcohol, forestry, and beer (art. 73-XXIX).[22] States theoretically still retained the capacity to levy an income tax, payroll taxes, sales taxes, and other taxes not explicitly stated in article 73. However, over time, the federal government came to monopolize almost all sources of revenue.[23] The federal treasury provided tax revenue shares (*participaciones*) to the states, which increasingly came to constitute the most important source of local government finance. The system of tax coordination that characterizes the Mexican federal system today was the consequence of this regional compromise struck between the federal and state governments after 1947.

The Mexican regional compromise required that local politicians delegate financial power to the president in exchange for sources of patronage through the federal bureaucracies, attractive careers in the federal government, and an active involvement of the federal government in state development. The arrangement took almost two decades to become stable. The solution was achieved through institutional rules and a peculiar political organization, the hegemonic party. The configuration of veto players at the local level made this system self-enforcing in the sense that local and national players were better off with this arrangement and therefore willing to abide by it. The losers in this arrangement were democratic politics and federalism.

In an insightful discussion of the centralization of politics in Mexico in the second half of the 20th century, Robert Scott argues that:

> [The weakening of the local machines] was coupled with the ever-increasing financial dependence of the formal state governments upon the central authorities, because just as the growing complexities of social and economic life called for greater expenditures by governmental agencies, the national government was busily preempting most of the major sources of tax revenue for itself. This forced the local officers to go to Mexico City, hat in hand, seeking grants from the national government to satisfy the demands of their constituents. (Scott, 1959:135)

Scott then goes on to discuss that there was a compensation for the loss of local financial independence and fiscal initiative in the form of electoral

---

[22] Municipal governments were granted in 1983 the exclusive right to levy the tax on land, but many of them had been exercising that right exclusively long before.

[23] At the end of the 20th century, the only taxes collected by the states were a payroll tax (usually one or two percent), a tax on license plates, and the tax on new cars – a federal tax transferred to the states. All other taxes were exclusively collected by the federal or municipal governments.

success. To others writing only a few years later, this trade-off was viewed in a clearly negative light because it reflected a federal government that was overawing the states. Pablo González Casanova, writing about democracy in Mexico, put it in the following terms:

The dependence of states with regard to the central government is a political, military, and financial fact. From the application of the Constitution to remove governors, passing by the political functions of the zone chiefs, the interior ministry agents, the deputies and senators who make a political career in the Capital city, the scarce finances of the states, the extreme dependence of state revenue on the federal one, and the possibilities for the oscillation of a hundred percent in federal aid, all the way to a political calendar that gradually accentuates the power of the president in the course of his presidential term, all these facts imply that the political instruments crafted to achieve a system of "checks and balances," like the one Madison proposed, do not function in the contemporary Mexican reality. (My translation, González Casanova, 1965:41)

Was this an exaggerated assessment? How complete was the sacrifice of state autonomy? What was the developmental consequence of the fiscal agreement? These questions are explored in the next two chapters.

4

Nominations, Veto Players, and Gubernatorial Stability

4.1. Stability in Political Ambition

This chapter explores the sources of stability of the Mexican regional compromise. An analysis of gubernatorial nominations allows me to show that politicians were in a political equilibrium: All major political players were willing to play within the rules of the game of progressive ambition established by the PRI because the system had become self-enforcing. Gubernatorial nominations were driven by a logic of unanimous approval by the main veto players, both at the national and local levels, which made the arrangement stable. The nomination game was underpinned by the peculiar crafting of institutional rules discussed in the previous chapter, including the no-reelection clause, federal control over electoral processes, and the staggered timing of elections. Hence, the purpose of this chapter is to explain why local political actors complied with the set of rules created by the PRI to structure political ambition, even as their fiscal authority was threatened.

In terms of the theoretical framework in Chapter 1, I show how the problems of commitment and redistribution were easier to solve once politicians found a way to channel their political ambitions at the local level. The analysis of gubernatorial stability sheds light not just on the dynamics of local politics but also on the way in which, notwithstanding disagreements and differing political preferences of the president and the politicians in the regions, they could agree on cooperating and respecting each other through the nomination process within the hegemonic party.

In contrast with the conventional wisdom among Mexico experts, I argue that presidential power in the process of governor nomination under the hegemonic party was limited because local and national veto players could counterweight his choices. The no-reelection rule allowed for a fluidity in the circulation of politicians that ensured that no politician or his clique (*camarilla*) would expect to be permanently excluded from the benefits of political power. Federal control over the electoral processes and vesting the authority over nominations with the president allowed for a solution of social choice dilemmas. The staggered timing of elections ensured that local politicians would remain in office even as presidents changed, providing a countervailing force to presidential power.

The chapter is organized as follows. The next section discusses the conventional wisdom on gubernatorial nominations in Mexico. Section 4.3 introduces a spatial model of gubernatorial nomination and veto players that sheds light on the nature of the stability in the game played by Mexican regional politicians. Section 4.4 provides empirical evidence for the model.

4.2. The Conventional Wisdom

Did governors have political authority once the hegemonic political system was established? According to Meyer: "The state governors are the center of the local political system, but all their important political decisions are made in consultation with the President and some of his ministers. The entire political life of a governor is controlled by the center, from his nomination by the Party to the selection of his successor" (Meyer, 1977:12). In Meyer's view, political control in the hands of the president was exercised through the removal of content in the electoral process; the centralization of resources in the federal sphere; a cult of personality that led to paternalism; the dominance of a political elite linked to the economic elite; and, finally, the occasional use of force by the federal government (Meyer, 1977). This "authoritarian" view of presidential power was already present in the classic work of Brandenburg, although he limited his judgment to the nomination process, not the actual exercise of power: "From pre-nomination to inauguration, the gubernatorial succession is controlled from Mexico City. The President of Mexico selects, the [federal] government minister oversees, and the defense minister enforces" (Brandenburg, 1964:150).

In a more nuanced analysis, Scott argues that the president used his corporatist power to enforce discipline among functional sectors, and this enabled him also to control local politics: "With this control [of the confederations] he could dictate nominations, elections, appointments and removals at all levels of government" (Scott, 1959:137). According to Scott,

"The sharpest interaction [within the political process] takes place in the struggles to influence nominations to executive posts, particularly the presidency and governorships" (Scott, 1959:198). Brandenburg also stresses that the "[p]ower transfer from a state governor to his successor follows the presidential pattern [because] the final word belongs to the head of the Revolutionary Family," while also conceding that "in several instances he [the head of the Revolutionary Family] merely rubber-stamps the selection by a regional strongman" (Brandenburg, 1964:150).

In spite of the prevailing view, it is not obvious that governors were simply presidential puppets. As mentioned in the last chapter, *cacique* governors who controlled extensive political machines in their states survived the corporatization of the party. According to Grindle, the control of political machines by those governors "earned them impressive bargaining power when dealing with the President and the national political leaders" (Grindle, 1977:126). Gubernatorial nominations in the single party were highly contested among state political leaders because they provided patronage, authority, and prestige to their holder. It is difficult to understand why politicians would devote valuable political resources on gubernatorial nominations and elections if the office were just a powerless part of the federal bureaucracy.[1]

The conventional view of candidate nomination within the PRI suggests that the president chooses a governor whose ideal point (i.e., his most preferred point in the policy space) is the same as his own. That is, because there is no check on presidential power, supposedly the president can nominate gubernatorial candidates as though they were appointed bureaucrats. As I will show, such a view is at odds with the empirical evidence. The president usually faced, and sometimes even nominated, governors characterized by ideological profiles different from his own. The institutional characteristics and procedures created by the hegemonic party system constrained those presidential choices.

In joint work with Joy Langston, I have analyzed the careers of governors in Mexico, showing that they tended to follow local ambition paths rather than achieving office through climbing the ladder of the federal bureaucracies. Performing a factor analysis of the career paths of 221 governors from

---

[1] It should be noted that not all accounts share this preconception. For example, although pointing out that governors can hardly challenge presidential leadership openly, to some extent because of the lack of financial resources, Grindle concedes that "the relations between the federal and the state governments are characterized by mutual attempts at manipulation and accommodation" (Grindle, 1977:127).

Table 4.1. *Factor Analysis of Governor Profiles*

	Factor 1 Federal Bureaucratic	Factor 2 Local	Factor 3 Federal Elective – Partisan
Deputy secretary	**0.92**	−0.05	−0.03
Secretary	**0.92**	−0.13	−0.004
Local deputy	−0.09	**0.67**	−0.02
Local PRI official	−0.15	**0.67**	0.24
Municipal president	−0.12	**0.63**	−0.24
Secretary of state government	0.16	**0.38**	0.09
National PRI official	0.12	−0.12	**0.74**
Federal deputy	0.02	0.23	**0.67**
Senator	−0.27	−0.22	**0.48**
Corporatist organization	−0.07	0.35	**0.46**
Eigenvalue	2.13	1.57	1.41
Percentage of variance	21.30	15.70	14.10
Cumulative	21.30	37.00	51.10

Highest values are in bold type.

1960 to 1995, we show that, although career paths often combined federal and local experience, the overwhelming majority of the governors achieved a nomination by following careers outside the main federal administrative posts (cabinet and deputy cabinet posts).

This factor analysis sheds light on what it meant to hold different types of experience before becoming a governor. The analysis was constructed through dummy variables indicating whether a governor had previously been a federal deputy, a local deputy, a mayor, a cabinet member, a deputy cabinet minister, a senator, a *Secretario General de Gobierno* in the state government, held leadership posts in the national or the local PRI, or belonged to the corporatist organizations. Table 4.1 reports varimax rotated factor loadings (i.e., the correlations evaluated in such a way that their structure is most simple) for each of the individual variables underlying the factor scores. The three factors cumulatively account for more than half of the variance in governor career profiles.

The first factor captures the career path of a governor whose career was constructed by advancing through top federally appointed bureaucratic posts. That pattern is distinct from the two others, as can be seen in the low loadings of the variables for belonging to the cabinet or the deputy cabinet with respect to the two other dimensions. The second factor instead

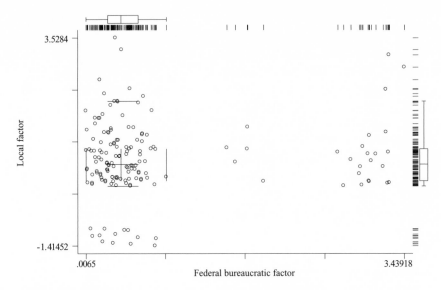

Figure 4.1. Governor career paths in Mexico, 1960–1994.

represents a "local" political career through both elective and bureaucratic posts at the state level, and the third factor represents an ambition ladder through the federal legislature and the holding of national partisan and corporatist posts. The factor scores suggest that politicians who became governors first by escalating the federal bureaucracy to enter the extended cabinet were distinct from those who followed localist or electoral careers. The career experience that helped individuals win a governorship was not necessarily a post through the federal bureaucracy.

Figure 4.1 graphs governors according to the first two factor scores, namely following a federal bureaucratic or a local political career. Clearly, there are some individuals with high scores on both dimensions, indicating that they followed careers that combined both types of posts. Hernández Rodriguez (1984) has argued that such combinations of career paths were a prerequisite for becoming a governor. In contrast to this view, the graph shows that the overwhelming majority of the governors followed careers with low scores in the federal bureaucracy. They fundamentally combined local career posts and posts in the federal legislature (the third factor, which the graph does not show). The box plots at the edges of the graph indicate that more than 50 percent of the governors are located in the area of a moderate local factor and a low federal bureaucratic one. When one plots factors 3 and 2, it also becomes clear that all governors had either local experience or federal elective experience, or both. There were virtually no governors without local *and* elective experience, whereas there were many governors without federal bureaucratic posts.

The conventional wisdom that conceives of governors as mere agents of the president in the states is hence probably wrong. There is surely some truth in the notion that the president controlled nominations, often choosing politicians who were more to his liking. But the president did not fill governor posts primarily by sending some of his close aides to become governors of their home states. In order to understand the logic of gubernatorial nominations in Mexico, the spatial model developed in the next section makes sense of the importance of local careers in governor profiles while showing that the power to nominate governors allowed the president to select local politicians with ideological preferences close to his own.

4.3. A Spatial Model of Gubernatorial Nomination

In a highly stylized fashion, the spatial model suggests that the presidential nomination of gubernatorial candidates within the PRI was determined jointly by the president's preferences, the status quo (personified by the governor inherited from the previous *sexenio*), and the preferences of "veto players" who were able to constrain the president's decision within some bounds. The inherited status quo is important because it takes into account the temporal mismatch between the presidential and gubernatorial electoral calendars and the elected nature of governors: The president cannot appoint governors but can only nominate them to win elections in a staggered calendar; and he inherits governors that he did not nominate. Consonant with the almost unanimous agreement of the literature on this issue (see Hansen, 1971:110–111), the president is the actor who chooses gubernatorial candidates within the PRI. But given the structure of political institutions, the game suggests that the president must respect the preferences of veto players.

Some political actors become "veto players" because the president requires their support in order to have his nomination accepted by politicians within the PRI. Such support would primarily entail mobilizing votes and political support, but it could also involve agreement by important actors within a state, such as business groups, labor unions, or local bosses (*caciques*). It should be clear that this is a de facto veto power, not a consequence of formal procedures or constitutional rules that vest authority in those players. The model assumes that veto players in each state behave as unitary actors. Because the gubernatorial candidate in each state must face an election, he requires the support of a local veto player, which one can think of as the local PRI organization, in order to command the votes to officially win the election. This is perhaps one of the most subtle aspects of the Mexican political system, which has often been attributed to the requirements of "legitimacy" of the regime. Rather than attributing elections to "legitimacy," the model developed here suggests that electoral processes were crucial at the local level as mechanisms that aligned governor preferences with the interests of the powerful local veto players.

Veto players, such as local politicians, are conceived of as different from the nominated governor. Local politicians seeking to advance their political careers might not be nominated by the president as the PRI candidates for the governorship, but, as I will show, they abide by the nomination.[2] I argue that this is what provided stability to the nomination system. Gubernatorial nominations, although controlled by the president, required respect for local political preferences, which had an underlying base of clienteles, business interests, and other forms of political support.[3] That did not mean governors were pure representatives of those interests. But neither were governors pure agents of the president.

In the model, veto players defer to presidential nominations because they hold a long-term perspective. If a gubernatorial candidate is selected who is far from the veto player's ideal preference, there is still the future possibility of having a governor selected who better fulfills the player's ideal policy position when in office.[4] A veto player maximizes the expected value of a stream of governors without heavily discounting the future. But perhaps more critically, a veto player defers to the president's nomination if the nominee is at least as good for the veto player and no worse than

---

[2] Veto players might be composed of the business interests of a state's producers as represented by a local chamber of commerce or industry. In some states, a specific powerful firm or a small group of landowners might be the interests that could effectively veto an unwanted gubernatorial nomination. It is important to repeat that, in contrast with much of the literature employing this concept, veto players in this case are not defined by a legal or procedural process. Informal practices within the PRI, including norms of deference toward other politicians, are what I have in mind, rather than any specific legal power.

[3] In a democratic setting, the relevant veto player could be the median voter, who would be decisive in an election involving such a candidate.

[4] This ensures that the nomination game does not become a zero-sum game in which each player tries to impose his most preferred outcome, which could degenerate into civil war. It is akin to the requirement in democratic settings that losers should perceive being able to win in the future and should value that future sufficiently (see Przeworski, 1991).

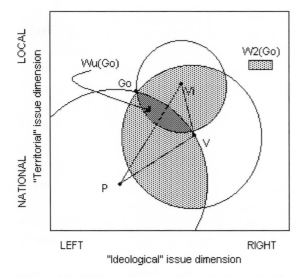

Figure 4.2. Winsets in a two-dimensional model of gubernatorial nomination.

the current governor, who is taken to be the status quo. Sitting governors cannot be reelected when their term ends.

I assume, however, that the status quo is the reversion point of the bargain. To the extent that no agreement is reached between the president and veto players, it seems reasonable to suggest that the current governor's closest and most trusted collaborator, the secretary of government, will become the nominee. In the game, the president nominates a governor using the logic of subgame perfection: Looking down the game tree, he will nominate only a candidate who would be acceptable to the veto player.[5]

Politicians disagree along different issue dimensions. Figure 4.2 shows a two-dimensional issue space. It is composed of a left–right ideological dimension on the horizontal axis and a local–national cleavage on the vertical axis. Each player will be described in this issue space by an "ideal

---

[5] This can be modeled as a sequential two-player game over an issue space. In a one-dimensional setting, players have single-peaked preferences. From a specific status quo, the president moves first, proposing a candidate. The veto player then either accepts or rejects this nomination. The payoff structure is given by the comparison of the loss functions of the distances from each player's ideal points to both the status quo (G_0) and the nominated candidate (G_n) if the nomination is accepted and zero if it is rejected. This game would only be zero-sum if the loss functions of both players were identical. The notion that the veto player has a longer temporal horizon than the president could be captured by greater tolerance to being far from the ideal point (and hence different loss functions), in which case the game is never zero-sum. For details, see Diaz-Cayeros (1997).

point" that represents his or her ideal combination of a left–right ideological position and a local–national position. The current governor can also be represented as a specific point. In this two-dimensional setting, there is no reason to assume that there should only be one veto player.[6] For the sake of simplicity, I propose that there are only two veto players in each state, a local one (V_i) and a national one (V). Both veto players can share the same right–left position but fall on different sides of the local–national issue dimension. The fact that they possess different interests on the second dimension makes them have separate ideal points. The presence of such a difference creates a nonempty set of alternative gubernatorial nominations the president can make.

If players have Euclidean preferences, their preferences can be represented by circular indifference curves in Figure 4.2.[7] The winset $W(x)$ of the status quo x is a set of points that a decisive set of players would prefer to the prevailing situation. If, for example, two players can make up a majority and the majority rules, the shaded area in Figure 4.2 represents the winset of the current governor when $x = G_o$, denoted by $W_2(G_o)$ (where 2 denotes that this winset requires a majority of two players). Under simple majority rule, the winset is (almost) never empty.[8] The winset of interest for the model is one requiring unanimous approval, denoted $W_u(x)$. The heavily shaded area represents that winset.

To close the model, let me define the Pareto set (P), which can be visually represented by the area contained in a triangle uniting the ideal points of the three players PV_iV. The Pareto set contains those issue positions where no player can be made better-off without making another player worse-off. The unanimous winset of any point in the Pareto set is empty. That is, veto players would not agree unanimously to something that makes at least one of them worse-off. But when the status quo lies outside the Pareto set, there will always be a nonempty unanimous winset.[9]

---

[6] In a one-dimensional case, it is only meaningful to include whichever veto player is decisive because any other would be redundant; or if two were decisive on opposite ends of the current governor, the status quo would remain.

[7] This implies assuming that preferences are separable and that both dimensions are weighted equally. On the implications of such assumptions, see Shepsle (1979), McKelvey (1986), Ordeshook (1986), and Shepsle and Bonchek (1997).

[8] Except when the status quo is the median in all directions (a rather exceptional case); see Ordeshook (1986).

[9] Formally, when x is a point in R^2, W_u is the unanimous winset, and P is the Pareto set, if $x \in P$, then $W_u(x) = \varnothing$; on the other hand, if $x \notin P$, then $W_u(x) \neq \varnothing$. Proof: The first expression is straightforward from the definition of the Pareto set, which is $P = \{x : \nexists\, y \succeq x\ \forall i\}$, and the

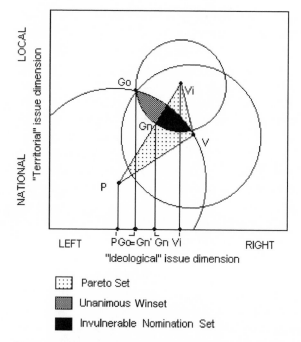

Figure 4.3. Pareto set, unanimous winset, and invulnerable nomination set.

The existence of a unanimous winset does not mean that a specific nomination that is unanimously preferred to the status quo will fall in the Pareto set. In fact, in the example provided, the winset includes points both outside and inside the Pareto set, as can be more clearly seen in Figure 4.3.[10] Nominations falling outside the Pareto set, however, would be "vulnerable" in the sense that the players would unanimously prefer some alternative to

definition of the unanimous winset, $W_u(x) = \{y : y \succeq x \; \forall i\}$, where $\succeq$ is a weak preference relationship, so that if $x \in P$, then $W_u(x) = \varnothing$. On the other hand, if $x \notin P$, then by definition $\exists \, y : y \succeq x \; \forall i$, which means that $W_u(x) \neq \varnothing$).

[10] That they might fall in the Pareto set is given by the condition that $P \cap W_u(x) \neq \varnothing$. If $x \notin P$, then $\exists$ some $y : y \succeq x \; \forall i$, so that $W_u(x) \neq \varnothing$; this, however, does not mean that because $y \in W_u(x)$ also $y \in P$. This property in fact depends on the specific assumption of Euclidean preferences, or at least preferences with the same A matrix. Under Euclidean preferences, through a geometric argument, one can show that since the sum of the two radii of the indifference contours of two players is never smaller than the contract curve that joins them, then $P \cap W_u(x) \neq \varnothing$. Moreover, the specific nomination always falls on the contract curve that joins the president with one of the other players. Moreover, Schofield, Grofman, and Feld (1988) have shown that as long as the space is two-dimensional, there is a nonempty core with a qualified majority rule of more than two-thirds, so that an invulnerable winset always exists under the most stringent rule of unanimity.

them. On the other hand, if a nomination falls in the Pareto set, no further unanimous change can be agreed on because at least one player would be worse-off by a change. In fact, any point inside the triangle of the Pareto set offers the possibility of having one player made worse-off while the two others could improve. Hence, if the president desires to make a nomination for a governor that will elicit support from all veto groups and the least resistance to attempts to change it at a subsequent point in time, he would presumably choose a point in the heavily shaded area labeled in Figure 4.3 as the invulnerable nomination set. Which point would the president choose among all the possible ones? The optimal one is the nomination at G_n, which is inside the invulnerable nomination set and the closest to the president's ideal point.

Notice also in Figure 4.3 that if one were to ignore the territorial dimension, the ideal points of the status quo governor, the president and the local veto player (V_i) could then be projected onto a horizontal axis. As compared with a one-dimensional model, in a two-dimensional setting, the nomination process is biased in favor of veto players. The same is true if the only relevant dimension is the territorial one, where the president ends up proposing a nomination that is not on the other side of the veto player with respect to the status quo. In this specific example, the president appears quite powerless to appoint his preferred governor on the left–right dimension (on that dimension alone, he would prefer to have the current governor reelected) and less capable of getting a favorable nomination in the territorial dimension. He is better-off than with the status quo, which is true of all the players as well. But the president has to trade off some left–right preferences in order to improve on the territorial dimension and hence achieve an indifference contour closer to his ideal point.

The nomination of G_n, as long as the president retains his nomination power, is not vulnerable, except if changes in the location of the president or the veto players occur. In principle, the positions of the veto groups could actually be fixed or only change very slowly.[11] The ideal point of the president, however, would change with each six-year term (*sexenio*). If a change in the president's ideal position occurs, G_n is vulnerable if it falls outside the now changed Pareto set. Hence, the next president can change the local status quo.

---

[11] If veto players are further away from the president but still on the same rays that join them, we know that the winset does not become larger. (For proof, see Tsebelis, 1995.)

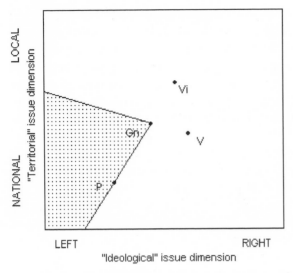

Figure 4.4. Invulnerability region for change in presidential position.

Figure 4.4 depicts the limits of the possibilities of these changes by showing the two areas where the next president could be located. The figure is constructed by extending a ray from each veto player that passes by the gubernatorial nomination in order to determine the region where that nomination lies inside the Pareto set. If the ideal point of the new president lies in the shaded region, the governor nominated by the previous president will remain invulnerable. That is, a successor who is more extremist than the former president, or at least lies in the same general direction relative to the governor as the last president, will allow the governor to remain in the Pareto set, and the next gubernatorial nomination will be invulnerable.

How likely is it that the new president will fall in an area like the shaded one? Except when the president and the veto groups are perfectly aligned in the same ray, the shaded area is always smaller than its complement in the issue space. The most likely outcome then is that with a change of president incumbent governors will fall outside the new Pareto set and therefore become vulnerable. Because by construction presidents and local veto players lie at opposite ends of the national–local dimension, the unanimous winset remains small. That means that swings in presidential ideology open up room for unanimous improvement, but those movements will tend to be over small issue distances.

109

A final point should be made regarding the possibility of governor removals. Even when a governor is invulnerable in the sense that he is in the Pareto set, if for any reason the president wishes to remove him, the winset between the two veto players with respect to the gubernatorial nomination generally is not empty (except when G_n falls along the contract curve of the veto players). Veto players would therefore be willing to go along with the appointment of a substitute governor. If the Senate, for example, were controlled by representatives located in the positions of V_i and V, and if the president requested that the Senate declare the dissolution of powers for governor G_n, there would always exist a substitute governor who would make the removal possible. Such a removal is costly for the president, however, because the substitute governor will be ideologically further away from him. Because of this cost, it is likely that removals of governors will occur primarily when the president is ideologically distant from the incumbent governor.

Thus, the model characterizes gubernatorial nominations as equilibria with the following features. First, the president cannot impose a nomination of his ideal point simply because he prefers it. Second, the dissatisfaction of the president with regard to the nominated governor depends on his relative position vis-à-vis the status quo and the veto player. Third, if presidents change through time and they swing according to a pendulum pattern (left–right), nominations will tend to shift increasingly less over time. Fourth, if local veto players do not change over time, they can increasingly obtain nominations that are better for them. Fifth, presidential power is limited to authority over party nominations; policies implemented by a governor during his term may differ from those of the president. Finally, the president is satisfied with this arrangement to the extent that it allows him to move the status quo closer to his ideal position, and local veto players are content to the extent that they face governors who are never further away from their ideal position, compared with the initial status quo. This is what makes the political equilibrium self-enforcing.

The implications of the simple model for understanding PRI hegemony are profound: Presidential nominations of governors in Mexico tended to be highly consensual because they implied improvements, for all veto players as well as the president, compared with the status quo. It was possible for a nomination to increase distance in one dimension in order to obtain a better outcome in the other dimension. The invulnerable unanimous winset became progressively smaller as the gubernatorial nomination moved toward the contract curve of the two veto players. However, this reduction in feasible nominations over time did not render the system completely immobile. Hence, the success of the Mexican regional political arrangement was predicated on the multidimensionality of political interactions. The territorial (national–local) dimension of politics gave room for gubernatorial nominations that could be highly consensual.

4.4. Evidence Drawn from Governors' Ideological Positions

In order to provide evidence for the model and to test the hypothesis derived from it, one should ideally possess a mapping of the spatial position of the president, governors, and veto players over the relevant dimensions. Unfortunately, the positions of the veto players are, in general, unobservable. The positions of governors and the president can be obtained from an ideological coding developed by Diaz-Cayeros (1997). Although I cannot perform a direct test of a formal model, much can be learned from testing hypotheses derived from its implications (Morton, 1999). The following hypotheses are tested in this section.

Hypothesis 1: Policy shifts through presidential nominations of governors will be small. This is because as long as the president and the local veto players are on opposite ends of the territorial issue dimension, the unanimous winset should be small.

Hypothesis 2: Presidents will usually be unable to nominate governors whose most preferred issue positions are identical to their own. This is because nominations can only be identical to presidential preferences when the presidential ideal point is between that of the incumbent governor and the veto players, which is a highly unlikely pattern in a two-dimensional setting.

Hypothesis 3: If the most common configurations of policy preferences are like the ones depicted in Figure 4.2, presidents will mostly show moderate power and will often appear powerless in their nominations. If true, Hypotheses 1, 2, and 3 refute theories of *presidencialismo* that predict gubernatorial nominations to be on the same ideal point as the president.

Hypothesis 4: Presidents should propose changes to the status quo only when they can nominate a more congenial governor. One should observe that if a president proposes a nominee whose policies are different from the previous governor's, the nominee should generally be closer to the president than the status quo. Because trade-offs across policies are possible, this should be viewed as a probabilistic statement. The greater the shift from the status quo, the more one should observe a bias toward gubernatorial nominees whose policies are closer to the president's.

Hypothesis 5: Governors who do not finish their terms because they are removed by the president will tend to be further away from him in the issue space; conversely, governors who do not finish their terms because they move into the federal cabinet should possess policy positions similar to presidential preferences.

If governors were mere creatures of the president, the power of the latter would be demonstrated if governors exhibited the president's preferences. My data suggest, however, that the ideology of governors strongly differed from that of the president. Although Mexico was governed by a single party, there is widespread agreement among scholars that the party was characterized by various ideological wings (see Hansen, 1971:110). The party claimed to represent a reformist revolutionary creed, but as the discussion in the previous chapters has shown, wide differences existed, for example between the "liberal" conceptions of property of President Calles and the more "collectivist" leanings of President Cárdenas. The party was able to accommodate, within the same "revolutionary family," politicians ranging from the radical left to the conservative right.

Each governor can be characterized as having a rightist, leftist, or centrist ideological position, depending on assessments and judgments drawn from biographical data. My governor database codes 485 governors from 1936 to 1994.[12] Although there are cases where it is relatively simple to determine that a protégé of, say, President Cárdenas was a leftist governor or to code Governor Maximino Avila Camacho in Puebla, the leader of the more conservative wing of the party during the 1940s, as a rightist, in most cases the coding depended on difficult judgment calls. My convention was to consider a governor to have an ideology code on the right when he was clearly associated with the political cliques (*camarillas*) of presidents Alemán, Avila Camacho, de la Madrid, or Salinas and to the left when associated with the *camarillas* of Cárdenas, López Mateos, Echeverría, and López Portillo. Such cliques usually are formed very early in a politician's career, and the assumption is that groups form around individuals with similar ideological positions. Some governors were coded according to their relationship with

[12] Of course, coding the "ideology" of politicians can be extremely tricky, especially in a system where one cannot use voting records, political platforms, or some other open behavioral trait for such a purpose. Lacking these, one must assume that career profiles and biographies tell us something about an individual's political beliefs.

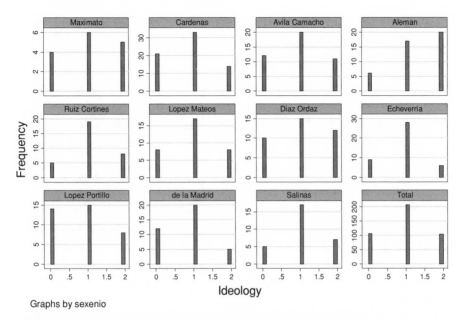

Figure 4.5. Ideological profile of governors by presidential period.

the *camarillas* of their states.[13] Another convention was that if a governor's ideology profile was known but there was no information about his successor, when the successor had worked under his predecessor's administration I considered the successor to adhere to the same ideology. Finally, leaders of labor and peasant organizations were coded as leftists. I did not have enough information to code 72 governors, who are treated as missing cases. A detailed report of the coding conventions and governors falling into each ideological profile is discussed in Diaz-Cayeros (1997).

The data summarized in Figure 4.5 suggest that the nomination of governors did not simply reflect presidential ideal policy positions. Although a rightist president such as, for example, Miguel Alemán nominated governors biased toward the right during his term, he also nominated many governors to the left. The converse is true for leftist presidents such as Lázaro Cárdenas and José López Portillo. Although the average nomination is consistent with what are generally regarded as the ideological leanings of the incumbent president, the most striking feature of Figure 4.5 is the spread of

---

[13] This relative coding means that, for example, a leftist governor in a state dominated by a rightist *camarilla* may be considered a centrist in a different state.

ideological profiles of governors nominated by each single president. The PRI was not an ideologically homogenous party.[14]

Table 4.2 provides evidence on the degree of ideological continuity in each state from one governor to the next. Continuity is measured through the difference between the ideological code of the new governor and that of the previous governor. I code whether there was no shift in ideology, a moderate shift (i.e., from the center to the left or right, and from the left or right to the center), or a radical shift (from one extreme to the other).

There is a large degree of continuity in state ideology because in 46.3 percent of the cases the subsequent governor shares the ideological position of his predecessor. In 42.9 percent of the cases, there is a moderate shift in the sense that, for example, a leftist governor is substituted by a centrist; and in only 10.8 percent of the instances are there radical shifts in which a leftist governor is substituted by a rightist or the other way around. This pattern is consonant with Hypothesis 1. Table 4.2 also shows that a large number of states (12) did not witness any radical shift at all.

To test the hypotheses derived from the model, however, it is crucial to show whether continuity is high compared with a counterfactual scenario of a purely random process. If a random process yields relative frequencies of no shift, moderate shift, and radical shift in 33.3 percent of the cases, the average value of no shift is significantly different (and higher), in a statistical sense ($t = 4.04$), from a haphazard event. However, the correct counterfactual scenario is one that takes into account the *actual* distribution of governors (both previous and current). Moderate governors cannot have anything but moderate shifts. Hence, the actual distribution of governor preferences yields a joint probability distribution of the form given in Table 4.3. The table reports in each cell the Markov chain probability of the distribution of governor ideologies, given the distribution at time $t-1$ and a random assignment of ideologies at time t. That is, because there is a specific proportion of each type of governor, a random change should produce some outcomes more often than others, depending on the joint

---

[14] The only exception occurs with Miguel de la Madrid (MMH). Although usually regarded as a rightist president, the governors that he nominated tended to be more leftist. This could be a consequence of his "lame duck" status as a president who had to accept conditions laid down by nontechnocratic politicians at a time of deep economic crisis. The other possibility is that because he included a disproportionate share of technocrats in his cabinet, he had to compensate traditional politicians with gubernatorial posts (see Hernández Rodriguez, 1992).

Table 4.2. *Continuity and Change in Governor Ideology (Compared with Previous Governor)*

	No Shift	Moderate Shift	Radical Shift
AGS	42.9	57.1	0.0
BC	42.9	42.9	14.3
BCS	77.8	22.2	0.0
CAM	36.4	45.5	18.2
CHIS	25.0	66.7	8.3
CHIH	53.9	38.5	7.7
COA	18.2	54.5	27.3
COL	50.0	50.0	0.0
DGO	83.3	16.7	0.0
GTO	41.2	52.9	5.9
GRO	33.3	53.3	13.3
HGO	36.8	63.2	0.0
JAL	60.0	30.0	10.0
MEX	28.6	50.0	21.4
MICH	45.5	54.5	0.0
MOR	33.3	66.7	0.0
NAY	28.6	42.9	28.6
NL	69.2	23.1	7.7
OAX	66.7	33.3	0.0
PUE	58.3	41.7	0.0
QRO	77.8	22.2	0.0
QR	50.0	37.5	12.5
SLP	53.3	40.0	6.7
SIN	40.0	40.0	20.0
SON	66.7	33.3	0.0
TAB	28.6	57.1	14.3
TAMS	18.2	63.6	18.2
TLAX	55.6	44.4	0.0
VER	55.6	0.0	44.4
YUC	22.2	22.2	55.6
ZAC	40.0	40.0	20.0
TOTAL	**46.3**	**42.9**	**10.8**

probabilities of each frequency. According to Table 4.3, the probability of observing no change in the ideology code of a governor with respect to the previous governor is the sum of the diagonals, which yields an expected frequency of no change in 37.72 percent of the cases. A continuity of 46.3 percent is still statistically larger than what would occur as a random event

Table 4.3. *Joint Probabilities of Governors Holding Similar Ideologies*

| | Current Governor | | |
| | Left | Center | Right |
Previous Governor	(0.2415)	(0.5085)	(0.25)
Left (0.25)	*0.0604*	0.1271	0.0625
Center (0.5)	0.1208	*0.2543*	0.1250
Right (0.25)	0.0604	0.1271	*0.0625*

No shift (marked in italic) = 37.72%.
Moderate shift = 49.00%.
Radical shift = 12.29%.

($t = 2.72$). Hence, gubernatorial nominations tend to exhibit relatively continuous ideological profiles.

To test Hypotheses 2 and 3, Table 4.4 provides evidence of the alignment of ideological preferences between the president and a newly nominated governor. It is constructed in the same way as the indicator of continuity, only in this case the interpretation of the indicators refers to the distance between the governor and the president. Only 32 percent of the governors nominated by the current president share his ideological profile, 50.3 percent are moderately distant from him, and 17.7 percent are on the opposite end of the ideological code. That is, consonant with Hypothesis 2, one observes that the exercise of presidential power generates gubernatorial nominations identical to the leanings of the president only occasionally. In terms of Hypothesis 3, half of the nominations are moderately distant from the president, and in almost one-fifth of the cases, the president had to interact with a governor who holds the opposite ideological profile. This pattern varies largely by presidential period, as Table 4.5 shows. Whereas presidents in the early years of the PRI, and more recently Miguel de la Madrid, often faced governors with ideological preferences radically different from their own, Adolfo Ruiz Cortines (1952–1958) and Gustavo Díaz Ordaz (1964–1970) faced no governor with whom they had great differences. This suggests that during the 1950s and 1960s the territorial cleavage was less relevant, which yielded ideological positions closer to the president, so no issue trade-off took place.

Making a calculation similar to that in Table 4.2, taking into account the distribution of preferences across governors and presidents, the counterfactual pattern of joint probabilities, as Table 4.6 reveals, shows that

Table 4.4. *Ideological Distance between President and Nominated Governor*

	Same Position $\|P - G_n\| = 0$	Moderate Distance $\|P - G_n\| = 1$	Great Distance $\|P - G_n\| = 2$
AGS	33.33	55.55	11.11
BC	46.67	40	13.34
BCS	40	50	10
CAM	16.67	50	33.34
CHIS	35.71	50	14.29
CHIH	38.46	53.84	7.69
COA	28.57	42.86	28.58
COL	30	60	10
DGO	28.57	50	21.43
GTO	50	38.89	11.12
GRO	37.5	43.75	18.75
HGO	31.58	52.63	15.79
JAL	41.67	50	8.33
MEX	26.67	46.67	26.67
MICH	35.71	50	14.29
MOR	33.33	44.44	22.22
NAY	44.44	33.33	22.22
NL	21.43	71.43	7.14
OAX	21.43	71.42	7.14
PUE	30.77	53.84	15.38
QRO	18.18	81.81	0
QR	0	90	10
SLP	37.5	56.25	6.25
SIN	33.33	50	16.67
SON	25	50	25
TAB	28.57	42.86	28.57
TAMS	38.46	38.46	23.07
TLAX	18.18	72.72	9.09
VER	33.33	8.33	58.33
YUC	33.33	33.34	33.34
ZAC	45.45	36.36	18.18
TOTAL	**32.09**	**50.25**	**17.67**

29.3 percent of the governors were in the same position as the president, 50.3 percent were moderately distant, and 20.5 percent were at a great distance. This profile results from the fact that moderate presidents should always get, at most, moderate governors. The pattern in Table 4.3 is hence

Table 4.5. *Ideological Distance of Governors by Presidential Period*

President	Same Position	Moderate Distance	Great Distance
Cárdenas	30.88	48.53	20.59
Avila Camacho	25.58	46.51	27.91
Alemán	46.51	39.53	13.95
Ruiz Cortines	59.38	40.62	0
López Mateos	24.24	51.52	24.24
Díaz Ordaz	40.54	59.46	0
Echeverría	20.93	65.12	13.95
López Portillo	37.84	40.54	21.62
De la Madrid	13.51	54.05	32.43
Salinas	24.14	58.62	17.24
TOTAL	**32.09**	**50.25**	**17.66**

no different from what would be observed under a random process. Although the empirical findings reinforce the evidence against presidential theories of governor nomination and are consonant with Hypotheses 2 and 3, the empirical evidence does not distinguish the implications of my spatial model of gubernatorial nominations from a random process, taking into account the actual distribution of preferences. But the overriding fact remains that presidents often nominated governors with ideologies opposite their own.

Hypothesis 4 suggests a stronger test for the model because it involves showing that the president chooses a pattern of nominations that generally does not make him worse-off, and in those cases when the status quo is changed, this should tend to improve the presidential standing. That is, the president might sometimes nominate governors that are far from his policy position simply because the feasible set of alternative nominations is completely restricted, but when changes to the status quo take place, this should be done in order to improve the president's welfare by nominating a more congenial governor. This hypothesis requires comparing the status quo the president inherits and the unobserved relative location of the national and local veto players simultaneously. Empirically, I need to combine the results from Table 4.2 with those of Table 4.4. That is, given a shift in the status quo, the nominations should lean more toward what the president desires than a random event, and nominations that change the status quo by making the president worse-off should be rather rare occurrences. Table 4.7 shows the relative frequency of nominations depending on the continuity

Table 4.6. *Joint Probabilities of Governors Holding Same or Different Ideology from President*

	President		
Previous Governors	Left (0.43)	Center (0.17)	Right (0.40)
Left (0.25)	*0.1075*	0.0425	0.1000
Center (0.5)	0.2150	*0.0850*	0.2000
Right (0.25)	0.1075	0.0425	*0.1000*

Same position (marked in italic) = 29.25%.
Moderate distance = 49%.
Great distance = 20.75%.

of local executives. That is, the rows represent the ideological continuity in local politics, and the columns provide the distance from the president. A random event would imply that the same percentage of nominations should occur under every row condition.

Given the actual distribution of presidential ideologies, a random distribution of gubernatorial nominations would have the president nominating governors at his exact position in 32 percent of the cases, moderately distant ones in 50 percent and very distant ones in 18 percent, regardless of local continuity. Table 4.7 exhibits more ideological similarity between the president and nominated governors as one moves down: The greater the changes, the more likely that nominees will be similar to the president. This finding provides supportive evidence for Hypothesis 4.[15]

Finally, to test Hypothesis 6, Table 4.8 shows the ideological difference between the president and the governors according to the way local executives finished their terms. There are no significant differences among governors who are very distant from the president. However, there is a distinct pattern among governors who were called by the president to join his cabinet: Almost half of these governors shared the same ideological code as the incumbent president. In the case of governors who were forced to

---

[15] Table 4.7 does exhibit an anomaly related to the presence of a large percentage of nominations (significantly different, in the statistical sense, from a random process), where there is a radical shift in local continuity and the nominated governor possesses exactly the opposite ideological coding as the president (the 35.14 in the table). That anomaly can probably be understood through case studies, in terms of breaks in the continuity of state politics. In most of these specific instances (which are distributed as one single occurrence in a few particular states), I believe the president made a trade-off on ideological grounds in order to achieve nominations closer to him on the territorial dimension, breaking the hold of a particular boss (*cacique*) in a state.

Table 4.7. *Percentage (Row) of Governors Nominated with Same or Different Ideology from President by Shift in Local Politics*

Previous Governors	President		
	Same Position	Moderate Distance	Great Distance
No shift	26.71	57.14	16.15
Moderate shift	31.79	52.32	15.89
Radical shift	43.24	21.62	35.14

Table 4.8. *Ideological Alignment of Governors Compared with President According to End of Term*

Ideology Compared with President	Finish Full Term	Resign / Dissolution	Leave Cabinet	Total
Same position	33.22	23.08	44.44	32.31
Moderate distance	50.17	59.62	37.04	50.51
Great distance	16.61	17.31	18.52	17.18

resign, or when "dissolution of local powers" was declared by the Senate, only around one-fifth of them shared the same ideological code as the president. This suggests that governors tended to be removed by the president for reasons different from ideological distance, but governors are, nonetheless, more likely to remain in place if their ideology is not too distant from the president's. When the ideologies of governors and presidents are very distant, this is probably for good reason. That is, the president is probably unable to exert his influence on those states governed by executives who are very distant from him, and he might even need to accommodate them.

The evidence provides further insights into how the political agreement between regional politicians in Mexico became self-enforcing. Ambitious local politicians were willing to pursue careers within the PRI, seeking nominations that were equivalent to reaching office. The rules that structured their political careers, including the prohibition of reelection, were acceptable because they made players collectively better-off, as discussed in Chapter 3. Of course, a sitting governor may have preferred to be reelected to the post, but the prohibition of reelection ensured that all local politicians had a real chance of reaching the highest prize in the future. Hence players were collectively better-off given the uncertainty concerning who was to occupy the governorship. Local politicians became professionalized, belonging to national or local cliques (*camarillas*), which competed against one another to secure nominations for both state and federal posts. At the local level members of the teams within the party cooperated with one another in the quest to attain the governorship in their home state. They did not use their entrepreneurial energies to seek office outside the party, which ensured hegemony. Local politicians who had not yet enjoyed the spoils of power had incentives to remain loyal to the sitting governor, the president, and the party hierarchy, because the political ambition ladder was highly structured. Although the eventual outcome of their careers was uncertain, they knew for sure that the no-reelection clause always gave them a real chance of arriving at higher office. Thus, ambitious politicians abided with party nominations even when they were not favored by them.

The governorship, moreover, was the end point to most political careers. Although some governors continued to exert influence in state and federal politics, the overwhelming majority of them retired from politics, engaging instead in highly profitable businesses. Government contracts, subsidized credit provided by federal and state developmental agencies, as well as tight business networks developed during their tenure in office ensured comfortable – in fact, often opulent – living conditions for the outgoing governor, his family, and his close collaborators.

The federal executive accepted limits over his authority vis-à-vis regional interests, recognizing the staggered timing of state elections and the resort to removal or appointment of governors only as exceptional strategies of governance. This was a price the president had to pay for the concentration of authority in so many other realms. The president still possessed authority in terms of setting the agenda within the party, subject to the acceptance of veto players, over the nomination of governors. This authority was only gradually exerted, however, because it was not until the fourth year of his term that the incumbent president would have nominated more than half of the sitting governors.

This peculiar system breaks down under a democratic setting. This is because once entry is allowed and a party nomination is not equivalent with the achievement of office, local politicians possess fewer incentives to comply with the arrangement. Once PRI candidates face challengers, a presidential nominee within the invulnerable unanimous winset is not better for the veto players if they believe that such a candidate will lose the election.

To be sure, the dynamics of entry and the triumph of opposition parties in local elections during the 1990s provoked a new pattern of gubernatorial nomination within the PRI. The party tried to field candidates with real prospects of winning in fair and clean elections (Diaz-Cayeros and Langston, 2004). Opposition parties were able to successfully remove the PRI from local office. State politics have been revitalized through this process, but, as the analysis shows, local politics were never altogether dead, even at the height of PRI hegemony.

5

Transfers and Redistribution in the Mexican States

5.1. The Consequences of Centralization

The political equilibrium generated through nominations within the hegemonic party became reflected in the willingness of Mexican regional politicians to accept a centralized fiscal bargain during the second half of the
20th century. The comprehensive revenue-sharing system that exists today
originated from a political equilibrium in which politicians at the local level
retained their local aspirations but were willing to cooperate with politicians at the national level. In this sense, the integration of a nationalized
party system in Mexico predated fiscal centralization.[1] It is often assumed
that the revenue-sharing system was always meant to be a redistributive
arrangement. Because Mexico's regime claimed as part of its revolutionary
credentials a quest for redistribution, scholars often assume that revenue-
sharing formulas would have been devised with redistribution in mind.
This chapter suggests instead that to a large extent transfers in the Mexican
federation have tended to be regressive rather than redistributive.

Two parallel developments converged to create the system that characterizes intergovernmental fiscal relations in Mexico today. The first was
the establishment of revenue-sharing between states and the federal government at the beginning of the 1940s, which gave states unconditional
transfers (*participaciones*) out of the collection of revenue from the exclusively federal excise taxes. This initial revenue-sharing system established
state shares on a case-by-case basis for each specific tax. The second development was the creation of a federal sales tax in 1947 (the *Impuesto Sobre*

---

[1] And in this sense has a different link of causality than that posed by Chhibber and Kollman
(2004).

123

Ingresos Mercantiles – ISIM). States could receive revenue from this federal tax if they agreed to keep a coordinated tax structure with a shared tax rate in which one part would be set by the states and another part by the federal government. By the early 1970s, all states had joined in the ISIM system, obtaining most of their local tax collection from this tax while also receiving some unconditional transfers through the revenue-sharing system.[2]

Centralized federal expenditures became the prime source of financing for development projects, which included irrigation, roads, and industrial districts. Decisions on the allocation of public goods were centralized in the federal bureaucracies and agencies and did not always take into account the needs of the local economies. But local politicians had few incentives to change the fiscal arrangement as long as entry into the electoral market of their home states was curbed. Local budgets increasingly were limited to covering the current expenditures of state administrations and the small fraction of local public works provided in each jurisdiction. The main consequence of the PRI's hegemony was that governors and local politicians had no control over the allocation of public expenditures by federal agencies and bureaucracies in their territories, nor did they seek it. Presidential priorities and bureaucratic inertias were reflected in the allocation of funds. The patterns of regional public good provision financed through federal public investment tended to reinforce regional inequality.

It is important to note that it was not until 1979 that fiscal relations between states and the federal government were merged into a single system with the introduction of the value-added tax (*Impuesto al Valor Agregado* – IVA) at the federal level: All states would receive general revenue shares from most of the federal tax collection according to previously agreed formulas. The unification meant that local budgets would be financed mostly through unconditional federal transfers (*participaciones*) contained in the revenue-sharing agreements, and the most important public works in the states would be financed through federal public investment funds. The consequence of this was the almost complete dependence of state governments on federal revenue or expenditure transfers for their current expenditures and financing of public works.

---

[2] It is important to note that the local taxes collected by ISIM were not revenue-sharing but local revenue generated through the part of the ISIM tax rate that belonged to state governments. However, states could not decide this state rate, it being set uniformly for all states belonging to the system.

This chapter discusses the creation of the revenue-sharing system in Mexico, its distribution across states, and the regional patterns of federal public investment (*Inversión Pública Federal*, or IPF, the most important fund financing public good provision). The next section discusses the creation of the General Revenue-Sharing Fund (*Fondo General de Participaciones* – FGP). Consonant with the historical account of the previous chapters, states were reluctant to embrace tax centralization and revenue-sharing. Other things being equal, they would have preferred to retain fiscal authority. However, by 1980 all had accepted the centralization of sales taxes through the IVA because the agreement made states recipients of some of the windfall revenue that was being collected at the federal level from the oil boom, and the electoral insulation the PRI afforded them made PRI state politicians feel invulnerable to electoral threats.

Section 5.3 then examines the allocation of federal public investment (IPF) among the Mexican states. In contrast with revenue-sharing funds, the resources financing IPF were not tied to local fiscal effort. The empirical evidence shows that the overriding imperative for the federal government when allocating investment to the states was to reinforce the patterns of economic growth and to reward PRI followers. On balance, that meant concentrating resources in the richest states. Thus, federal transfers in Mexico did not constitute a flow of resources to compensate for regional inequality but were concentrated precisely in those regions that were already rich.

Section 5.4 shows that redistribution was limited by the underlying economic strength of each state and the bargaining power of governors vis-à-vis the federal government. In particular, this section tests hypotheses emerging from a bargaining model in Chapter 1 that suggests that revenue-sharing, at its origin, will not be redistributive. The model suggests that when federal tax collection depends on state effort, redistribution cannot be carried out in revenue-sharing arrangements. It is only when federal financial resources are unrelated to local fiscal effort that it is possible to transfer funds in a redistributive manner. The final section discusses how democratization has influenced the revenue-sharing agreement since the 1990s.

5.2. Tax-Sharing Agreements and the Rise of Participaciones

The constitutional reforms of 1940 and 1942 established (or reasserted) exclusive federal authority over foreign trade, financial institutions, and natural resources under federal jurisdiction (oil and mining) in addition to federal excises on oil and fuel products, electricity, tobacco, matches, the beverage *pulque,* and forestry products (Retchkiman and Gil Valdivia, 1981:77).[3] The 1942 reform also established the constitutional precept that states were to receive shares from the revenue the federal government collected from those excises (*participaciones*) according to the dictates of a federal law yet to be drafted. According to Octavio Sentíes, at the time a senior state official in the Estado de México, the tax reform of 1942 was the death sentence for the Mexican federal arrangement:

Who will assure that future presidents of the Republic, less aware of their responsibilities, will not take reprisals against the governors, "withholding" their revenue shares, forcing them into the loss of face by being unable to cover their economic liabilities? Who will prevent, under such conditions, turmoil and discontent, for example due to the nonpayment of wages? This is possible, and there will be someone who shall profit from the new procedures to obtain the perfect political control of the local executives. (My translation, Sentíes, 1942:63)

The underlying assumption of this diagnosis was that financial dependence through revenue shares would lead to political control. Many governors were reticent about accepting the centralized deal, as can be witnessed by the open objections to the reforms by the states of Morelos, Zacatecas, Hidalgo, San Luis Potosí, and Yucatán (quoted in Sentíes, 1942:41–51). By 1947, however, the federal government had obtained a large degree of fiscal coordination among the states. In the Third National Tax Convention, which took place that year, states confirmed their commitment to the system of *participaciones* and accepted the creation of a national sales tax.

The national sales tax, or *Impuesto Sobre Ingresos Mercantiles* (ISIM), represented a major achievement for the federal government. It taxed consumption through a general indirect tax instead of the multiple product-by-product excises. The federal finance ministry hoped that all states would be brought under the ISIM, eliminating their local taxes and keeping a unique national federal sales tax with a local rate surcharge. This second goal met with only limited success. States would establish their ISIM surcharge on a voluntary basis, so in 1948 only the federal territories of Baja California Sur and Quintana Roo, together with the Federal District, adopted it.

---

[3] This constitutional reform was a watered-down version of a law initiative sent by President Cárdenas in the late 1930s that attempted to keep under exclusive federal authority not only those items but also the income tax and the excises on beer, alcoholic beverages, honey, textiles and threads, gambling, lotteries and raffles, wood, railroads, and transportation. The reform was not approved by Congress (Sentíes, 1942:39).

Aguascalientes joined the ISIM in 1949; Morelos, Querétaro, and Tlax-cala the following year; and Michoacán and Sinaloa the year after that. That is, during the term of Miguel Alemán (1946–1952), the president who sponsored the Third National Tax Convention, only one-third of the states accepted a unified federal sales tax.

The purpose of the ISIM was to tax sales at a uniform 3 percent rate across the country. The rate was made up of a 1.2 percent rate that was kept by those states that accepted the new tax and 1.8 percent to remain in control of the federal government. If states did not agree to the ISIM, the 1.8 percent rate was collected by the federal government, and consumers and producers would also be subject to local taxes (Servín, 1956:70). The ISIM had the advantage of requiring only one administrative apparatus for its collection. Theoretically, a unique state or federal collection agency would be established in each state. In practice, states became collection agents, while the federal government carried out the administration and surveillance (auditing). In order to join the new system, states had to elim-inate all their taxes on sales, industry, and production. States collecting important sources of revenue from their own sales taxes were not willing to adopt the ISIM. The 1.2 percent rate was not enough to compensate for their loss in revenue and tax authority, particularly considering the risk, noted in the quotation from Sentíes (1942) earlier in this section and the credibility model discussed in Chapter 1, of federal promises not being fulfilled.

Fiscal coordination and centralization had advanced to some extent by 1948. The *contribución federal* (the financial transfer from the states to the federal government) had been eliminated. All states received federal trans-fers in the form of *participaciones* as a reward for accepting the exclusive federal authority over federal excises. For the first time in the century, states refrained from taxing the products under exclusive federal jurisdic-tion. This was a concrete result of the recommendations issued by the Third National Tax Convention. A committee run by the states was also created as a result of this convention to oversee and decide the distribution of federal revenue-sharing funds (see Servín, 1956:66–67). The statutory rate of *par-ticipación* funds was different for each specific product, ranging, for example, from 10 percent for oil products, 15 percent for tobacco, and 20 percent for forest products to 40 percent for salt (Secretaría de Hacienda y Crédito Público, 1973:8). The criteria for determining the shares received by each state were never transparent, but federal authorities had moved the system significantly beyond the failures of the 1920s and 1930s.

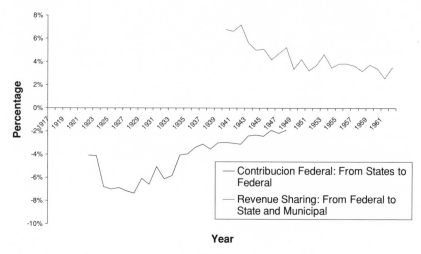

Figure 5.1. Revenue transfers as share of federal government revenue.

Mexico was moving away from local tax authority to a fiscal system in which federal transfers would play an increasingly important role. Figure 5.1 graphs the evolution of revenue-sharing transfers as a percentage of federal revenue. The negative transfers before 1948 represent the *contribución federal* (i.e., funds received by the federal government from the states); positive numbers denote *participación* transfers received by state and municipal governments. Before 1947, most transfers went from states to the federal government through the *contribución federal*. In the 1930s, the system of revenue-sharing on federal excises was created. As the graph indicates, for a time both transfers coexisted.

The creation of the sales tax in 1948 did not bring about an increase in revenue-sharing, measured as a percentage of federal finances. Federal revenue collection in taxes that were not subject to revenue-sharing was increasing. Hence, although states were sharing the rate of the ISIM, this was not the backbone of state finances. In fact, revenue-sharing only increased dramatically after 1970. By the end of the 20th century, the federal government unconditionally transferred around 20 percent of its revenue to states and municipalities.[4] The dramatic shift from a fiscal system in

---

[4] This rise of federal transfers is more dramatic if one considers the expenditure side, where the federal government made massive investments in the states, particularly since the 1960s, through IPF. Moreover, since the 1990s, the federal government has transferred most of its expenditures for education, health, and the provision of local public goods to states and municipalities.

128

which states were self-sufficient in tax collection and the federal government depended on states for around 10 percent of its revenue needs to one in which states depend on the federal government for around 90 percent of their revenue is crucial to understanding the political economy of Mexico during the 20th century.

What were the effects of this new arrangement? According to an assessment by a federal government committee formed in 1954, the "success" of the revenue-sharing system in Mexico had been insufficient. In their judgment, the lack of success was evident in that the system of *participaciones* had not produced redistributive effects. It is not clear why a tax-sharing system should be redistributive because from a bargaining perspective, as discussed in Chapter 1, tax shares must be somewhat proportional to the opportunity cost of states belonging to the revenue-sharing system. Nonetheless, the federal government explicitly considered redistribution a goal that had failed. Perhaps more tellingly, the government attributed the failure mainly to political factors:[5]

One might say that the revenue-sharing regime prevailing in Mexico has operated, until now, in the opposite direction from what is desirable, namely, signifying greater federal help for the richer states. One cannot say that this was a purposeful policy but rather a consequence of the fact that some states and municipalities are stronger from a political point of view and hence better organized to make their needs known. (My translation, *Comisión de Inversiones*, 1954:836)

Far-reaching fiscal reforms were carried out at the beginning of the 1950s, including a major overhaul of the federal income tax (see Urquidi, 1956; Ortíz Mena, 1966; both reprinted in Solís, 1973). After an adjustment to the exchange rate in 1954, Mexico witnessed a period of moderate growth under fiscal stability commonly known as the "stabilizing development." In 1953, the federal government drafted a Fiscal Coordination Law (*Ley de Coordinación Fiscal*), the secondary law meant to give coherence and transparency to the arrangements for revenue-sharing that had already been enacted a decade earlier. The main consequence of this law

---

[5] The assessment was made by a federal commission in charge of the investment programs of the federal government under the *Inversión Pública Federal* funds. The technocratic flavor is evident in the quote: A political determination of the flow of funds was not viewed as a purposeful choice. González Casanova argued in 1965 that federal transfers (*participaciones*) to specific states were determined basically by economic criteria, giving more resources to the more developed states. He speculated, however, that variations in transfers over time, which were often very large, would be mostly politically determined.

was that the committee on fiscal relations overseeing shares of revenue transferred to the states would be composed of three representatives of the federal government (from the finance, trade, and interior ministries), five state representatives, and three citizens with no vote (Retchkiman and Gil Valdivia, 1981:79). Nonetheless, this committee did not make the rules governing the allocation of *participaciones* to the states any more transparent than they had been before.

As part of these reforms, the federal government coaxed the states of San Luis Potosí, Colima, Yucatán, Hidalgo, Campeche, and Tabasco to adopt the ISIM and abandon their local sales taxes. Puebla joined the next year, and Guerrero in 1957. Thus, by the end of the 1950s, half of the states belonged to the federal sales tax system. The other half kept their local sales taxes so that their consumers and producers were subject to both federal and state sales taxes. The 13 states that did not become part of the ISIM system – namely Baja California, Coahuila, Chiapas, Mexico, Guanajuato, Jalisco, Nayarit, Nuevo León, Oaxaca, Sonora, Tamaulipas, Veracruz, and Zacatecas – included all the large rich states and almost all border states. But they also included the two poorest states, where local bosses were powerful. Still, during the coming years, states were enticed to join into revenue-sharing arrangements with the federal government in what Careaga and Weingast (2003) have aptly called the "fiscal pact with the devil."

The reluctance of the stronger states to accept the ISIM is clear in retrospect: Even though everyone in the system would have benefited from the 1.2 percent rate, that rate did not yield enough revenue to compensate for what these states were obtaining by themselves (Secretaría de Hacienda y Crédito Público, 1973:123). Moreover, the risks involved in losing fiscal authority were not trivial. States were powerful enough, even as the hegemonic party system became consolidated, to retain their fiscal authority. In the larger, richer states, a major concern was the loss of the revenue they could attract from industrial activity concentration; among the border states, it was because many subsidiary firms located production in those states for export into the U.S. market, but the federal tax would be assessed in Mexico City, where their corporate headquarters were located.[6]

---

[6] For the poor states, it was because even though economic activity was limited, their tax rates were so high that the lower rate with a broader base would not compensate for their loss in revenue.

In the 1970s, the federal government pursued an ambitious fiscal reform, which was largely unsuccessful. This failure has been attributed mostly to opposition by business interests to changes in the income tax and, more generally, to the deterioration in the relationship between the administration of President Echeverría and large firms. The reform failed to transform the ISIM into a value-added tax. One element of the reform that did succeed, however, was the incorporation of all states into the federal sales tax. The federal strategy was simple: It proposed increasing the tax rate by one percentage point, granting almost all of the additional revenue to the states (1.8 percent of the rate would go to the states, whereas the remaining 2.2 percent would go to the federal government). This was complemented by the introduction of a special 10 percent rate of the ISIM for luxury items, for which 40 percent of the revenue was to be kept by the states; the transfer of *participaciones* on 45 percent of the income tax generated from producers involved in agriculture, cattle raising, and transportation (the so-called *causantes menores*); and providing greater surveillance authority to the states. In spite of these carrots, Milton Everardo Castellanos, then PRI governor in Baja California, claimed that he was "forced" to accept the new arrangement through pressures from the federal government (quoted in Campuzano Montoya, 1995:214).[7]

By 1974, all states were part of the ISIM. For the first time since 1925, there was a unified tax system with no jurisdictional overlap. This was consolidated in 1979 with the creation of the *Sistema Nacional de Coordinación Fiscal* (SNCF), which allowed for the substitution of the ISIM with a federal value-added tax, the *Impuesto al Valor Agregado*, or IVA (Jannetti, 1989). The success at coordination was not a result of a government more committed to transforming the status quo. It was the reflection of a federal system that had been centralized through the PRI. Economic forces alone could not account for this outcome. Mexico was experiencing the peak of federal and presidential power.

The SNCF was accepted by the states with almost no resistance. This was attributable to the political conditions, the timing of the reform, and, most importantly, the state of federal finances. The dominance of the PRI during the late 1970s was overwhelming: President López Portillo ran unopposed in the 1976 election because the Communist Party was still banned and the

---

[7] Baja California resisted coordination until the very end, as can be seen in its dissenting state position presented in the meeting where these matters were agreed; see *Secretaría de Hacienda y Crédito Público* (1973).

PAN was unable to agree on a candidate. The reform was timed skillfully, playing with the temporal horizons of governors: During 1980, when the reform would come into effect, most of the "inherited" governors (i.e., those who were not nominated by the sitting president) would be just finishing their terms according to the staggered timing of local elections.

Finally, and most crucially, the country was in the midst of an oil boom. The federal government was obtaining a substantial amount of revenue from the windfall gains of the nationalized oil company, PEMEX. Because taxation of natural resources, and oil in particular, was exclusively federal, state governments were not directly profiting from the expansion in available resources. They did receive more resources and projects through *Inversión Pública Federal*, but those transfers were ultimately controlled by the president and his bureaucracies. The SNCF offered the opportunity for states to reap part of the benefits of the oil boom as unconditional tax transfers, although the arrangement made state governments more dependent on the federal government.

Although every state had been encouraged (or forced) to join in the federal sales tax, the introduction of the value-added tax in 1979 produced a major redistribution of resources among states. On the one hand, the VAT was now collected where value was added, not where sales occurred; when the tax was paid by the final consumer in one state, a tax credit had to be issued for the taxes paid in other states, with a consequent redistribution of where revenue was accrued. On the other hand, the success of the VAT required the elimination of some remaining state-level excises in order to bring about more horizontal equity among regionally dispersed producers. These issues were addressed through the negotiation of the SNCF among states and the federal government, including the Federal District. The arrangement tied *participaciones* to explicit formulas that considered population, education expenditures, revenue collected in the past, and indicators of state performance in tax collection. The overhaul of the revenue-sharing system through the SNCF eliminated the last vestiges of local tax authority and weakened the derivation principle in the allocation of fiscal resources. Henceforth, fiscal transfers to states and municipalities were for the most part detached from their local capacity to tax.

The federal finance minister tinkered with the formulas almost every year since 1980. At first, the main ingredient in the formulas was the assurance that states would receive the same revenue they were previously collecting from local taxes. This suggests that the main constraint at that moment was to ensure that all states participated in the new system. Later on, an attempt was made to tie formulas to some measure of effort at tax collection, either in local taxes, VAT collection in each state, or federal taxes transferred to the state administrations collecting them (namely, the tax on new cars, the *Impuesto Sobre Automóbiles Nuevos*, or ISAN). This suggests that the system moved toward a greater concern for incentive compatibility and performance. At the beginning, formulas also included what was called a "complementary fund," which attempted to compensate the states that were receiving the least resources. This introduced an equalizing tendency in the shares, which was further reinforced in later years by giving a greater weight to population factors. (For discussions of the formulas and their changes, see Chapoy Bonifaz, 1992; Díaz-Cayeros, 1995; Aguilar Villanueva, 1996; Arellano Cadena, 1996).

Thus, abstracting from the subtleties of each individual formula, the overall pattern over time has been that at the beginning of the SNCF states received revenue shares much in line with the revenue they were collecting beforehand from their own taxes, their rate in the federal ISIM, and their *participaciones*. That meant, in fact, that poorer states had much smaller per capita *participaciones* than richer states (Díaz-Cayeros, 1995:94). It also meant that the oil-producing states received a disproportionate share of resources because they had previously been receiving high *participaciones* on federal oil taxes. However, as formulas have changed, there has been a slight tendency toward per capita convergence because poorer states have witnessed larger increases in *participaciones* than richer ones, consonant with the larger weight given to population in the calculation of revenue shares (Díaz-Cayeros, 1995:95).

The revenue-sharing arrangement of the SNCF was a contract between states and the federal government. There was no constitutional provision that forced states to give up their authority over taxation: States belonged to the system by agreeing to withdraw their own taxes and receive *participaciones* in exchange. When the system was created, governors also signed administrative collaboration agreements, which involved working closely with federal authorities on issues of federal tax compliance. The shares distributed to each state through the formulas of revenue-sharing have differed widely, depending on the specific characteristics of each state. Notwithstanding the common tinkering with the formulas, revenue shares have remained fairly steady over time. What determined the amount of funds each state received out of the total pool of federal resources to be distributed? The next section provides an answer focusing on expenditure transfers, while Section 5.4 returns to revenue-sharing.

5.3. Discretion in Federal Public Investment in the States

Although much discussion of Mexican fiscal federalism tends to concentrate on the revenue-sharing system, these funds have been small when compared with the most prominent financial flow at the regional level: federal conditional grants to states earmarked for specific projects, contained within the so-called federal public investment (*Inversión Pública Federal* – IPF).[8] During the 1960s, *participaciones* represented less than 10 percent of state budgets, although they have steadily increased in importance until they accounted for half of the gross state revenue during the 1980s and 1990s. State-collected "own revenue" and debt gradually played a negligible role in local finances. But the IPF represented, during the 1980s and 1990s, between twice and four times the sum of all state budgets.[9]

These territorial funds were crucial to federal finances. Around one-third of the federal government's consolidated programmable budget (that is, the total budget of the federal government, excluding *participaciones* and interest payments on the federal debt) was allocated territorially within the IPF from 1965 to the mid-1990s. Almost all local public goods in Mexico were financed through these federal funds. The money was allocated to subnational jurisdictions through a wide variety of federal agencies, programs, and bureaucracies, with the collaboration of local governments.[10] Funds were sometimes directly exercised by the local

---

[8] It is important to distinguish in analytic terms that *ingresos propios* and *participaciones* are tax revenues (although *participaciones* appear as a budgetary item on the expenditure side for the level of government that is transferring them), whereas IPF is a budgetary expenditure of the federal government in the regions. This analytic distinction suggests that whereas *participaciones* and *ingresos propios* will be complicated primarily by incentive problems, IPF issues are mostly concerned with accountability of the level of government that decides on and carries out such expenditures.

[9] Financial resources are fungible, so a full depiction of transfers between the federation and the states would take account not only of the specific federal program that comprises capital expenditures on social welfare – funds for infrastructure, industry, and agriculture – but also the allocation by the federation of current federal expenditures and unconditional transfers. Bargains might be struck where an allocation in one area (say, infrastructure) allows for the transfer of a state's own funds otherwise devoted to that use to another area (say, social welfare). To get the full picture, one would hence require territorial allocations not only of investment but also current federal expenditures and other transfers. There is no estimate of current expenditures by the federal government in each region (although it is obvious that a large share is taken by the Mexico City bureaucracy), although a sizable amount is accounted for by budgetary items related to education, including the teachers' payrolls decentralized in 1993.

[10] Federal spending in what constitutes the so-called *Ramo XXVI*, the poverty alleviation program (PRONASOL), commanded substantial attention in the 1990s, not just because

governments, but under very strict federal guidelines and oversight. That is, federal funds were controlled by the federal bureaucracies, although they were spent, especially since the 1970s, jointly with the lower levels of government according to "development agreements" (the *Convenio de Desarrollo Social* and *Convenio Unico de Desarrollo*, the Social Development Agreement and Single Development Agreement, respectively).

The federal government often publicized its investment projects in terms of the development generated wherever they were carried out. Job creation and promotion of economic activity were emphasized as central benefits. It is difficult to judge the effect of those projects on social well-being and the standard of living of the population where they were carried out, but what lies beyond any doubt is that they created sources of patronage and private benefits for federal bureaucrats, governor, local politicians, and the president himself through kickbacks, real estate speculation, and outright corruption (Scott, 1959:250; Hansen, 1971:125).

Corruption usually occurred through privileged access to public contracts, where politicians often became major partners of the firms carrying out the projects.[11] Thus, the use of public office and federal projects for personal enrichment became one of the most prominent features of Mexican political activity. As the powerful politician Carlos Hank González put it in his famous dictum: "*un político pobre es un pobre político*" (which translates into something like "a poor politician is a bad politician"). Or consider Jesús Silva Herzog's[12] more critical view: "Politics is the easiest and most profitable profession in Mexico" (quoted in Hansen, 1971:125).

In the context of the fiscal bargain, regional politicians in Mexico abdicated their budgetary authority over these funds.[13] As McCubbins and

of the amount of money involved but also because a whole bureaucratic apparatus was put together to make the program an instrument of the federal executive; but it is just one of the smaller parts of IPF.

[11] See, for example, the candid assessment by Ramón Beteta, former minister of finance, in an interview with James Wilkie (1978): "There are many ways through which a public official can become rich without necessarily being illegitimate, even though they might not be ethical. For example, a public official knows that a new highway is going to be opened, or it could be the contractor who will build it, or whoever will order its construction. This individual could, either directly or in a roundabout way, buy land that is going to be affected by the highway and thus obtain some benefit. This is not ethically correct, but it is not a crime either" (my translation, Wilkie, 1978: 40).

[12] This was the prominent PRI member, grandfather of the political commentator Jesús Silva Herzog Márquez.

[13] It is important to distinguish that this would not be a "delegation" relationship between the assembly and the bureaucracies. Abdication means that the effects of budget appropriations

Noble (1995) point out, abdication cannot be straightforwardly inferred from observed behavior: If a political agent does not openly exert influence to change an outcome generated by a bureaucracy, that does not necessarily mean that it failed to approve of the output produced by bureaucratic behavior. Bureaucracies might have real advantages in processing information, providing expertise, or generating public goods and services for politicians, and it might be rational for the legislature to grant them a free hand.[14] However, abdication of authority can be inferred if although local politicians have information and resources concerning the effects of federal budgets in their regions, they nonetheless fail to act on them. The administrative procedures followed in Mexico for the disbursements in federal funds suggest that local politicians had information and expertise that was useful to the federal bureaucracies. Federal agencies and projects were carried out in collaboration with the local authorities through the so-called development agreements. Because of the scarcity of local finances, state–federal collaboration involved matching funds only to a limited degree; it involved primarily local surveillance and administration, which opened opportunities for corruption among local politicians. Regional leaders knew the effects of federal expenditures, but their incentives were such that they were willing to follow presidential initiatives and projects.

Figure 5.2 plots the relationship between the relative shares of IPF that each state received during each presidential administration between 1970 and 1994 and the state's share of population. Each presidential administration is matched with the closest census data.

Obviously, the shares of IPF were highly correlated with the share of population because public goods and services are required in a direct proportion to the population being served. However, the graph in Figure 5.2 shows that the match is by no means perfect ($r = 0.7159$). There are significant deviations in the relationship, which means that per capita investment in each state was not constant.

In order to understand the determinants of the deviations from proportionality observed in each state during each presidential term, I performed a pooled cross-sectional time series estimation. Care must be taken in considering the nonstationarity of the series because observations are correlated

---

can be systematically unfavorable to the states and still no legislative oversight would be exercised, either before or after the fact.

[14] In order to prove an abdication hypothesis, one must show that political agents were worse-off than they would have preferred if they had information, agenda control, or some other resource that bureaucracies held (McCubbins and Noble, 1995:58).

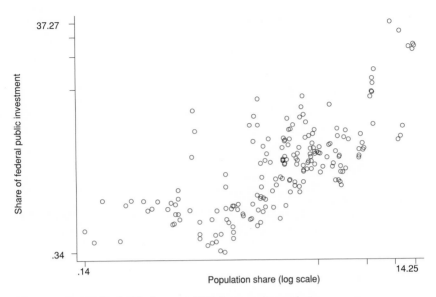

Figure 5.2. Relationship between IPF shares and population.

between years. In order to make the series stationary, I used the lagged value of the deviation from proportionality of each state (DEV_{t-1}), a standard procedure. I also use the share of IPF a state had in the previous period (IFP_{t-1}) to control for the total share of resources that historically has been received from the previous presidential term. I include as independent variables the size of each state proxied by population (POP_t), the level of development of each state as measured by its per capita gross state product (GSP_t), and the support received by the PRI in the presidential election ($VPRI_t$).

The deviations from population proportionality should be explained by the presidential priorities in the pursuit of coalition-building strategies, which may shift each presidential term. Because the estimates control for past values, this is an allocation at the margin. Both the lagged variables should be positive. The population control should be negative because, other things being equal, disproportionality will be larger in smaller states than in larger states. This is because in a local jurisdiction public goods might have some fixed costs.

The more important determinants for the purposes of understanding the federal bargain in Mexico are GSP and VPRI. A positive relationship between per capita GSP and disproportion in relative shares would mean

Table 5.1. *Determinants of Deviations from Equal Per Capita Shares Dependent Variable:* $DEV_t = IPF_t / POP_t$

	Random-Effects GLS	Fixed-Effects OLS
IPF_{t-1}	0.0753***	0.1218**
	(3.155)	(2.211)
DEV_{t-1}	0.4786***	0.122
	(6.123)	(1.219)
$logGSP_t$	0.7955***	0.8979***
	(5.050)	(4.684)
POP_t	− 0.1184***	− 0.1266
	(3.208)	(1.111)
$VPRI_t$	0.0137***	0.0115***
	(3.195)	(2.672)
C	−3.405***	−3.33***
	(4.239)	(3.271)
Overall R sq	0.5819	0.4854
	chi2(5) = 197.79	F(5,123) = 8.02

$n = 160, t = 5, i = 32$. Hausman test: chi2(5) = 52.86.
t statistics are in parenthesis.
* Significant at the 90% level.
** Significant at the 95% level.
*** Significant at the 99% level.

that richer states tended to have a larger share of public investment than poorer ones.[15] This would occur because the president would give a greater priority to states that can reinforce his national objectives. I expect a positive relationship between PRI support and the deviations of proportionality in IPF because public investment was used to reward supporters.[16] The first column of Table 5.1 provides the results of running a GLS random-effect estimate of the deviations from proportionality.

In this GLS estimate of the pooled data, all the signs are as expected and significant. However, the Hausman test reported at the bottom of Table 5.1 reveals that if the specification of the model is correct, a random effects model is not appropriate because the error terms are correlated with the

[15] In terms of Hirschman's (1958) classic terminology, federal investment in Mexico would follow an entrepreneurial rather than a reform function.
[16] As pointed out by an anonymous reviewer, it has become relatively common to use the malapportionment in the legislature as a good measure of the political determinants of transfers across states in federal systems. The Mexican legislature has generally been well apportioned, however, so I do not include such a variable in the estimation.

independent variables (Kennedy, 1996). Hence, a fixed effects model is called for, which takes into account the different pattern followed by each state. The second column of Table 5.2 reports the fixed effects model. The variables of interest, GSP, and VPRI retain significance and have the expected sign. All presidents targeted a disproportionate share of resources toward the richer states, notwithstanding that such a strategy increased regional inequality.[17] They also gave disproportionate allocations to PRI supporters, regardless of the development impact of the projects.

5.4. The Distribution of Revenue-Sharing across States

In order to assess the distributional consequences of the revenue-sharing agreement struck in 1980, I use as dependent variables the per capita federal revenue-sharing transfers to the states in the years 1982 and 1992. Those years are chosen for various reasons. The "founding" moment of the revenue-sharing system is 1982, when all states became fully integrated into it. It is also a year of federal elections; if electoral considerations played a role in the allocation of *participaciones*, they should be captured in that moment. In terms of governor time horizons, 1982 was also a year when most governors had a fair amount of their term still to go because the staggered electoral calendar in the states had only two elections coming during the following two years. The 1992 estimate reflects a year when governors possessed relatively long time horizons because almost half of them were just beginning their constitutional terms but well into the years of more intense political competition.

The independent variables for the estimation include the revenue-collecting capacity of the states (as an indicator of opportunity costs) and several political indicators of the temporal perspective of governors (as indicators of their bargaining power). I control for the revenue collection base of each state with a variable measuring state per capita income (*Gross State Product* – GSP) for the years 1980 and 1988 (the closest years for which

---

[17] There is no straightforward pattern in the share of IPF (as opposed to the disproportionality of the share given a state size) that each state receives and electoral support for the PRI in the presidential election. The PRI vote should not be reflected in the share of IPF for three reasons. First, large states will remain with large shares, regardless of PRI support, simply because in those states a "fair share" seems to be kept. Second, a marginal decline of PRI support during the years of party hegemony, say from 95 to 90 percent, will probably have no effect on budget shares because such a decline poses no real challenge to the political survival of the federal executive. Third, the overall patterns throughout the six-year term might be hiding specific temporal effects during the electoral year.

official estimates at the state level were available). I expect that the richer a state is in terms of its GSP, the larger the per capita federal transfer it can bargain for.

I also add a dummy variable that measures what could be thought of as the bargaining strength of oil-producing states ($Oil = 1$ for Campeche, Tabasco, Tamaulipas, and Veracruz). Although oil revenue is strictly federal (and constitutes a rather substantial share of government revenue), its collection depends on the cooperation of local governments. The *Oil* variable should be positive because oil-producing states would have a greater opportunity cost of belonging to the revenue-sharing system because they control the territorial location of oil.

To measure local time horizons, I use a simple measure (*Time*) of the percentage of the constitutional term left for each governor. *Time* in 1982 is different from that in 1992. I expect *Time* to have a positive effect, reflecting larger time horizons and hence less discounting for governors who have most of their term ahead of them. As a measure of the discount rate caused by executive instability, I introduce the historical variable *Instability*, which measures the number of governors that each state has had on average since 1935. The larger the *Instability* variable (which is measured for simplicity as an index, where the federation equals 0), the more likely it is that a governor might not finish his or her constitutional term in office and so the less that state should receive through *participaciones*.

Finally, I include electoral variables in order to test whether there is an electoral bias in the allocation of these resources. *PRI Vote* measures the percentage of the PRI vote in the federal elections of 1982 and 1991. *Governor* measures local-level electoral support for the governor holding office in 1992, who might have faced election some years earlier, in order to test whether the particular popularity of the executive of each state might increase his or her bargaining strength vis-à-vis the federation in the era of greater electoral contestation. Table 5.2 reports the results of the estimations.[18]

---

[18] An OLS assumption of normally distributed errors is not satisfied for the dependent variables of the estimation, the per capita revenue shares in 1992 and 1982. An appropriate procedure is a maximum likelihood (ML) linear estimation using the gamma distribution. This general distribution – of which the chi-squared and the exponential distributions are special cases – has been used extensively because of its mathematical tractability and substantive flexibility (King, 1989: 51). For my purposes, the density function can be written as

$$f_\gamma(y \mid \alpha\beta) = \frac{y^{\alpha\beta^{-1}} e^{-y\beta^{-1}}}{\beta^{\alpha\beta^{-1}} \Gamma(\alpha\beta^{-1})},$$

Table 5.2. *Estimation of Allocations in the Revenue-Sharing System*

	(1) 1992	(2) 1992	(3) 1982
C	928.56 (2.48)***	553.54 (1.00)	− 175.36 (0.44)
Gross state product	0.0152 (3.08)***	0.0168 (3.18)***	0.0299 (8.55)***
Instability	−752.48 (1.96)**	−660.39 (1.64)*	−512.3 (1.79)*
Time	169.70 (0.87)	175.79 (0.89)	−286.63 (1.12)
Oil	410.80 (2.57)***	397.43 (2.38)**	210.46 (1.33)
Governor	−262.69 (0.67)		
PRI vote		200.71 (0.31)	448.78 (0.90)
$\bar{R}^2$	0.3180	0.2393	0.7789
log L function	222.98	223.15 (sum: 220)	217.14 (sum: 226.5)
est. param. α	21.58	21.35	18.29
Wald test	14.77	14.76	14.56

t statistics are in parentheses.
* Significant at the 90% level.
** Significant at the 95% level.
*** Significant at the 99% level.

For the estimates of 1992, reported in columns (1) and (2), there seems to be good evidence that the revenue-sharing system in Mexico is a contract resulting from a bargain rather than a discretionary allocation controlled solely by the federal authorities. Richer states receive larger transfers, and the effect is large. In per capita terms, for every additional 1,000 pesos of per capita GSP (in constant 1980 pesos), a state received 15 or 17 additional pesos per capita in revenue transfers. In U.S. dollar terms, this would mean an additional dollar transfer per capita for roughly every 60 dollars of per capita GSP.

where $y > 0, \alpha > 0, E[y] = \alpha, V[y] = \alpha(\beta + 1)$, and $\Gamma(.)$ is the gamma function (see King, 1989: 46, 51).

As expected, the *Oil* variable is positive and significant. Oil-producing states could bargain for more resources because they possessed a very valuable resource in terms of potential revenue. Although the oil-producing states would be unable to threaten the federal government by withholding oil, they have other less confrontational ways to make it clear that they control this resource. For example, during the late 1980s, many "accidents" in oil pipelines allegedly were in fact political pressures on the federal government exerted by the powerful oil workers' union. If a state government wanted to disrupt oil production, it had the means to do so.

The *Instability* variable is negative and always significant, which suggests that "risky" states received less resources. That means that governors who were less likely to finish their terms did not have the same bargaining position as those who were quite secure in office. The reason that governors do not finish their terms is usually related to political conflicts that run out of their control, sometimes related to local postelectoral conflicts.

The temporal horizons of governors measured by *Time* suggest that the more of the governor's term is left, the more revenue the state receives. The result is not statistically significant, however. This could be attributed to several reasons. It might be that the overriding consideration of risk is only the historical instability of a state, not the years left in the constitutional term of a governor. Or it could be that the linear measurement of the variable is not appropriate. An exponential time discount would imply that the last years in office are more heavily discounted. A popular saying in Mexico calls the last year of executives in office the *año de Hidalgo*, which refers to the practice of governors and bureaucrats alike to "steal" as much as they can in that last year.[19]

The electoral variables, which measure the electoral strength of the PRI in both federal and local (gubernatorial) elections, are negative but not significant, so there is no evidence of a partisan bias in the allocation of funds through revenue-sharing. An unreported specification verifies whether states governed by the PAN opposition party have a pattern different from PRI-governed states by including a dummy variable for Baja California, Chihuahua, and Guanajuato. Consonant with estimations by Arellano Cadena (1996), this variable is not significant. This result contrasts with the electoral determinants found in the last section for *Inversión Pública*

---

[19] The saying refers to the founding father of the nation, and it comes from a rhyme: "El año de Hidalgo, ch—— su madre quien deje algo," which translates into something like: "The year of the founding father, f—— whoever leaves anything behind."

Federal (IPF) and with those of other studies that have found that components of IPF, such as the widely publicized poverty alleviation program The Program Nacional de Solidaridad PRONASOL, were electorally motivated (Dresser, 1991; Molinar and Weldon, 1994; Diaz-Cayeros, Estévez and Magaloni, forthcoming). This difference is not surprising, however, if one considers the different logic in each of these transfers. Revenue shares are mostly stable over time, and they have been dictated by the evolution of taxation and the bargaining power of governors in that realm. The IPF instead varies dramatically from year to year according to bureaucratic and presidential choices, with some degree of influence played by local politicians who seek to influence investment projects toward their regions.

Column (3) of Table 5.2 reports estimates for the founding year of the revenue-sharing system in 1982. In this estimation, only *GSP* and the *Instability* variable are significant. The nonsignificance of the *Oil* variable suggests that 10 years earlier the system of revenue-sharing was not particularly biased in favor of the oil-producing states – apart from the bias captured by the *GSP* variable. It is also noteworthy that although 1982 was an electoral year, there is no evidence of a partisan allocation of funds, which probably reflects that the electoral threats at the time were not so significant.

The basic insight obtained from this statistical analysis is hence that resource allocation in Mexico depended, as posited by the bargaining model in Chapter 1, on the opportunity cost of local governments belonging to the federal arrangement and on the risk faced by local executives, as determined by the uncertainty of their tenure in office. The results suggest that even within a cooperative coalition, governors could bargain for resources rather than act merely as administrative agents of the federal government.

5.5. Democracy and Fiscal Federalism

In July 1989, for the first time since its founding, the PRI admitted defeat in a gubernatorial election. In the northern state of Baja California, Ernesto Ruffo, a businessman and a popular mayor before his candidacy, was sworn in as the first governor belonging to an opposition party, the *Partido Acción Nacional* (National Action Part, PAN). At his first press conference, he announced that he had received a bankrupt state administration, which to some extent was attributable to the abuse of state public funds for the campaign of the PRI candidate. He suggested that there would not be enough money to pay the wages and Christmas bonuses to the local bureaucracy, composed mostly of members of the PRI (Campuzano Montoya, 1995:73).

143

In a highly controversial move, the local government issued debt in order to finance its deficit. The governor commanded the greatest attention, however, when he challenged the president to keep the promise he made before the election, that the federal government would give equal financial treatment to governors whose party affiliation differed from his own. He protested, moreover, that the federal government was not transferring to Baja California its proper revenue share (*participación*) in keeping with the prevailing revenue-sharing agreements.

The governor's accusations were threefold: that the finance ministry claimed to have handed over funds that the state administration never received; that the federal finance ministry was not complying with the formulas of revenue distribution; and that Baja California was not receiving transfers in proportion to its yield in federal taxes. The governor threatened to sue the federal government in the Supreme Court (a symbolic rather than a real threat) and to withdraw from the national system of tax coordination (*Sistema Nacional de Coordinación Fiscal* – SNCF). The threat of withdrawal was taken seriously by the federal government: PRI governors were also starting to complain (in private and off the record) about the prevailing system of revenue-sharing. If Baja California rejected the system, other states could follow suit.

The complaints of Baja California resonated powerfully with state politicians in Mexico because most political actors believed that the federal government had behaved opportunistically, withholding resources from the states when the federal finances so dictated. In the context of the aftermath of the "lost decade" of the 1980s, in which there was virtually no growth, local politicians were less willing to passively accept only those funds that the federal government willingly gave them. The electoral protection that the PRI had given them in the past was no longer assured, given the mounting challenges of parties both on the left and right, which became all too evident after the 1988 presidential elections in which Cuauhtémoc Cárdenas, the son of former President Lázaro Cárdenas, split from the PRI, running a highly popular candidacy. Although it is impossible to know for sure who won the election, the PRI resorted to electoral fraud.

Revenue sharing was supposedly less subject to manipulation by the federal government than federal public investment. But a clear indicator of the discretion exercised by the federal government with respect to revenue sharing is the difference between the funds that were actually disbursed each year and the statutory rate in the revenue-sharing law. Figure 5.3 attempts to reconstruct the gap between the statutory rate and the percentage of

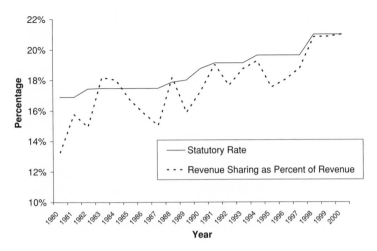

Figure 5.3. Revenue sharing vs. statutory rate in Mexico.

federal revenue that was transferred to the states through *participaciones* each year since 1980. One of the difficulties in holding the federal government accountable for the funds that should be distributed to the states in Mexico is that not all federal revenues are "shareable": Only the federal government knows the exact amount of the federal shareable revenues, and that amount is the one to which the statutory rate applies. But if one assumes that shareable funds remain a relatively constant ratio with respect to total federal revenues, the indicator in the graph in Figure 5.3 is a good proxy of how compliance with revenue-sharing has evolved over time. The graph suggests that the federal government in Mexico has often failed to give states as much revenue as it was legally obliged to.

Ruffo's rebellion marked the start of a new phase in federal–state relationships: He challenged the secrecy in the way that financial resources were allocated by the federal government. His challenge was not limited to a critique of the way in which federal resources, through the *Inversión Pública Federal* (IPF), were spent but encompassed taxation as well. The alleged partisan bias of financial flows allocated to regions by the federal government became one of the most controversial topics, both among politicians and in academic research (see Dresser, 1991; Molinar and Weldon, 1994; Rodríguez and Ward, 1995; Mogollón, 1996; Acevedo Monroy, 1997). But the opposition governor went beyond a demand for steady federal financial resources: He opened up the debate on fiscal authority and federalism, calling for greater transparency in the way tax revenues were shared among states within the centralized system of taxation.

This chapter has shown that the distribution of financial resources was linked with the relative bargaining strength of states vis-à-vis the federal government. The distribution model in Chapter 1 suggested that resource allocation games in federal systems are not zero-sum strategic interactions. If they were, cooperative arrangements such as federalism would be unreasonable and a territory would only be held together by organizations resembling an empire more than a federal pact (Riker, 1964). For many critics of the long years of PRI hegemony, the Mexican system was just a step short of empire. According to this view, under the hegemonic party system, states were mere administrative units always ready to obey presidential mandates. The discussion of this and the previous chapter should suggest a more restrained view. Although the Mexican federal system was undeniably characterized by a large degree of centralization of financial resources, and local politicians were willing to sacrifice their parochial state interests in the pursuit of national political careers within the PRI, the evidence of state bargaining strength suggests that the germ of state autonomy, which is a precondition for any federal arrangement, was not lost throughout these years.

Governor Ruffo's challenge was met by the president in an innovative way through the creation of an academic committee that would determine whether the PAN governor's complaints were true. The committee was headed by Luis Aguilar, an expert at a prestigious academic institution.[20] The committee produced a report in the middle of 1993 that was not publicly released. The panel of experts determined that Ruffo's allegations were unfounded. It argued that in 1987 Baja California received more resources through the *Sistema Nacional de Coordinación Fiscal* (SNCF) than it would have obtained if the previous system had not been changed and that in 1991 the state received 13.5 percent more federal transfers than the federal revenue collected in the state (Campuzano Montoya, 1995:217). The governor gave up, although he claimed "that it had been impossible to reach the truth of fiscal justice" (Campuzano Montoya, 1995:218).

Ruffo lost the battle, but he won the war. He obtained an increase in federal discretionary resources to his state. The finance minister visited

---

[20] The nonpartisanship of the head of the committee is somewhat suspect with hindsight because Aguilar went on to occupy a subcabinet post in the interior ministry after 1994 as part of the PRI administration of president Ernesto Zedillo.

the state at the same time that the panel produced its report, announcing an increase in conditional transfers to the state through *Inversión Pública Federal* (IPF). The finance ministry also agreed to increase transfers to the state for educational expenditures. BANOBRAS, a federal government development bank, agreed to grant new credits at low interest rates to finance public works in the state, and the opposition governor created the most important precedent of openly debating the issues of fiscal federalism. In 1995, even before the PRI lost control of the Chamber of Deputies in the 1997 midterm election, legislators modified the presidential budget initiative, increasing the pool of revenue shares transferred to the states.

After 1997, the federal budget in Mexico was radically transformed in all matters related to fiscal federalism. The future of the *Sistema Nacional de Coordinación Fiscal* depends on the way in which governors bargain with the federal government over the allocation of financial resources. It took until the year 2000 for the PRI to lose the majority of the governorships and for an opposition party to win the presidency. Will democracy bring about radical changes to the way federalism works? This question cannot be answered within the confines of the case of Mexico, so we need to look elsewhere for experiences regarding the role of political regime change in revenue-sharing.

PART II

Centralization and Revenue-Sharing in the Latin American Federations

T he second part of this book seeks to shed light on the variation in the centralized federal compromises that were established in the Latin American federations. The emphasis lies on the moment of creation of revenue-sharing systems rather than on contemporary events and debates on fiscal federalism. The creation of a centralized fiscal bargain differed among the Latin American federations depending on the resources available to the central government, the credibility of the threats made by the states, and the way in which promises by the federal government were enforced. If a bargain was struck, it had distributional consequences. The benefits of cooperation could be shared among the participants in multiple ways.

The theory in Chapter 1 suggested that in order for revenue-sharing systems to become established, a credible "federal fiscal compromise" must be reached in which the federal government commits to making a financial transfer to the states and provinces. The empirical evidence suggests that the commitment is hard to fulfill because Latin American federal governments have often breached fiscal compromises by withholding resources from their states and provinces. On a more positive tone, the evidence suggests that democratic accountability improves the compliance of federal governments with revenue-sharing. The analysis of Venezuela, Argentina, and Brazil shows that democracy matters for fiscal federalism.

The effect of democratization of fiscal authority and centralization is an issue that could not be assessed in the case of Mexico because of the absence of a regime change until 2000. The future evolution of centralization in Mexico can only be assessed by looking at the logic of what has happened in the other Latin American federations. Moreover, in order to really test the potential of the theoretical account in Chapter 1 as an explanation of the process of centralization and the construction of fiscal authority, it is necessary to provide evidence suggesting why some countries followed paths that were different from Mexico's and, in those cases where the paths were similar, whether the same types of explanatory variables account for the similar outcomes.

Latin American federations were established early in the history of federal regimes: Mexico in 1824, Venezuela in 1830, Argentina in 1853, and Brazil in 1889. Riker (1964) argued that they were constituted as federal regimes in order to hold vast territories together in the face of external threats. The liberal elites in Latin America also adopted the federal form of government out of a desire to imitate the success of the United States. Much has been discussed about the "centralist tradition" in Latin America noted by Veliz (1980). Notwithstanding such a cultural predisposition, the fact is that federalism was vibrant and alive as a form of political organization in the newly independent nations.[1] Federalism in Latin America, however, was politically more centralized from the outset than the one found, for example, in the United States. Latin American federalism was more about "hanging together" than about "coming together" (Stepan, 2004).

The viability of Latin American countries during the 19th century was far from assured because of external threats and domestic challenges. Argentina, Mexico, and Venezuela experimented with unitary and federal constitutions, punctuated by bloody civil wars, during their first decades as independent nations as they sought an institutional design that would keep their countries together. Brazil was different. Its federation emerged as a compromise solution after the empire to balance the interests of Minas Gerais, Sao Paulo, and, to some extent, Rio Grande do Sul (Love, 1971).

In the realm of taxation, the Latin American federations inherited their local tax structures from colonial times. At the national level, state consolidation was only achieved once a solid financial footing for the federal government was established through the control of customs duties and the establishment of creditworthiness in the international environment. In Mexico and Venezuela, customs duties became the most important source of revenue for the federal governments in the late 19th century. Royalties and taxes on mining complemented this revenue. Taxation of land was an important source of state-level revenue.

---

[1] See, for example, the essays in Carmagnani (1993).

The most controversial revenue for the subnational level in all four countries came from the taxation of the circulation of merchandise across jurisdictions. In Argentina and Brazil, federal control of customs duties came relatively late. Provincial and state governments levied taxes on the circulation of merchandise both within the country and in world markets (i.e., customs). The liberal flow of goods and services through the assurance of interstate commerce was in fact one of the most contested issues in the 19th century throughout Latin America. Even in countries where the central government controlled customs and liberal elites had established provisions in their constitutions forbidding barriers to the circulation of goods, the free flow of interstate trade was not a reality until the last decades of the 19th century. Mexico eliminated the colonial tax on the circulation of merchandise, the *alcabala*, officially in 1884, although de facto only until 1896, and Venezuela eliminated taxes on transit only after 1881.

Nevertheless, at the dawn of the 20th century, all the Latin American federations had established relatively strong federal governments and had integrated national markets. Some countries had been more successful than others in freeing, in accordance with their liberal creed, the internal flow of commerce. Some had also succeeded in creating the conditions for an incipient process of industrialization, attracting foreign investment and exploiting world markets. Entrepreneurship spirits had become manifest in all countries, as demonstrated by the thriving domestic capitalist classes that lived in the cosmopolitan capital cities or in the rich provincial capitals. Although living conditions were precarious for the vast majority of landless laborers in the agricultural sector, a middle class of merchants, artisans, and professionals had gradually emerged. Except for Argentina, the countries were poor, but their prospects were very promising.

The global depression in 1929 produced a common international shock that created a "critical juncture" (Collier and Collier, 1991) that would put a halt to this liberal export-oriented phase of economic growth. The response of each federal government to the international crisis would determine its future development paths and the centralization of fiscal authority. During the 1930's all the federal governments in the region shifted their development strategies. In all countries, momentous transformations took place in the political realm, and the relationship between the federal government and the states or provinces was redrawn in accordance with the political changes. In particular, the imperative for the federal government to collect taxes from sources different from the dwindling customs and export taxes led to the creation of national income taxes and efforts to unify excises and sales taxes. The success of such efforts depended on the specific articulation of national and regional politics in each country.

Compared with the direct collection of taxes by each territorial unit in a federation, revenue-sharing implies a radical transformation in the nature of fiscal authority. First, the responsibility (and blame) for tax collection is shifted from the local level of government to the national one. Second, if there is greater collection efficiency in the centralized administration of taxes, subnational units can receive more funds than they would have obtained from their direct exercise of tax authority.[2] Third, because the recipient government does not exercise potential tax authority, the central government can carry out redistribution through the way in which funds are allocated across units. On all of these grounds, revenue-sharing arrangements are usually considered to make everyone better off: Local governments obtain additional revenue without political costs, and the national level of government can carry out redistributive functions.

The Achilles heel of revenue-sharing systems is, as the first part of this book has shown for the case of Mexico, that promises by the central government are not always credible. It is possible for the central government to renege on making transfers, and redistribution can make a territorial unit a net loser from the arrangement. A recipient government with high economic activity might not only receive less revenue-sharing funds than what is collected in its jurisdiction, but it could receive even fewer funds than what it could have generated had it not joined the revenue-sharing system and instead kept a tax system of its own. In federal regimes, where constituent units control their constitutional tax authority, revenue-sharing can be established when a regional bargain is struck in which states or provinces are willing to abdicate their tax authority.[3]

The chapters in this part of the book address four major questions. First, I ask whether and under what conditions a centralized fiscal pact creating revenue-sharing was reached in each country. The model in Chapter 1 suggests that such a pact is more likely when the central government is

---

[2] Blankart (2001) sees this as a monopolistic practice in which states prevent fiscal competition.

[3] A second issue, which economists tend to stress, is that revenue-sharing breaks the benefit principle of taxation because the funds to finance public goods do not necessarily come from the same citizens who obtain the benefits. This is a general problem in all transfer systems and is not unique to revenue-sharing.

more powerful than those of the states. My analysis suggests that in Brazil a centralized pact did not come about because the states had the military power to threaten the federation. Not even the military governments were able to impose a unitary system by force. In Venezuela, in contrast, military dictators established initially a centralized pact that over time turned into a unitary imposition. Argentina reached a centralized bargain early on, but the lack of federal compliance undermined the system until it collapsed in the last decades of the 20th century.

Second, I ask what determines the level of resources that were transferred to the states and provinces. This is reflected in the statutory rates of the revenue-sharing systems. These statutory rates are the consequence of pressures from local politicians that become articulated in the party system. In Venezuela, where the party system became highly centralized and oil revenues were centrally controlled, the statutory rates remained relatively low. In Argentina and Brazil, in contrast, where careers were more localist and states and provinces controlled sizable resources for patronage, statutory rates tended to be high.

Third, I ask whether the statutory rates in the revenue-sharing systems were respected. It turns out that in each country there is less opportunism on the part of the federal government during eras of democracy. This suggests that democracy does produce some accountability of the federal government to local interests.

Finally, I ask what kind of distributional consequence emerged from the creation of the revenue-sharing arrangements. Although fiscal federalism systems in Latin America have differed in the way they have evolved, they have all tended to shift the distribution of revenue transfers to benefit small states to the detriment of the richer, more advanced, or more productive regions, including the central metropolitan areas. This trend has made the systems more "redistributive" over time. Thus, although centralized fiscal bargains might at the outset involve respecting a "derivation principle" in the allocation of funds (i.e., in the absence of a fiscal bargain, rich states could have taxed themselves and retained more resources than the poor ones), as those systems evolve through time, redistribution plays an increasingly more prevalent role. In Mexico, neither revenue-sharing nor federal investment were particularly redistributive. Funds were allocated to give preference to the richer regions and the hegemonic party strongholds. The federal governments in the other Latin American countries instead used revenue-sharing as a way to redistribute resources toward the poorer states and provinces, although they also kept a partisan logic in the distribution.

Median voter models of income redistribution, such as the Meltzer-Richards framework (Acemoglu and Robinson, 2001; Boix, 2003), hypothesize that democracies should tend to equalize the availability of public goods and incomes across regions. Latin American federations offer variation both in terms of the democratic nature of their regimes and the degree of redistribution they have achieved. A simple conjecture would suggest that the difference between Mexico and the other Latin American federations can be attributed to the regime type. However, the discussion of Latin American fiscal evolution suggests that the relationship between democracy and regional redistribution is rather complex (see Eaton, 2004). Stepan (2004) has argued that federalisms differ according to their "demos-constraining" features and that those variations result in different policy outcomes. According to his argument, the most demos-constraining federations are likely to exhibit more unequal (personal and regional) distributions of income.[4] Tracing the regional redistributive process in Latin America over time shows that in all countries revenue-sharing systems gradually become detached from the so-called derivation principle (i.e., the territorial origin of the revenue), in which funds were allocated primarily as a function of the economic base of each state, toward systems favoring the small and poor regions in each country. This expands the scope of redistribution. This trend has also been true of Mexico's revenue-sharing system since the 1980s. The redistribution achieved varies in each revenue-sharing system. The most redistributive federalism in Latin America turns out to be the Argentine one, followed by Brazil and Venezuela (Mexico being the least redistributive). However, when the regional distribution of public funds is calculated taking into account not just revenue-sharing but also federal transfers on the expenditure side and the retention of fiscal authority

---

[4] Beramendi (2003) has argued that federalism can be devised so that regional elites can "protect" inequality from the redistributive efforts of a national government. The Latin American experience suggests that the relationship among democracy, the strength of the federal units, and redistribution might evolve through time in unexpected manners. Authoritarian rulers can use redistribution to preempt regime change, whereas democratic governments might limit redistribution in order to appease powerful challengers. Hence regional redistribution is neither more nor less likely when a regime is democratic. However, to the extent that strong states control sources of taxation, the scope of redistribution is limited by federalism.

over the VAT by the Brazilian states, it turns out that Venezuela is far more redistributive than Brazil. Surprisingly, the Brazilian system is not as redistributive as suggested by the literature. The Brazilian overall distributive pattern is in fact similar to Mexico's, although through very different mechanisms.

The chapters in this second part of the book are organized as follows. The next chapter discusses the Venezuelan process of consolidation of federal tax authority. It argues that a process of centralization that started in the 19th century led to the virtual disappearance of the federal arrangement. Consonant with this, the fiscal bargain between states and the federation was one where the states gave up their capacity to collect revenue and the federal government allocated funds to them with vast discretion. To a large extent, windfall resources from oil were responsible for this outcome. Democracy improved the Venezuelan fiscal compromise by compelling the federal government to fulfill its transfer promises. But democracy did not ensure that federalism would yield greater redistribution toward poor regions. Venezuela shares with Mexico the features of a party system in which the control of nominations was highly centralized and a transfer system that was made possible by oil windfalls, but fiscal centralization in Venezuela predates the consolidation of a regional compromise through political parties.

Chapter 7 discusses Argentina, where the process of centralization of tax authority was quite parallel to Mexico's. The Argentine fiscal arrangement in the 1930s bears a striking resemblance to Mexico's in the effort to create a unified system of excises and sales taxes. The feature that distinguished Argentina, in stark contrast with Mexico, was the coming and going of different political regimes and federal administrations. This instability made the system of intergovernmental relations incredibly complex. In Argentina, democracy had a positive effect on compliance, but the process was far less linear than in Venezuela. Throughout, Argentine local politicians retained more fiscal authority than their Venezuelan or Mexican counterparts. Argentina's revenue-sharing system was highly redistributive, although autocratic governments were just as likely to benefit poor regions as democratic ones.

Finally, Chapter 8 discusses the case of Brazil, where a centralized federal bargain was rejected by the states. States in Brazil, particularly Minas Gerais and Sao Paulo, had enough power to credibly threaten the federal government and resist the pressures toward centralization. In fact, not even the military governments of the 1960s and 1970s were able to take fiscal authority away from the states, even though they centralized fiscal resources and created a revenue-sharing system. Hence, Brazil remained a peripheralized federal system where although revenue-sharing played a redistributive role, the most important source of revenue, the value-added tax, is controlled by the states, limiting the scope for regional redistribution.

6

Venezuela

UNITARIANISM IN DISGUISE

6.1. The Abdication of Fiscal Authority

Venezuela is the most centralized of the Latin American federations and was the first to strike a centralized fiscal bargain. To a large extent, the centralized fiscal bargain in Venezuela involved the abdication by the states of all tax authority and the virtual abandonment of federalism. Venezuelan governors were appointed rather than elected in each state jurisdiction. The lack of strong state representation and power meant that the federal government could avoid complying with promised transfers to the states. Such an arrangement was only viable because the federal government had massive revenue from oil.

As the country established a democracy in the second half of the 20th century, compliance with revenue-sharing improved. The democratic governments that emerged from a compromise reached in 1958, the so-called *Pacto de Punto Fijo*, were able to compromise for the peaceful alternation in political power and respect partisan electoral strongholds in the states. Governors remained unelected, and the system was not highly responsive to territorial interests. Thus, regionalism in Venezuela became relatively unimportant by the second half of the 20th century. Most of the regional differences in political attitudes could be subsumed under a rural–urban cleavage (Baloyra and Martz, 1979:87). However, federalism retained a residual character that was not eliminated by the modernization forces. Federalism reemerged after 1989 with the process of decentralization and the reform that allowed for the direct election of governors. The collapse of the duopolistic compromise of Venezuelan democratic politics can be attributed to a large extent to the resurgence of those regional forces (Penfold-Becerra, 2004:221).

This chapter discusses federalism in Venezuela, contrasting the evolution of this highly centralized regime with that of Mexico and the other Latin American federations. The next two sections provide a brief account of the history of fiscal federalism in Venezuela and the processes that gave birth to the revenue-sharing system. Section 6.4 discusses the problem of compliance with federal promises in the context of the centralized fiscal arrangement. Section 6.5 provides an econometric account of the trends in revenue-sharing and tests for the effect of democracy on fiscal compliance. Section 6.6 discusses the evolution of redistribution trends across states and over time. Section 6.7 concludes with a discussion of some of the contemporary debates on Venezuela's federalism.

6.2. The Venezuelan Fiscal Pact

As in Mexico, Venezuela's 19th century was characterized by violent conflicts over the role of the church, control of national taxation (the so-called *patronato* rights), and agrarian issues that were reflected in controversies over whether a federal or a unitary form of government was best suited for the country. Even after centralization of political authority was achieved by Antonio Guzmán Blanco (who ruled the country on and off from 1870 to 1888), regionally based *caudillos* remained key actors in the political system.

The "Basis of the Union" section of the 1864 Venezuelan Constitution established the division of tax authority between the states and the federal government. The constitution explicitly declared that, upon joining as a Federation, states were obliged "not to establish taxes, before the consumption phase, of products or articles already subject to national taxes."[1] Since 1858, the constitution had stipulated, moreover, that consumption of products from other states could not have taxes different from those established on local products. Hence, issues related to interstate commerce and fiscal barriers to the movement of goods were constitutionally settled earlier than in Argentina or Brazil.

Guzmán Blanco successfully centralized fiscal authority by fulfilling a federal obligation that had been established in the 1864 Constitution but had not been met until he came into power (Suárez, 1965). The constitution provided that the federal government would grant subsidies to the states that did not have mines as a source of revenue. In 1881, Guzmán Blanco struck a deal with the regional *caudillos* in which federal control over all

---

[1] Article 3, Section 5.

mining and salt taxes was exchanged for the transfer of federal subsidies to *all* states (Floyd, 1992). This revenue-sharing agreement proved to be quite consequential for the future evolution of Venezuelan federalism. The 1881 Constitution guaranteed to the states two-thirds of any revenue collected in the national customs for the transit (territorial) tax and two-thirds of taxes on mines, salt, and vacant land (Mariñas Otero, 1965).[2]

The constitution also determined the distribution of the funds to each state according to population. The per capita distributional rule became an important precedent for the distribution of funds in subsequent decades. In contrast with revenue-sharing systems in the other Latin American countries, which were established in the 1930s (Argentina and Mexico) and the 1960s (Brazil), Venezuela introduced a centralized fiscal bargain in the 19th century. This was a reflection of the weakness of federal institutions. Venezuela also established the simplest formula for the distribution of funds across constituent units.

With the 1881 compromise, revenue-sharing was explicitly protected by the constitution. Decades before the oil booms that would mark Venezuela's development, mining taxes had become explicitly federal instead of exclusively under the jurisdiction of the states (as had been previously established in the 1864 Constitution). This federal pact originated from conditions of the 19th century, when regional strongmen credibly threatened the federal government with violence. Guzmán Blanco consolidated power in the central government but did not succeed in eliminating the existence of local armies (Mascareño, 2000:21). The federal government was willing to transfer resources in exchange for states' agreement to curb their tax authority. But the scope of the agreement was relatively limited. Mining taxes were not the most important source of revenue – had oil revenue been constitutionally controlled by the states in the early 20th century, the history of Venezuelan federalism might have been very different.

According to Floyd (1992), the compromise of 1881 was possible because Guzmán Blanco accommodated the regional *caudillos* through measures such as the creation of the Federal Council in 1879 to be in charge of naming "presidents" to the states. This council was composed of regional *caudillos* (Floyd, 1992:193). This suggests that, lacking articulated political parties, Venezuelan elites used the council as an institutional device whereby they could ensure guarantees of federal respect for their regional authority. By

---

[2] Article 13, Section 32.

refraining from using the presidential prerogative to name state executives, allowing the governors themselves to negotiate those appointments, an important precedent was established: The selection of governors would respect local political forces rather than being a mere imposition from the center. This informal practice continued throughout the 20th century, particularly after 1958.

In addition, the federal government initiated a public works program. Guzmán Blanco made sure that regional *caudillos* headed the development boards (*Juntas de Fomento*) in charge of road construction in their states, which gave them access to jobs for patronage, a budget to administer, and rents (Floyd, 1992:172–173). Guzmán Blanco coaxed states to eliminate taxes on transit (*peajes*), which used to be the main source of financing for public works at the local level. From then on, the general (federal) tax on transportation became the main source to finance public works in the states. Hence, Floyd notes that "with the help of the regional caudillos, Guzmán Blanco had despoiled the states of most of their independent economic power" (Floyd, 1992:177). States would not exercise taxation but would receive both unconditional and conditional transfers through revenue-sharing and the development boards.

The federal transfer to the states constituted between 30 and 50 percent of state revenues at the end of the 19th century (Floyd, 1992:175). In 1893, the size of the subsidy was increased from two-thirds to 100 percent of the mining taxes, plus a provision guaranteeing a minimum lump sum if mining taxes were to be eliminated sometime in the future (Suárez, 1965:32). In 1901, these sources of revenue were constitutionally determined to be the only allowable ones for the states except for local taxes on documents (*papel sellado*) and taxes on natural resources. A minimum fixed transfer to each state was also guaranteed by the 1901 reform.[3] These developments suggest that by the turn of the century, efforts were being made to ensure federal compliance with revenue-sharing, which at the time was based, as in Mexico and Argentina since the 1930s, on specific taxes.

The fiscal arrangement remained in place during the next couple of decades, particularly following the stable authoritarian regime established by Juan Vicente Gómez in 1908. Gómez promoted a liberal trade regime, which allowed for a boom in the export of coffee, cocoa, and hides. He

---

[3] In 1903, alcohol (and tobacco for a brief number of years) was added as a state source of revenue, on the basis of a federally determined tax base and rate, to be distributed across states according to production.

also weakened regional *caudillos* through the use of force. But most crucially, Gómez took advantage of foreign investment to develop the oil sector. By 1925, oil was the most important Venezuelan export, even above coffee (Sullivan, 1992:258). Venezuela became the world's most important oil exporter in 1928 (Karl, 1997:80). Oil became an unprecedented source of revenue, controlled not by the state governments but by the federal executive.

6.3. Oil, Federal Transfer Shirking, and the Loss of Federalism

Federal authority over all matters related to natural resources became the cornerstone of the centralized fiscal pact once Venezuela became, in Karl's (1997) terms, a "petro-state." The 1925 Constitution (the fifth of seven made by Gómez) established strict federal jurisdiction over virtually all taxes. This constitution "reserved to the jurisdiction of the Federal Power . . . everything relative to the organization, collection and investment of stamp taxes, cigarettes, title deeds, matches, alcoholic beverages, and all the rest that may be established by law with a national tax character" (my translation, Mariñas Otero, 1965). This constitution also formally created the *Situado Constitucional* (Constitutional Appropriation).

The *Situado* was a revenue-sharing fund established as a fixed sum for the next three years, and it subsequently made up 12 percent of the revenue collected at the federal level. In 1925, together with the creation of revenue-sharing, consumption taxes were explicitly put under exclusive jurisdiction of the states. But this provision was short-lived. Had this provision remained in place, perhaps Venezuelan states would have evolved in a manner similar to Brazil some years later. The oil boom gave a final blow to any effort by the state administrations to retain important sources of revenue at that level. There was no reason to make efforts to collect revenue from consumption tax bases given the windfall revenue from oil, which in the 1930s made up more than 50 percent of federal revenue (Kornblith and Quintana, 1981, quoted in Karl, 1997).

In terms of the model in Chapter 1, Venezuela seems to go through two different phases. In the first one, which occurs during the 19th century, a successful compromise is established among the *caudillos*, who agree to create a very early system of revenue-sharing. This is a form of federal bargain in which the *Juntas* were the institutional solution devised to provide credibility to the federal promises. The second phase, during which the *Situado* was created, occurred in an era when states were so weak that a unitary

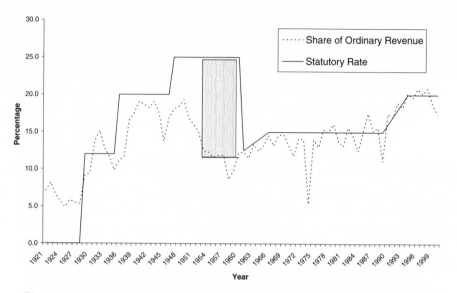

Figure 6.1. Venezuela: Revenue-sharing as percentage of federal revenue.

imposition succeeded and gave rise to a new system in which federalism virtually disappeared.

Figure 6.1 shows the evolution of the *Situado Constitucional* in Venezuela during the course of the 20th century. The dotted line plots the percentage of funds that were effectively transferred from the federal government to the states in accordance with the constitutional mandate. The solid line represents the statutory rate of revenue-sharing, explicitly mandated in the constitution. The shaded area represents a period when the federal government was given discretion to determine the statutory rate within the large band between 12.5 and 25 percent. The mismatch between both lines represents the degree of compliance by the federal government with the revenue-sharing agreement. Funds effectively transferred are measured by dividing the *Situado Constitucional* funds actually disbursed by federal ordinary revenues. Between 1937 and 1953, that share was calculated as a percentage of the previous year's collection, in accordance with the legislation, that lagged the base for the calculation of revenue-sharing.[4]

---

[4] As with most Latin American official statistics, there are important variations in the amounts reported by various sources. The data were constructed on the basis of Kornblith and Maingón (1985) and *Oficina Central de Presupuesto* (OCEPRE) (undated), coupled with reports from the *Ministerio de Hacienda*, the *Oficina Central del Presupuesto*, and the *Banco Central de Venezuela*. From 1936 to 1975, the data appear to be relatively reliable in that at

The graph in Figure 6.1 suggests that the 1925 reform represented a real increase in funds transferred to the states, although the federal government was, in practice, not bound by the statutory rate. This is consonant with Karl's (1997) account of how Gómez used the power of the presidency to selectively grant funds to his cronies, thus extending a clientelistic network in the federal bureaucracy that passed through the regional *caudillos*. The regional forces were subdued, although not eliminated. The timing of national consolidation prepared the country to face the international challenges of the coming years. The global depression in 1929 meant a sharp shock for any country relying on international markets for their growth. However, Venezuela was not hit too hard by the depression because oil exports and prices quickly recovered.

Perhaps because of these favorable conditions, the authoritarian regime survived the death of Gómez in 1935. There were some efforts, however, to introduce a political opening at the time. In particular, the 1936 Constitution legalized political parties and electoral competition. In the tax realm, consumption taxes became exclusively federal, removing this vestige of tax authority from the states in exchange for the state's abdication of consumption taxes. Federal authority over sales taxes meant that the one source that could have become important in the future, as it did in Brazil and Mexico, was no longer under the control of the states. The *Situado* was increased to 20 percent. The original proposal the federal government wanted in the constitution was to have a *Situado* rate of 17 percent for most states and an additional 3 percent for states with natural resources (Suárez, 1965:59), but different treatment across jurisdictions raised more problems than it solved.

It is clear from Figure 6.1 that the administrations of Generals Isaías Medina Angarica and Eleazar López Contreras between 1935 and 1945 did not fulfill their transfer commitments. Nonetheless, the reform meant that funds transferred effectively did increase. By the 1930s, states had become completely dependent on the *Situado* for their local finances. According to Betancourt (1940:436–437), states on average received 95 percent of their revenue from the *Situado*,[5] a dependence that has remained since then. The

---

least two independent sources coincided in the statistics reported. The reported compliance with the statutory rate differs from that of Kornblith and Maingón (1985), most markedly after 1958 because whereas they continued to use lagged revenue collection as the base of their percentage, starting in that year I use the current period, as provided by the legislation.

[5] The dependence might be somewhat exaggerated. According to the finance ministry, the dependence in the 1940s was at around 60 percent. However, this is an artifact of including the Federal District as a state. In fact, when Caracas is excluded from the figures, states

increase in the statutory rate brought about an increase in transfers to the states, but the process was controlled by the federal government and subject to its discretion. The increase in funds lagged behind the legal change, and when the federal government was in a more stringent financial situation in the 1940s, it reduced the transfers accordingly.[6]

In 1945, a short-lived government was led by *Acción Democrática* (Democratic Action, AD), a multiclass party founded in 1940. The AD's administration of the so-called *trienio* tried to use the revenue-sharing arrangement as a mechanism to cement its bases of support in the rural periphery (Powell, 1971). The 1947 Constitution explicitly prohibited double taxation by the states (*Memoria de Hacienda*, 1948:43), and further increased the *Situado* to 25 percent of national revenue. The rules for the distribution of funds were changed to favor the more backward peripheral regions.[7] Moreover, the finance ministry offered matching funds for those states that would coordinate their expenditure programs with those of the federal government.

Figure 6.1 shows, however, that the evolution of funds transferred to the states did not match the statutory rate increase in the years of the *trienio*. What appeared in the law to be an increase in transfers to the states was only a symbolic gesture. The federal government transferred only as much funds as its budgetary conditions and its own priorities allowed. The problem was that Venezuelan politicians had not created a commitment mechanism to hold the federal government accountable for its promises, and Venezuelan state executives could not credibly threaten to exit the fiscal arrangement in retaliation.

had been dependent, as suggested by Betancourt, on the *Situado* for around 90 percent of their income up until the 1990s. By the 1950s, state fiscal authority had in fact virtually disappeared: The federal government was collecting 90 percent of all revenues in the country, whereas states only collected directly 3 percent of them (*Ministerio de Hacienda*, 1955; Carrillo Batalla, 1968), the rest being made up of municipalities' own revenues.

[6] In 1943, the federal government transformed the fiscal structure of the state, establishing the Hydrocarbons Act and creating a modern corporate income tax as the mechanism for taxing the oil sector. Although Karl (1997) argues this was "perhaps the most important piece of legislation in the history of Venezuela" (Karl, 1997:85), from the point of view of the history of fiscal centralization, this was not a qualitative change: It made the extraction of federal revenue more efficient, yielding a larger pool to be shared. But the authority to tax either domestic consumption or specific products through excises no longer belonged to the states. The disincentive effects of the prereform tax structure were not at the state level but at the federal one.

[7] The reformed Constitution of 1947 established that 30 percent of the *Situado* would be distributed in equal parts to each state, and the rest would be transferred according to the old population criteria. As discussed in Section 6.6, this was part of the coalitional strategy of AD, trying to appeal to rural interests in the periphery.

The AD government was overthrown by the armed forces. During the rule of Pérez Jiménez, the federal government made efforts to eliminate any remaining regional and state autonomy. Starting in 1949, an annual Convention of Governors was established to settle any controversial matters related to the *Situado*. Those conventions were mostly an instrument of the federal government to further centralization. They were not, as the *Juntas* of the previous century had been, a source of credibility for the federal government. For example, an agreement was reached in 1951 to centralize all accounting practices. Kornblith and Maingón in fact suggest that both dictators Gómez and Pérez Jiménez can be seen as sharing a centralization goal (Kornblith and Maingón, 1985:64). However, there is no firm evidence suggesting that the democratic governments that came after these dictators were more likely to decentralize revenue, as I will explore further. Regime type does not seem to drive tax centralization in terms of the statutory rates. As I discuss, however, democracy does influence compliance with those legal provisions.

In 1953, the *Situado* was further reformed, with the apparent goal of increasing funds to the states but a de facto reduction in them. The 1953 reform created enormous leeway for the federal government by establishing that between 12.5 and 25 percent of federal revenue would be transferred by the *Situado*, depending on a decision made every year by the Convention of Governors. This room for federal discretion is depicted in Figure 6.1 as a gray area in the statutory rate. Because governors were not elected independently but were appointed by the dictator, in practice the variable statutory rate meant that transfers would be kept at the lower bound. Authoritarianism, coupled with the lack of a direct election of governors, rendered the federal system all but inoperative, notwithstanding the institution of the Convention of Governors.

However, and in contrast with his predecessors, Pérez Jiménez transferred funds that closely matched the lower bound of a 12.5 percent minimum statutory rate. Apparently, federal discretion had been eliminated. This compliance was, however, creative accounting, not de facto compliance. As discussed by Suárez (1965), the 1953 reform allowed the federal executive to determine the amount of the *Situado* not according to the ordinary revenue collected the previous year but in terms of its budgeted figures. The dictatorship's budgetary practice was to formulate a moderate budget and then add extraordinary expenditures, which would come to represent up to 50 percent of the budget actually spent. The budget was therefore essentially meaningless as an instrument for federal accountability.

The process for determining the *Situado* since 1953 suggests that compliance with the statutory rate was met, as it was not difficult for the autocrat to do so. In an environment with moderate inflation, referring the base of calculation of the revenue shares to the previous year's tax collections broke the derivation principle in the determination of the *Situado*.[8] By 1958, the failure to comply with revenue-sharing was clear. Even the official figures showed that the *Situado* represented only 8 percent of ordinary revenue (Suárez, 1965:88). This can be seen in the deep dip in the graph for that year in Figure 6.1.

Venezuelan politicians and scholars have repeatedly argued that a federal system of government was adopted as a copy of an ideal, laid out in the U.S. Constitution, too far from the legal traditions and cultural predispositions of the country. The dictatorship of Pérez Jiménez took this notion to heart, moving Venezuela to a unitary form of government. The *Memoria* of the finance ministry for 1956, in fact, goes to the extreme of expressing that "the native form [unitary] has been recovered, through the steady but progressive incorporation into the federal treasury of the revenue and assets that had been [wrongly] recognized to the states" (my translation, *Ministerio de Hacienda*, 1982:128).

6.4. Democracy and Federal Compliance

The Pérez Jiménez dictatorship did not last. Radical political change was coming to Venezuela. In spite of the windfall gains from an oil boom, the Pérez Jiménez regime was not able to construct a progressive coalition, like the one the Brazilian military rulers created during the 1970s, to stay in office. Led by the leaders of AD, the party in office during the *trienio*, a phenomenal challenge was mounted against the intentions of Pérez Jiménez to stay in office indefinitely. Karl (1997) argues that what emerged in Venezuela was the "construction" and "consolidation of complicity" by political elites. Venezuelan authors have, perhaps more generously, called the arrangement an "elite conciliation" (Urdaneta, Olavarria, and Maya, 1990:49) or a "populist conciliation" system (Rey, 1989, quoted in Mascareño, 2000:28).

---

[8] Kornblith and Maingón argue that this was acceptable because states expected that budgeted revenues would be higher than those actually collected (Kornblith and Maingón, 1985:64). This does not make sense, however, given that the norm had been precisely the opposite. For example, between 1920 and 1942, budgeted revenue was always below the sums actually collected, in a low-inflation environment (see *Banco Central de Venezuela*, 1942).

Democratic representation and competition were substituted by a "pacted democracy" (Karl, 1997:101). In 1958, all the major Venezuelan elites agreed, in the *Pacto de Punto Fijo* (named after the ranch belonging to Rafaal Caldera, where it was signed), to share a common economic policy platform regardless of the electoral outcomes and to incorporate losers into cabinet positions (Kelley, 1977). Together with other peak-level agreements, this elite compromise maintained political competition but constrained it within programmatic and substantive bounds.[9] The two main political forces, AD and the *Comité de Organización Política Electoral Independiente* (COPEI), agreed to keep political competition in place but to temper what they saw as its destabilizing elements. The agreement involved the allocation of offices according to the voting strength of each party. The pact dramatically transformed the political system. Oil allowed politicians to keep the pact in place. As noted by Karl, "oil creates a politician's dream – a positive sum game that permitted democracy without losers" (Karl, 1997:111).

The 1961 Constitution was a direct consequence of the political compromise that created the new regime. In the fiscal realm, the federal government would transfer 12.5 percent of its ordinary revenue, to be increased by half a percent each year until it reached 15 percent. Figure 6.1 shows that the gap between the statutory rate and the actual funds transferred was very small in those years. Democracy had a real positive effect in enhancing the credibility of federal promises. From then on, although macroeconomic conditions and the international oil price could lead to sharp decreases in revenue-sharing during some years, compliance with the centralized federal arrangement became the rule rather than the exception. Thus, regime type had an effect on compliance with the federal pact, although the democratic governments did nothing to decentralize (either by devolving tax authority or increasing the statutory rate) the federal bargain they inherited from their authoritarian predecessors. The statutory rate was fixed at 15 percent, and virtually all tax collection remained federal.

Venezuelan governors were appointed rather than elected officials. Hence, compliance with revenue-sharing after the establishment of Venezuelan democracy remains somewhat puzzling because it is not clear which political actors were pressing the federal government to keep its side of the bargain. It is then worth devoting some attention to the role

---

[9] The literature on this agreement is substantial, but see Daniel Levine (1978), Collier and Collier (1991), and Karl (1989).

of governors in the system. In the 1961 constitutional debates, a major controversial issue was related to the nature of the federal pact and the role of governors in the system. Political elites seemed not to have been interested in keeping elected governors. In the debate over the 1961 Constitution, Senator Ambrosio Oropeza, for example, expressed this position in the following terms:

What the states are interested in is not whether they will be given the right to appoint their governors; what the states are interested in is their revenue, and that such revenue should not be . . . alms giving. The *Situado Constitucional* is a euphemism disguising those alms. What states are interested in is that the *Situado Constitucional* shall be provided in abundance and justice, but above all justice, because nothing can be more equitable and just than establishing that if their authority to create their own taxes has been stripped away, they should be compensated in a sufficient and generous way for this infringement on their autonomy, and thus it might be that their state finances might actually be strengthened. (My translation of quote in Olavarría, 1988:316)

The main argument for keeping nonelected governors was the notion that central appointments would bring about political stability. The *Pacto de Punto Fijo* might have been impossible if governors had challenged the president, claiming a legitimacy of their own. The historical precedent that the AD politicians had in mind when rejecting elected governors was a factional disruption that had led to their first internal fracture within the party in 1948, precisely concerning the direct election of state executives.[10] Regardless of whether one can prove such a counterfactual scenario, the basic point is that Venezuela's political elites agreed that the construction of political authority would be done through highly nationalized political parties, not local political forces.[11] Venezuelan politics was based on a national democratic system, but there was no local-level democratic practice.[12] Although the 1961 Constitution envisaged the direct election of governors, such a provision was left in "suspension."

[10] On the factional struggles within AD and Venezuelan parties, see Coppedge (1993).

[11] According to Levine, "Venezuelan politics can be described as a party system. The basic vehicles for political action are parties, the fundamental legitimate power resource is mass consult and votes, and power is transferred through elections (Levin, 1973: 8)."

[12] The basis of support for the dominant "partiarchy" was mainly rural. As pointed out by Levine and Crisp, "The Venezuelan system is predicated on the dominance by two parties which have their strongest historical roots in the rural periphery, and . . . this dominance has tended to alienate more individuals in urban and metropolitan sectors of the Center and of more modern regions." (Quoted in Louis Goodman, 1995:99). See also the excellent analysis of the correlates of AD support by Coppedge (1993).

An important element that allowed parties to reduce the incentives for politicians to cater to territorial or state interests was the electoral system. In particular, a closed list system meant that nominations were hierarchically controlled by the national party leadership in the center (Coppedge, 1993). A fused ballot structure ensured that there would be no split tickets, and the reelection clause, which only allowed candidates to run again in a district different from the previous one, made sure that politicians would not become too attached to territorial interests. In fact, Venezuelan politicians were similar to PRI politicians in Mexico because they did not seek to retain their office but rather to advance in their careers toward appointed posts controlled by the federal bureaucracy and agencies (Kelley, 1977:38).

The years of democratic stability after the *Pacto de Punto Fijo* were also years of profound centralization. In 1966, half of the revenue-sharing funds became conditional, to be "coordinated" with federal programs. This meant that 50 percent of the funds would have to be allocated to the states according to federal investment priorities (see Contreras Quintero, 1966; Carrillo Batalla, 1987:142). This so-called *Situado Coordinado* (Coordinated Appropriations) meant a reduction in the discretion of governors over the use of revenue-sharing funds.[13] On the other hand, particularly since 1973, public enterprises have become one of the most important sources of patronage and political exchange (see Kornblith and Maingón, 1985; Karl, 1997), a fiscal resource that states could not use. Hence, for most of the 20th century, Venezuela was a federal regime in name only.

6.5. Statistical Analysis of the Evolution of Revenue-Sharing

To buttress the argument made in the previous section, this section provides econometric estimations of the relative importance of democracy and compliance with statutory rates in the evolution of revenue-sharing funds in Venezuela. I use as the dependent variable the share of fiscal resources transferred to the state governments, as a percentage of federal revenue collected, as an indicator of the importance of fiscal transfers.[14] I provide

---

[13] As discussed in the next chapter, a similar measure was enacted by the military governments for revenue-sharing in Brazil at practically the same time.

[14] The empirical analysis in this and the following chapters relies on federal sources of revenue-sharing information. Although it would be important to reconstruct revenue-sharing patterns from the recipient government's point of view, state or provincial public finance data in Latin America are less reliable than federal-level data. State and provincial governments

two operationalizations of this dependent variable: one that directly calculates how much revenue-sharing is being transferred out of the "shareable" federal taxes, and a second measure that calculates the relative importance of revenue-sharing as a percentage of total federal revenue from any source.[15] I hence use revenue-sharing divided by total ordinary revenue (*situado/ordinario*), which is the data depicted in Figure 6.1; and the share of revenue-sharing divided by total government revenue, including debt (*situado/total*).

One could argue that revenue-sharing is uniquely determined by the statutory rate contained in the law. The pairwise correlation between the statutory rate and the actual funds disbursed, as a percentage of "shareable" revenue, is 0.63 in Venezuela. As discussed in the previous section, the political process that establishes the statutory rate and the degree of compliance with it are the central pieces in the story of the centralized fiscal bargain. In Venezuela, the federal government was not under the same scrutiny from independently elected state authorities as in the other Latin American federations. In fact, as I have argued, it was not until Venezuela was able to articulate regional interests through a stable two-party system after 1958 that the mismatch between revenue-sharing and statutory rate was reduced.

The gap between the revenue share actually transferred over time and the legal *statutory rate* indicates the extent to which the federal government complied with the centralized federal bargain. In Venezuela, the statutory rate comprised all the ordinary federal revenues, but it did not include debt.

Revenue-sharing systems are characterized by a strong temporal inertia, so the *lag of the dependent variable* is an indicator of the stability in the evolution of revenue-sharing. This independent variable is used not only to statistically correct for problems of autocorrelation in the estimation

often vary within the same country in terms of their professionalization, bureaucratic capacity, and general accountability in the publication of public finances. The federal government might use revenue-sharing information strategically in its interaction with states or provinces, but there are reasons to believe that this is the best information available. Because federal administrations change over time, the data reported by various governments allow for the verification of sources and estimates. On the other hand, because states and provinces are interested in having reliable information from the federal government to determine whether the federal government is complying with the revenue-sharing system, it is likely that this pressure generates a built-in mechanism to produce more reliable data.

[15] In the years when revenue-sharing was determined by the previous year's tax collection, an appropriate temporal adjustment is made to take into account the lag in the calculation of revenue shares.

but on substantive grounds as a measure of the temporal resilience and continuity of the revenue-sharing system. The larger the coefficient of this lagged dependent variable, the more predictable the revenue-sharing arrangement has been through time. Thus, when the federal government is complying with its side of the fiscal bargain, the evolution of revenue-sharing through time should be clearly defined by the revenue shared the previous year and the statutory rate.

The *statutory rate* indicates how much revenue *should* legally be transferred to states. This is not just a technical decision but embodies a political compromise that lies at the core of the federal pact. It is a consequence of the political bargains made by the states and the federal government. For compliance to occur, revenue-sharing trends should respond, at least at the margin, to shifts in the statutory rate. If they did not, this would suggest that the federal government was not keeping a minimal requirement of the centralized fiscal bargain in the sense of granting more (or less) transfers when a political decision is made to increase (or decrease) the statutory rate.

Because the estimation includes the lagged dependent variable, as well as other control variables besides the statutory rate that reflect political and economic circumstances, I do not expect the coefficient of the statutory rate to be equal to one. In Venezuela, statutory rates often were not respected. I do expect, however, that when statutory rates increase, one should observe an increase in the share of revenue actually going to the states.

There are at least two mechanisms through which federal governments circumvented a direct match between the statutory rate and the actual funds disbursed in the form of revenue-sharing. It was possible for federal governments simply not to pay out the correct amounts to states or provinces. Federal governments can in general make it difficult for provinces or states to know beforehand exactly how much funding they are entitled to receive. A second major mechanism was through inflation, which allowed governments to distribute revenue shares according to underestimated projected budgetary tax collections, leading to shortfalls in revenue-sharing, when compared with the statutory rate. The inflationary tax primarily benefited the federal government, which controlled the money supply.[16]

Beyond the political compromises embodied in the statutory rate, the regime type might determine the provision of funds to the states. I code

---

[16] Finally, the statutory rate can differ from the revenue shares actually distributed, even without deception from the federal government, because of differences in accrual and cash flow estimates made by the bureaucracies in the finance ministry or the central bank for the collected revenue and the actual reality of such collection.

regime as a dichotomous variable for whether the country was *democratic* in a given year. As previously discussed, there is no compelling reason to expect democracies to decentralize more funds in the form of revenue-sharing because there is no necessary link between greater accountability or local representation and revenue-sharing (Eaton, 2004). In fact, a state or province that receives more funds in the form of revenue-sharing is fiscally more dependent on the federal government than one that controls its own sources of revenue.[17]

However, the argument about a credible commitment to revenue-sharing systems suggests that democracies should have an advantage in making states believe that the federal side of the bargain will be kept. Moreover, to the extent that democratic rule also involves, beyond frequent elections, checks and balances on the power of the executive and the federal government, the gap between revenue-sharing and the statutory rates should be smaller under democracies than under autocratic rule.[18]

In order to control for the temptation of the federal government not to comply with the centralized fiscal bargain, reducing revenue-sharing to the states, I use two control variables, one reflecting the overall *size of the federal government*, as measured by federal government revenue collection as a percentage of GDP, and the *federal budget deficit*, also measured as the difference between expenditures and revenues of the federal government over GDP. These indicators were obtained from the Oxford Latin American History Database, which updates Thorp (1998).[19] Finally, in order to make sure that there is an economic control for the performance of the economy, I include the *level of development*, as measured by the per capita GDP stated as purchasing power parity dollars of 1970, also using data from the Oxford Latin American History Database.[20]

---

[17] A high reliance on revenue-sharing might be a political outcome that is not desirable from the point of view of the median voter in a province or state.

[18] Unreported estimations were also carried out with a more continuous measure of democracy, as reflected by the Polity index, but the dichotomous regime type indicator gives a sharper substantive interpretation to the findings while the main results hold.

[19] OxLAD, http://oxlad.qeh.ox.ac.uk/, accessed June 8, 2004.

[20] The effect of the level of development on revenue-sharing is ambiguous. On the one hand, there might be a tendency for greater decentralization as a country becomes richer because there is a greater need to tailor public goods to the specific heterogeneous preferences of different regions. However, on the other hand, fiscal centralization seems to accompany the development process. Hence, the effect of this variable is ambiguous. Unreported estimates were also carried out using alternative control variables, such as the level of urbanization, the growth rate, or the degree of openness to international trade. Because there were no theoretical expectations about what the effects of these variables should be, and they never

Venezuela

Table 6.1. *Revenue-Sharing Compliance in Venezuela (Standard Errors in Parentheses)*

	(1)	(2)
L1	0.63**	0.61**
	(0.09)	(0.09)
Statutory	0.18**	0.15**
	(0.06)	(0.06)
Democratic	2.24	2.57*
	(1.36)	(1.39)
N	79	79
F	31	21
Durbin-Watson	2.21	2.14
R-squared	0.724	0.640

Economic controls: Size of federal government (REV/GDP), federal deficit, GDP per capita.
* Significant at the 95% level.
** Significant at the 99% level.

The results are presented in Table 6.1. The first column presents the restricted definition of ordinary revenue, which comprises strictly the pool of funds to be shared. In this sense, this first estimation provides a direct test of the degree to which the Venezuelan federal government complied with revenue-sharing. The second column shows revenue-sharing as a percentage of total federal revenue, including debt. Table 6.1 reports only the coefficients for the lagged dependent variable, the statutory rate, and the regime type variables. The control variables were not statistically significant, although they had the expected sign.

The temporal inertia in the evolution of revenue-sharing is not too high, particularly when compared with the analyses of the Argentine and Brazilian systems in the next two chapters. The fact that the governors were not elected until 1989 probably made the revenue-sharing system more vulnerable to federal discretion than those of the other Latin American federations. There is a statistically significant effect of the statutory rate, which means that when rates increased, the overall share of resources transferred to the states also increased. However, the relationship suggests that each additional percentage point of statutory rate increase only becomes reflected in 0.18 of a percent larger share.

achieved any statistical significance, the only control variables kept in all the estimations are the size of the central government, its deficit, and the level of development.

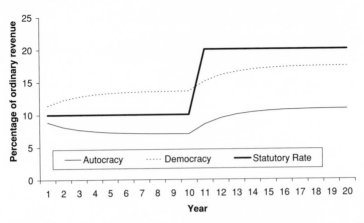

Figure 6.2. Simulation of effect of democracy on revenue-sharing in Venezuela.

Democracy had the effect of transferring two and a half additional percentage points of effective revenue-sharing to the states after 1958. This means that democratic governments influenced a larger transfer of funds beyond the indirect effects that democracy might have on the choice of particular statutory rates. To see the specific effect of regime type, Figure 6.2 makes a simulation of the effect of regime type on the sharing of funds in Venezuela. The graph assumes that for the first 10 years there is a 10 percent statutory rate and that over the next 10 years the rate has increased to 20 percent. Those statutory rates are marked as a bold line. The simulation is made with the coefficients of total resources in column 2. Under autocracy, the response to the statutory rate was rather muted. Moreover, the temporal inertia under autocracy in Venezuela made the share of revenue decrease as the years went by, when the statutory rate was low. This inertial effect looks very different under democracy. Not only is the compliance with the system much better under democracy, but the inertial elements keep revenue-sharing at increasing levels, although in the case of the 20 percent statutory rate, never at quite that level.

6.6. The Distribution of Revenue-Sharing among States in Venezuela

Many studies have analyzed the allocation of revenue-sharing funds across states and provinces in Latin America, particularly for the cases of Argentina and Brazil, which are discussed in the next two chapters. The Venezuelan fiscal system has tended to shift the distribution of revenue transfers to benefit small states to the detriment of the richer, more advanced, or more productive regions, including the central metropolitan areas. This trend made the system relatively "redistributive." Although centralized fiscal bargains might at their inception involve respecting a "derivation principle" in the allocation of funds (i.e., in the absence of a fiscal bargain, rich states could have taxed themselves and retained more resources than the poor ones), as those systems evolve over time, redistribution plays an increasingly more prevalent role. In Venezuela, the derivation principle was preserved in the 19th century, but by 1924 the distribution system had become detached from revenue collection.

Subnational governments in Venezuela have been fully dependent on federal transfers since the early 1900s. The federal government has been able to carry out widespread redistribution of resources through the centralized control of oil revenue. The early political compromises between center and periphery were responsible for such an outcome. Notwithstanding the stability of the Venezuelan fiscal arrangement, the federal government has had a wide margin of discretion in the allocation of funds among the constituent federal units, even in eras of federal compliance.

For most of the 20th century, Venezuela distributed its revenue-sharing funds according to a formula that allocates equal per capita resources to all states and a minimum lump sum to each state.[21] The constitutional provision containing this distributional rule was enacted in 1947. The pool of resources available was tied to revenue collected by the federal government (mostly from oil receipts). But the specific shares each state received were detached from fiscal effort or underlying economic activity indicators. It might seem obvious from this fact that the evolution of the allocation of funds should simply reflect population trends. However, political actors have discretion in the way they apply even fixed rules, and compliance with promises is imperfect. Hence the distribution of funds across Venezuelan states has varied over time, beyond reflecting demographic trends.

Figure 6.3 shows the evolution of the distribution of *Situado Constitucional* transfers received by a selection of Venezuelan states since 1948.[22] Obviously, population changes over time as a result of demographic factors and migration. These demographic forces depend on differential rates of

[21] Establishing 70 percent on the population principle and 30 percent in equal parts.
[22] OCEPRE, based on *Oficina Central de Presupuesto* (undated), "40 años de Presupuesto Fiscal 1948–1988." I thank Francisco Rodríguez for making these data available.

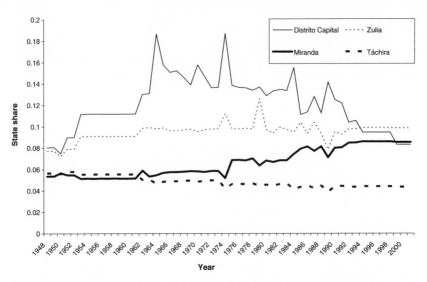

Figure 6.3. Evolution of revenue-sharing for selected states in Venezuela.

economic activity in each state, among other things. Because population censuses are not carried out every year but usually once each decade, there are fluctuations in the shares that are attributable to discrete population changes when estimates are adjusted and biases in the estimations used to measure population in the intercensus years are eliminated. However, these factors alone cannot account for the patterns in Figure 6.3. In particular, the trend and spikes in the share of the federal capital can only be explained by the exercise of discretion on the part of the federal government.

The graph in Figure 6.3 shows that the share of the federal capital surged during the 1960s, even though the formulas for the allocation of funds remained formally unchanged. Of course, this was an era of urbanization, but the share of Caracas gradually declined over the subsequent decades. The rich state of Zulia experienced a rather steady coefficient, reaching allocations very similar to those of the federal capital in the 1990s. Miranda was a state where the share of revenue-sharing could be accounted for by the increase in population it experienced; and the same might be true of Táchira, the region that produced the Venezuelan leaders during much of the first half of the 20th century, which shows a declining share over time, as reflected in its population trends. But population trends cannot account for the patterns of Caracas or Zulia.

Venezuelan critics have noted that there were wide discrepancies between the shares of funds that states were allocated and what they should

Table 6.2. *Gini Coefficients of Revenue-Sharing Distribution*

	Venezuela	Argentina	Brazil
1930	n.a.	0.5174	
1940	0.2337	0.4990	
1950	0.2658	0.5114	
1960	0.2957	0.5159	0.6632
1970	0.3048	0.4681	0.6499
1980	0.2980	0.4121	0.6125
1990	0.2916	0.4028	0.6157

have received on the basis of population. For example, Carrillo Batalla notes that Miranda's larger population in the 1970s was not reflected in its allocation of *Situado* funds when compared with Táchira (Carrillo Batalla, 1987:140). The graph shows that Miranda and the federal capital did not receive *Situado* allocations that reflected their similar population shares until the 1990s. These deviations in the distributional rules suggest that the allocation of funds in Venezuela has been a consequence of ad hoc political compromises.

Because states in Venezuela received 30 percent of the funds in equal shares, regardless of their population or production, and given that the population distribution across the Venezuelan states is relatively more equal than that observed in the other Latin American federations, the inequality in the distribution of funds in Venezuela is not very high. This can be seen in Table 6.2, which reports the calculation of the Gini coefficient in the allocation of the *Situado* funds since 1948. At around 0.3, this Gini coefficient is quite low when compared with Argentina or Brazil, which are also depicted in the table.

The Gini coefficient is calculated in such a way that perfect equality would imply that all states receive the same amount of funds. This does not mean that such equality would be desirable from several normative perspectives, but it provides a clear benchmark from which one can compare both the Latin American distributions across each other as well as over time.[23] The Gini coefficient suggests that Venezuela is relatively close to giving out the same amount of funds in the *Situado* to all states, regardless

[23] In this calculation, the coefficient takes the province or state as the relevant unit of comparison, not the household, the individual, or the value of production.

of any other consideration. The population-weighted Gini coefficient for Venezuela in the 1990s lies at around 0.25, which means that the distribution is egalitarian in population terms also. The Gini coefficient when weighted by economic activity in the states, as measured by total GDP, is also in the same range, at around 0.23.

In theory, the *Situado* should not differ in its distribution except in matters related to the population figures used for its calculation because no change has been made in the allocation formula since 1947. The Pérez Jiménez administration provided funds with strict coefficients that did not vary the allocation across states during the years of his rule. However, after the 1958 democratization, and more specifically the 1961 constitutional reforms that increased the *Situado*, the allocations became somewhat volatile. Thus, the allocation of funds across states exhibited more flexibility when Venezuela became democratic.

Every 10 years, there is a spike in the distribution that reflects an adjustment to the federal capital shares to account for updated population census figures. However, it is interesting to note that as soon as that adjustment is made, the next year the allocation reverts to the distribution that was previously observed. This suggests that the federal government was compelled to make redistributive adjustments when "objective" population figures were publicly known, but it could revert to the historical patterns of allocation once it recovered the discretion to "estimate" population during the intercensus years. Nevertheless, compared with the other Latin American federations, in Venezuela there have not been major changes in the dispersion of funds across states.

6.7. Recent Developments

More recent developments in Venezuela have revitalized the federal pact. In 1989, the direct election of governors was established (which had already been considered in the 1961 Constitution but had remained in "suspension"), and a major process of decentralization was set in motion. Consonant with this process, as can be seen in Figure 6.1, the *Situado Constitucional* was increased by 1 percent each year, reaching 20 percent by 1994, where it has remained since. Conditionality on the use of *Situado* funds was virtually eliminated (Barrios Ross, 1998). Urdaneta, Olavarria, and Maya (1990) suggest that the reason elites in the "hegemonic parties" accepted the election of governors was because they believed it would have no effect on the political system to the extent that administrative processes remained highly centralized. They were wrong, which suggests that fiscal behavior probably responds to political configurations rather than the contrary.[24]

Penfold-Becerra (2004) argues that the 1989 changes that instated gubernatorial elections activated the federal arrangement and explain to a large extent the demise of the party system that had been so stable since 1958. Governors began to construct local bases of political support, and local elections opened the gate for the entry of new parties. In the founding election, three of the governors were not from the established AD and COPEI; by 1998, almost 50 percent of the mayors and 12 of the 23 governors were from the less established parties (Mascareño, 2000:48). Most governors were easily reelected for a second term, which suggests they quickly constructed local bases of support. The creation of single-member districts for the election of regional representative assemblies strengthened the localist effects of the reform. The centralized structure of the traditional political parties, AD and COPEI, proved ineffective to compete in local elections, paving the way for the ascent of Hugo Chávez.

In the late 1980s, when the presidential commission for the reform of the state (Comision Para la Reforma del Estado, COPRE) was considering the decentralization reforms, Gonzalo Barrios, leader of AD, was in total agreement with Luis Herrera Campins, one of the top leaders of COPEI, in opposing the election of governors (Mascareño, 2000:24). Both argued that the direct election of governors would weaken the president's capacity to act – and hence was undesirable. They were wrong. As President Hugo Chávez proved, presidential capacity in Venezuela has not been diminished: It was the party system that collapsed. Although fiscally centralized and marked by a high dose of presidential dominance, federalism in Venezuela has been renewed.

---

[24] The causal hypothesis proposed by Chhibber and Kollman (2004).

7

Argentina

REGIME CHANGE AND FRAGILE CREDIBILITY

7.1. Coalition Formation in the Midst of Instability

The Argentine federation was formally constituted in 1853, to be joined by Buenos Aires in 1860. It was preceded, after independence, by what Gibson and Falleti (2004) call a "hegemonic confederation." That confederation, dating to 1831, subdued the interests of the dominant province, Buenos Aires, through the iron-fist rule of Juan Manuel de Rosas. The subsequent "unity by the stick" of Argentine federalism (Gibson and Falleti, 2004) was achieved when provinces joined together in a centralized but asymmetric federation, with Buenos Aires keeping a privileged position. When the federal capital was created in 1853, control over the most important source of taxation, international trade through customs, became federal. The provinces, however, retained more fiscal authority than states in Venezuela or Mexico. To a large extent, the characteristics of the fiscal pact in Argentina are accounted for by the distrust of the "peripheral" interior provinces toward the "core," represented by the federal government and Buenos Aires.

Fiscal centralization was always feared on the grounds that it would privilege the outward-oriented port city and the beef- and grain-producing Pampas vis-à-vis the regional interests of the "interior." The political coalition that emerged triumphant in the 20th century involved the urban workers countering the influence of the export-oriented Pampas through the construction of a coalition with the more backward periphery (Gibson, 1996). This coalition was cemented through several devices, including the redistributive transfer of financial resources toward poorer regions and the establishment of highly malapportioned representative assemblies (Sawers, 1996; Porto and Sanguinetti, 2001; Tommasi, 2002).

The revenue-sharing system (*coparticipación*) created in 1934 was meant to establish a simple framework for the unification of income, sales, and excise taxes in the country, but political changes throughout the years, including swings between democratic and authoritarian regimes as well as bargains among the provinces, resulted in the creation of complex rules and transition mechanisms for the transfer of funds between levels of government. This produced a "fiscal labyrinth" (Saiegh and Tommasi, 1999), which characterizes Argentina's fiscal federalism framework to this day.[1] Arguably, the Argentine system is the most complex fiscal federalism arrangement in Latin America.

The superposition of various ad hoc fiscal arrangements accumulated over time generated an array of laws that comprised an unwieldy system. Specific revenue-sharing rules were established for each federal tax, and those rules were full of exceptions. This contrasts with the Venezuelan, Mexican, or Brazilian revenue-sharing systems, which are broadly based on sharing the most important taxes through relatively simple rules.[2]

In the 1990s, efforts to simplify the system resulted in a peculiar institutional arrangement: Although revenue-sharing was constitutionally mandated and protected, the distribution of resources across states (the so-called secondary distribution) was fixed according to constant coefficients. The fixed-share rules limited federal discretion in the allocation of funds to the states but eliminated the flexibility of the fiscal arrangement to respond to changes in the economic environment (Tommasi and Spiller, 2003). Hence, in Argentina the fundamental dilemma of fiscal centralization was settled through a complex, inflexible, and multilayered system that rests on a constitutional mandate to provide transfers but in practice consists of ad hoc political arrangements that arose over decades of alternating political regimes.

The Argentine system has also been characterized by very dramatic shifts and changes in the distribution of funds between the provinces. This is consonant with regime instability and the consequent shifts in the

---

[1] This complexity is recognized by the government itself. An updated fiscal labyrinth is posted on a Web page of the Comisión Federal de Impuestos: http://www.cfi.gov.ar/leyes/LaberintoCoparticipacion032002.ppt (accessed April 2004).

[2] Mexican revenue-sharing in excises, which was also started in the 1930s, shares some features similar to Argentina because it is also based on provisions and rates for specific products.

revenue-sharing system as a whole. Given that authoritarian rulers in Argentina often did not comply with the rules for the primary distribution of funds, it might not be surprising to find that they did not comply with the so-called secondary distribution either. But an interesting feature is that instead of simply allocating funds with no formula, different regimes repeatedly changed the secondary distribution formulas in order to justify their varying goals.

Nonetheless, the hallmark of Argentine fiscal evolution has been that, in the midst of all the instability, federal governments resorted to the transfer of resources to the provinces in an effort (often unsuccessful) to keep a ruling coalition in place. The frequent authoritarian interludes and regime changes in the country did not determine the degree of decentralization in the fiscal arrangement. Democracy, however, improved federal compliance in the sense that a commitment to transfer funds was more likely to be kept by democratic administrations than authoritarian ones. As in the Venezuelan case, it is important to note that democracy did not impact the degree of decentralization as measured by the statutory rate. Authoritarian governments were just as likely as democratic ones to increase that rate (Eaton, 2004). However, the transfers effectively delivered were affected by democracy because democratic federal governments were more likely to comply with the fiscal pact. In terms of the distribution of funds across provinces, throughout the second half of the 20th century both authoritarian and democratic governments cultivated a coalition of the periphery by granting more resources to the poor interior provinces vis-à-vis the export-oriented Pampas.

The next section outlines the trends in revenue-sharing in Argentina over the 20th century, measuring the degree of decentralization generated by those transfers. Section 7.3 discusses the inception of the centralized fiscal pact in the 1930s. Section 7.4 then discusses the era of Perón, which shifted the distribution of revenue-sharing in favor of the poorer provinces of the interior. Section 7.5 addresses the effect of authoritarianism on revenue-sharing. Military governments often shirked their fiscal promises. This resulted in the collapse of a system that when it was first established had achieved a relatively high level of compliance. Section 7.6 provides an econometric analysis of the trends and patterns discussed in the previous sections, and Section 7.7 discusses the distributional patterns of allocation of funds across provinces. Finally, Section 7.8 briefly sketches some of the more recent developments and prospects for the future of the fiscal pact in Argentina.

7.2. The Argentine Fiscal Pact

The Argentine fiscal labyrinth finds one of its clearest expressions in the frustrating inconsistency of fiscal accounts and financial figures of transfers to and revenue-sharing with the provinces. Argentine fiscal indicators are radically different when using, for example, contemporary sources for the 1930s, compilations of data done in the 1960s, or reconstructions with uniform accounting criteria carried out in the 1990s. As noted by Rock, since Argentine bureaucracies weakened in the 20th century and data became a tool of propaganda, after the 1940s "statistics and quantifications in Argentine history are thus better treated as illustrating trends and relationships" (Rock, 1987:xxix). With this caveat in mind, Figure 7.1 shows the trends in the evolution of the revenue-sharing arrangement in Argentina during the 20th century.[3]

Figure 7.1 shows, in a form analogous to Figure 6.1 for Venezuela, the statutory rate for revenue-sharing and the share of taxes transferred to the provinces and the municipality of Buenos Aires. Given the complexity of the fiscal system, the statutory rate (known in Argentina as the "primary" distribution because it divides revenue between the provinces and the federation) that is shown in the graph in Figure 7.1 corresponds to the most important taxes subject to revenue-sharing each year. The break in the series reported in the graph corresponds to a period when the revenue-sharing system broke down and was substituted by federal discretionary transfers. Although the statutory rate (the solid line) has generally increased over time (as stressed, for example, by Cetrángolo and Jiménez, 1998), a somewhat different reading of these data suggests that sharp changes characterized revenue-sharing over time (Eaton, 2001).

Figure 7.1 depicts two measurements of federal revenue-sharing transfers. Because not all taxes are subject to revenue-sharing (i.e., *coparticipables*),

[3] The graph is constructed based on figures by *Ministerio de Hacienda* (1938), Blanco (1956), Consejo Federal de Inversiones (1965, 1991), Vázquez-Presedo (1976), Nuñez Miñana and Porto (1983), Pirez (1986), *Administración Federal de Ingresos Públicos* (AFIP) (1999), *Dirección Nacional de Análisis e Investigación Fiscal* (2002), Porto (2003), and *Anuario Estadístico* (various years). Most of the time, figures reported from different sources do not coincide. In order to settle on a series, when two or more different sources report the same figures, this was taken as an indication of more reliable figures. The most reliable figures with this criterion are those for 1959–1963 and from 1970 onward. However, it should be noted that all of these sources rely on federal reporting, which is different from provincial data. Figures of revenue-sharing according to the federal government, for example, are quite different from data since 1983 reported by the provincial governments and compiled by the *Dirección Nacional de Coordinación Fiscal con las Provincias* (2002) in the Ministry of Finance.

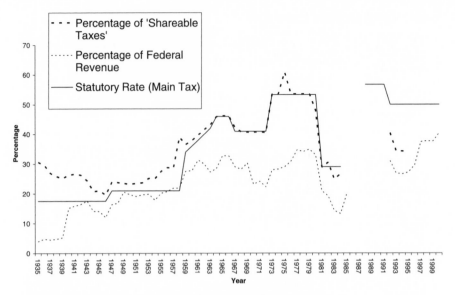

Figure 7.1. Argentina: Evolution of revenue-sharing.

one ratio (the bold dotted line) indicates the share of resources transferred out of federal taxes subject to revenue-sharing. The second ratio (the soft dotted line) indicates the transfers to subnational governments out of total federal revenue (including both federal tax administration and customs but excluding debt and the social security administration contributions). Because the statutory rate in Figure 7.1 does not cover all the shared taxes, the line for the share of *impuestos coparticipables* is sometimes above the statutory rate. The graph does not include all the discretionary transfers provinces received from the federal government but only those comprised by the revenue-sharing agreement.

Notwithstanding dramatic shifts between democracy and authoritarianism, the statutory rate in Argentina has usually been respected (which can be seen in the graph as the gap between the statutory rate and the percentage of "shareable" taxes). This contrasts with Venezuela, where authoritarian governments did not transfer the promised sums to the states. This does not mean that the Argentine federal governments did not try to shirk their obligations in the revenue-sharing agreements. Whereas in Venezuela all taxes were subject to sharing, so that shirking can be more easily measured as gaps in Figure 6.1, in Argentina federal discretion took the form of withholding revenue sources from the general pool, hence making them not subject to revenue-sharing. Despite sharp increases in the statutory rate since the late 1950s, the provinces in Argentina kept receiving around 20 percent of federal revenue, as indicated by the percentage of federal revenue (light dotted) line in Figure 7.1.[4] This is a far cry from the generous rates (above 50 percent) indicated by the statutory rate during the last decades of the 20th century.

Hence, the instability of Argentine fiscal federalism, with its frequent changes in rules, abuses through federal interventions in the provinces, violations of the constitutional mandate for the federation to collect only customs duties, and an overall discretionary allocation of funds from the federal to the provincial level, has been reflected in dramatic shifts in the revenue-sharing arrangements. However, in the midst of such instability, the federal government was able to get away with only transferring a fraction of the funds, mostly funds that it historically had been giving out to the provinces.[5]

The Argentine historical experience provides an example of how a commitment by the federal government to transfer resources to the states that was initially credible eventually broke down, most notably after 1983. Notwithstanding shifts in political regimes, provinces were less subject to

---

[4] It is worth mentioning how this graph differs from the somewhat misleading graph provided by Eaton (2001) in his otherwise excellent account of revenue-sharing in Argentina. By joining each change in revenue-sharing ratio with a line, Eaton's graph visually exaggerates the effect of the Perón administrations, making it seem as though Perón dramatically increased revenue-sharing in his first term whereas the largest increase was made by the Frondizi administration, and the fall in revenue-sharing during the administration of General Jorge Videla seems to happen in the second Perón term. To be fair, Eaton is careful to explain in his text which administration made each change, but the graph he uses (as well as a table where he reports percentage changes in revenue-sharing) are visually rather deceiving. His graph suggests that revenue-sharing rates have been very unstable in Argentina. My graph suggests instead that, except for the period when the military governments decreased the statutory rate between 1980 and 1988, Argentine provinces have basically experienced steady and increasing rates of revenue-sharing. My graph also includes the actual transfers received by the provinces, which tell a different story than the statutory rate, which is central to the credibility issues of transfer systems I want to highlight.

[5] The overall level of decentralization in Argentina remains relatively large compared with the other Latin American federations, even though scholars have discussed a process of "recentralization" in the 1990s (Falleti, 2001; O'Neill, 2001; Wibbels and Remmer, 2000; Eaton, 2004). Decentralization is attributable to two different factors: On the one hand, fiscal transfers from the federation to the provinces through revenue-sharing are substantial, and on the other, provinces in Argentina have retained more tax authority than have states in Mexico or Venezuela. This chapter is mostly devoted to discussing the revenue-sharing aspects, but it is important to remember that there is residual tax authority lying in the provinces.

abuse from the federal government than states in Venezuela or Mexico. To a large extent, this is a reflection of the vitality of state politics and the fact that, in spite of a trend toward tax centralization, political incentives in Argentina remained relatively decentralized. However, the federal government systematically withheld resources from the provinces, and this became reflected in a deep-seated distrust by the provinces toward the center. In the end, the system collapsed when provinces would no longer believe federal promises. In what follows, I will stress the developments at the inception of the revenue-sharing system between the 1930s and the 1960s. Although the story of the collapse of the revenue-sharing system in the 1980s and its subsequent reconstruction is critical to understanding developments today, I will touch on this process more briefly.[6]

7.3. The Fiscal Bargain

Most scholars agree that Argentina's political and economic development was profoundly shaped by the events taking place in the 1930s as a response to the Great Depression (Rock, 1987). Before 1934, there had been several efforts at centralizing the internal taxes that had been created in 1890 and reserved exclusively to the provincial jurisdiction. The bargain that created the system of revenue-sharing only became possible because of the economic dislocations generated by the disruption of international trade. Like most other governments at the time, Argentine federal finances relied primarily on customs duties. Although import duties were exclusively federal, states could impose tariffs on exports, which provided a very dynamic source of revenue, given the high demand for Argentine products worldwide.

Revenue-sharing was not an innovation brought about by a democratic government.[7] Argentina had introduced universal male suffrage in 1912 and witnessed a transition to democracy in 1916. But the second *Radical* government (i.e., from the Unión Cívica Radical Party, UCR) of Yrigoyen could not withstand the impact of the global crisis in 1930 (Rock, 1987:212). As argued by Eaton (2001, 2004), one should not assume that democratic governments are more prone to transfer fiscal resources to states in a federation.

---

[6] This story is well covered by a host of excellent work by Argentine scholars (see, for example, Cetrángolo and Jiménez, 1998; Jones, Sanguinetti, and Tommasi, 2000; and Tommasi, 2002).

[7] It is important to note that Argentine regime changes often pose a challenge in terms of figuring out whether the government in office is democratic. Although elections were held after 1932, the regime was plagued with electoral irregularities and the president was not controlled by Congress (see Smith, 1974).

In fact, the dilemma of fiscal centralization discussed in Chapter 1 suggests that the creation of revenue-sharing depends on the credibility of the alternative threat of a unitary imposition. To the extent that military governments have a greater capacity to threaten to crush rebellious provinces, it is more likely that provinces will accept a centralized federal bargain (i.e., one in which transfers play a bigger role and states refrain from collecting their own taxes) when offered one in order to avert a unitary imposition.

Given that the Argentine economy was so closely tied to world markets, most studies of the political economy of Argentina in the 1930s focus on the external developments: the controversial Roca-Ruciman agreement, which attempted to provide a sure external market with the British, and tariff policies for import substitution (see Rock, 1987). The construction of domestic fiscal institutions, however, is crucial to understanding the external developments. A reformist finance minister, Federico Pinedo, created a system of exchange-rate controls in 1933 that initiated policies of agricultural support through regulatory boards (*juntas*). These boards were not unlike the marketing boards extensively used in Africa in the second half of the 20th century with the stated goal of stabilizing agricultural prices.[8] As noted by Bates (1981), marketing boards are best understood as instruments politicians use in the construction of government coalitions. Pinedo also created an independent central bank in 1934 (headed by Raúl Prebish), which allowed the government to regulate the money supply and in fact cleared the way for Keynesian monetary policies.

The finance minister sought to redesign the fiscal arrangement between the federal government and the provinces through the unification of excises (the so-called internal taxes), the establishment of a national sales tax, and a permanent income tax. According to Rock, "This amounted to a fiscal revolution, which swept away a system that dated from colonial days" (Rock, 1987:222). Before 1934, the provinces and the federal government had increasingly relied on taxes that were not constitutionally separated among jurisdictions. Whereas customs duties on imports were exclusively federal and internal taxes belonged exclusively to the states, the sources of revenue that had increased in importance in the early decades of the 20th century were the concurrent ones (i.e., state and federal sales taxes).

---

[8] They are, however, quite different from the Brazilian valorization boards, discussed in the next chapter, which were controlled by coffee producers and purchasers, not the government.

In a statement that resonates with discussions in Venezuela, Brazil, and Mexico in the 19th and early 20th centuries, Federico Pinedo made this assessment of the need for tax unification: "Every day the trend for each of the states in the nation to defend their own production becomes more evident, and with this purpose provincial internal taxes have become protectionist duties." He then went on to assert that internal taxes had become a "trade policy weapon" that "as true customs duties, will prevent interprovincial trade and will profoundly divide" the country (my translation, *Ministerio de Hacienda*, 1938).[9]

The revenue-sharing system was initially constructed on the basis of specific taxes, each of which had its own "secondary distribution"; that is, the allocation of transfers to each province. The income tax, which had been created in 1932 as an extraordinary measure of the *Concordancia* government (a coalition of conservatives, a faction of the *Radicales* and independent socialists), became a permanent fixture in 1935. Gasoline taxes (dating from 1933), a surcharge on wine, and an excise on yerba mate were also included, as well as the newly created national sales tax. Revenue-sharing was also established on new taxes created after 1935, such as the profits tax in 1946, the tax on windfall profits, and a presumptive tax on inheritances.

The advantages of revenue-sharing, according to the Ministry of Finance, were that the new system would allow for greater equality in the tax burden, reduce collection costs by eliminating conflicts over jurisdiction, and provide for more equality in the distribution of revenue – "benefiting poor regions with surplus resources from the regions with easy and abundant resources" (my translation, *Ministerio de Hacienda*, 1938). This assessment of the benefits of the system suggests that redistribution was considered from the outset as one of the goals of revenue-sharing on the part of the federal government. The certainty in the flow of resources would also allow for financial planning by the provinces.

However, the rules for the secondary distribution of excises (*impuestos internos*) provided guarantees that no state would be worse off with revenue-sharing than with its previous exercise of tax authority. This meant that the system could not be redistributive. A fixed amount would be transferred, to be determined on the basis of the average 1929–1933 revenue collected by

---

[9] This same assessment was echoed by Eugenio Blanco, the finance minister of the government that deposed Perón two decades later: The system of revenue-sharing was seen as an answer to "the interprovincial economic war in critical moments for the country" (my translation of Blanco, 1956:34).

the provincial internal taxes. That amount was to be increased by 10 percent each year over the coming five years. The statutory rate between the federal government and the states would then be fixed at whatever distribution would have been reached in 1938–1939. The distribution among the provinces would gradually shift as the fund became larger from a derivation-based principle in which shares were allocated according to the location of production to a criterion based on equal per capita transfers after 10 years.[10] For the income and sales taxes, on the other hand, the distribution for the provinces and the city of Buenos Aires was to be fixed at 17.5 percent, which is the statutory rate graphed during those years in Figure 7.1.

The crucial question that emerges from such a complex system, involving promises and transition mechanisms that had to be enacted in the future, is to understand why provinces believed the federal government would keep its transfer promises. The political dynamics that made a fiscal compromise possible can be traced to the cleavages dividing the federal congress, which in turn reflected the regional interests at the time. As discussed by Smith (1974), the *Concordancia* period was characterized by discordant voting patterns in the Congress, reflecting the instability of partisan alignments. In particular, before 1936 (when the so-called *Personalist* wing of the *Radicales* decided to participate in electoral contests), notwithstanding the frequent practice of electoral fraud during this period, the ruling coalition of conservatives was rather incoherent as a voting group. This opened up a window of opportunity for the government to propose wide-ranging changes in the fiscal arena.

Smith's (1974) analysis suggests that the most important factors underlying voting patterns in the Argentine Congress in the first half of the 20th century were partisan attachments and regional cleavages. For the most part, partisan attachments were the overwhelming consideration. Regional cleavages became subdued, playing a limited role only on specific votes (Smith, 1974:67). But the regional origin of a legislator was a predictor of voting patterns in the 1930s, precisely as the revenue-sharing reform was being debated.[11] The roll call votes taken involved a decision as to whether Buenos Aires would be included in revenue-sharing, the general reform of provincial taxes and autonomy, the duration of the law for 10 years, and the

[10] The production criterion benefited the wine- and sugar-producing regions of Mendoza, San Juan, Tucumán, Salta, and Jujuy.

[11] This is reflected in Smith's (1974:140) data as an $R2$ of 0.21 between region and voting scores from 1932 to 1935, one of the highest correlations in the roll calls he analyzes.

establishment of the sales tax. All these roll calls reflect a regional cleavage rather than a partisan one (Smith, 1974:177).

But why would provinces believe the federal government would comply with a complex transition process in the course of the next 10 years? From the point of view of provincial governments, in which *Radical* party leaders were still powerful, it was not obvious that the *Concordancia* government could credibly make such a long-term commitment. Pinedo found a creative institutional solution by using a third-party enforcer. The central bank was used as a crucial credibility-enhancing mechanism by the federal government. The specific mechanism to give credibility to the transfer system embodied in revenue-sharing was that the payments would be made not by the federal government but by the independent central bank on a daily basis. As stated by the Ministry of Finance, "The Bank cannot stop [paying the daily quotas of revenue-sharing to the provinces] under any pretext, not even if commanded by the National Government" (my translation, *Ministerio de Hacienda*, 1938:n.p.).

The finance minister explicitly stated that the solution to create the revenue-sharing agreement would need to have a "contractual" character, in that provinces belonged to the system through their "adhesion" to it, rather than a constitutional mandate (*Ministerio de Hacienda*, 1938). This highlights that the federal government understood all too well that success in establishing a transfer system and the centralization of taxation could only be achieved by giving procedural guarantees and creating something akin to a fiscal contract.[12] This is precisely the insight highlighted by the model of credibility through time provided in Chapter 1. In contrast to Argentina, when the Mexican finance ministry tried to impose centralization in 1925 and 1933, without safeguards for the states, it failed.

An additional "carrot" was included in the deal that created revenue-sharing: Because many provinces were having trouble paying their debts as a consequence of the Great Depression, the federal government undertook debt bailouts for Jujuy, Mendoza, San Juan, Salta, Tucumán, Buenos Aires, Corrientes, La Rioja, and Santa Fé. For half of the provinces, the bailout was not unconditional but would have to be paid back through discounts from revenue shares in the coming years.[13] This opened the door for the

---

[12] It is not necessarily clear why politicians chose a contractual agreement, in terms of what is now called in Argentina a *Ley Convenio*, rather than a constitutional change that would imprint the system into the basic law of the country. Brazil and Venezuela followed the constitutional route, whereas Argentina and Mexico went the contractual way.

[13] Those debts were covered under article 9 of law 12.139.

federal government to withhold revenue-sharing transfers from the states in the future, which would become an important practice in subsequent years.

7.4. Revenue-Sharing under Perón

The revenue-sharing law was given an explicit duration of 10 years. By the time it was to be renewed, vast changes in the political landscape were taking place. The *Concordancia* government ended in a coup, from which Juan Domingo Perón emerged as the charismatic leader who swept the democratic election of 1946. Although the *Concordancia* era was a limited form of democracy, military rule turned out to be a breaker of the federal commitment: 1943 witnessed the first time (but not the last) that the federal government broke its transfer promises. A fixed maximum of shareable revenue was established for the income tax (Porto, 2003:15), and the federal government became the residual claimant of any additional revenue above that threshold. The abuse by the federal government can be clearly seen in Figure 7.1 in the dip in revenue shares after that year and that lasts until 1947.

When Juan Domingo Perón came into office as a democratically elected president, he convoked a convention of ministers of finance to meet and discuss the revenue-sharing arrangement. The federal government's goal was to make states comply with the agreement of 1934 because many of them were in practice levying internal taxes (excises), which violated the fiscal contract. For many provinces, most prominently Mendoza, the convention was a chance to voice their grievances about fiscal centralization as it had been enacted in 1934 "because [revenue-sharing] emerged from governments with no legitimacy" (my translation, *Ministerio de Hacienda*, 1946:331). Despite some provincial complaints, the convention agreed to keep the revenue-sharing system in place, including the unification of taxes. It also increased the provincial shares in the primary distribution.

The First Argentine Convention of Finance Ministers provides a counterexample of successful provincial bargaining when compared with the failed Mexican fiscal conventions of 1925 and 1933. There are striking similarities between both countries' conventions. For example, in both countries, a substantial amount of time was devoted to discussing procedural issues as well as the nature of the decisions (i.e., whether they were binding or just recommendations) and the voting mechanisms that would be used to reach them (*Ministerio de Hacienda*, 1946:157–187). The agenda of proposals for the conventions in both countries was relatively similar, including the approval of specific changes to the revenue-sharing systems, the configuration of federal taxes, and the agreement of administrative mechanisms to make the fiscal system more effective.

But the outcome in Argentina was starkly different from Mexico's: The convention successfully produced a set of unanimously approved reforms, which were ratified both by the provincial legislatures and the federal congress, whereas the Mexican conventions largely failed. The Mexican conventions, as discussed in Chapter 2, were characterized by an effort by the federal government to use majority rule and the composition of committee assignments in the convention as a device to railroad approval of its proposals. In Argentina, convention delegates instead agreed on recommendations through a rule of unanimity; they created a larger committee (seven members instead of four) for the discussion of tax issues because this was the biggest priority for all of them; and the finance minister explicitly made an effort to balance committee assignments in a way that was agreeable to all provinces.

The convention increased revenue-sharing to 21 percent (one more percentage point than what was originally envisaged by federal authorities when delegates arrived at the convention). The provinces, in turn, refrained from imposing illegal taxes. The incremental resources allowed the delegates to agree on a rule for the distribution of funds that paved the way for provincial redistribution through revenue-sharing.[14] Although the formula itself was not highly redistributive, it allowed redistributive criteria in the allocation of funds across provinces, which would become more important in subsequent years.

The Perón administrations generally kept promises in sharing revenue. In fact, these years are the only ones when the line depicting the share of general revenue is virtually the same as the statutory rate, which means that the Perón governments kept almost no sources of finance outside of the shareable revenue pool. A careful reading of the debates in the Convention of 1946 suggests an explanation: At the beginning, the provinces were relatively strong vis-à-vis the federal government. However, a most

---

[14] They kept a derivation principle in the formula for distributing funds across provinces. Nineteen percentage points would be distributed through a formula with three elements: 30 percent according to provincial revenue; 30 percent according to provincial ordinary expenditures; 30 percent according to population; and 10 percent according to federal tax collection of income and sales taxes. But they reserved the two additional percentage points to be allocated in a redistributive manner, allocating funds according to the inverse of population (thus rewarding small, backward provinces in the periphery).

critical aspect of Perón's strategy toward the provinces was the gradual use of federal discretion in the allocation of revenue-sharing and other federal funds across regions. In 1947, rules for the secondary distribution of funds were changed in favor of the city of Buenos Aires and the smallest states. This was part of a strategy to create an alliance with the regional *caudillos* of the poorer provinces as a counterweight to the Pampas (Gibson, 1996; Tommasi, 2002).

Perón's compliance with the revenue-sharing agreement contrasts with Rock's assessment claiming that Perón's 1949 Constitution "eliminated the sectional and regional weightings that were legacies of 19th century federalism" (Rock, 1987:288).[15] Rock argues that with Perón "the long process by which power had become increasingly centralized and also personalized here reached its acme" (Rock, 1987:289). There is no question that Perón's constitution allowed for "widening presidential authority to intervene in the provinces" (Rock, 1987:289).[16] However, in terms of the flow of financial resources to the provinces, Perón kept his federal promises.

Perón's rule was personalistic and centralized, but he used this popularity and charisma to increase federal revenue collection and spending, which benefited the provinces as much as the federal government. With increased federal revenue, substantial increases in federal largesse to the regions in the form of new federal programs became available. The provinces effectively received their statutory rates of revenue shares and increased the available funds in real terms. The most significant development in this respect was that in 1949 the federal government increased the sales tax rate from 1.5 to 8 percent. This was a shareable tax, so it provided windfall revenues to all provincial governments. Although inflation was creeping in, revenue from the sales tax quadrupled (Blanco, 1956). Moreover, Perón's administration successfully eliminated most of the remaining provincial taxes that restricted trade, which was important for the articulation of internal markets and set the stage for import substitution industrialization (ISI). The fiscal history of federal–provincial relations suggests that Perón's base of support in the provinces was in fact contingent on keeping the federal bargain.

The first finance ministers' convention, in 1946, agreed that meetings would be held every year in order to discuss issues of fiscal federalism.

---

[15] Through the elimination of the Electoral College for the election of the president, the extension of that term, and the establishment of direct election of senators rather than their appointment by provincial legislatures.

[16] However, federal intervention was not something invented by Perón (see Ministerio del Interior, 1933; Gibson and Falleti, 2004).

In 1951, the sixth such meeting centered around the demand by some of the producer provinces to revise the rules for the distribution of revenue shares to be more in accordance with derivation principles. Provinces were still willing to put countervailing pressures on the federal government in this meeting, albeit in a muted form. By the seventh meeting of finance ministers, in 1952, however, the records of the convention suggest that Perón had indeed centralized political power to an unprecedented degree. The meeting became an opportunity for a public display of allegiance to Perón rather than a debate concerning the interests of the provinces.

It is quite telling that the publication of the meeting is prefaced by pictures of Perón and his wife, Evita, in the front pages. Perón himself closed the meeting by delivering a speech urging that all provincial actions be coordinated in the fulfillment of his Five-Year Plan. He suggested that states had benefited from the then current fiscal arrangement to the extent that the federal government had bailed them out, had financed massive public works, and was collecting federal taxes effectively.[17] The speeches of the ministers in that meeting mostly concentrate on praising Perón and discussing the creation of two new provinces, Chaco and La Pampa, which were initially to be called Presidente Perón and Eva Perón!

The creation of new provinces allowed Perón's *Partido Justicialista* (Party of Justice) to reinforce its control of the Senate, while malapportionment in the lower chamber gave it an edge as part of a coalition involving the periphery. Rock's (1987) assessment of Perón's power concentration is hence correct, but his timing for the abdication of provincial power is premature. Had Perón been able to stay in office after 1955, he would have probably turned toward much greater centralization in the fiscal realm. But this assumption is difficult to test because Perón could not hold on to power.

The most significant change to revenue-sharing in the last years of the second Perón administration, which was to have a lasting impact to this day, was that in 1954 the federal government excluded the collection of a fraction of federal taxes from the pool of the "shareable" taxes (*coparticipables*). The 1954 reform established that taxes earmarked for investment and public works with a national impact would not be included in the revenue-sharing pool. That was justified on the grounds of the national developmental impact of federal expenditures in the provinces. This was

---

[17] In this sense, Perón made the first massive use of the instrument of conditional transfers, or *Aportaciones del Tesoro Nacional* (ATNs), which became most prominent in recent years.

similar to the creation of the *Situado Coordinado* in Venezuela because it removed resources from the discretionary use by provincial governments, even if the funds would eventually be spent in the states. Revenue-sharing in excises was also fixed at 46 percent for the provinces (without the city of Buenos Aires), an important ratio to keep in mind because it would become the focal point for discussions about the primary distribution of funds in the coming years.

7.5. *Authoritarianism and Shirking of Revenue-Sharing Promises*

Despite promises of "social harmony, balance, justice, and solidarity" (Rock, 1987:313), by the 1950s the Perón regime had become increasingly repressive, clashing with all sorts of interests, including the Catholic Church, the metalworkers union, and even manufacturers who benefited from the state-led import substitution industrialization (ISI) strategy. Perón was forced out of power in 1955, leaving the economy in shambles. The revenue-sharing system also went through a profound transformation at the end of the 1950s, although unrelated specifically to the process that led to the downfall of Perón.

The fiscal contract that underpinned revenue-sharing on sales and income taxes was to expire in 1955. Hence, a pressing issue for the new military government was to redraw the revenue-sharing agreement. From a perspective clearly hostile to the previous administration, the secretary of finance of the administration succeeding the Perón administration summarized the problems of the prevailing revenue-sharing system as twofold: The system did not transfer enough resources to the provinces; and there was a need to "agree on greater automatism in the distribution system, so that the delivery of resources to each province shall not be a discretionary act by the central power that it can use for its political speculations" (my translation of Blanco, 1956:34).[18] Despite the apparent antagonism of the new military government toward the previous fiscal pact, it did not make changes in the revenue-sharing system. Revenue-sharing was simply extended by decree for a few more years under the status quo rules.

As discussed by Eaton (2001) and Pirez (1986), the most important increase in the statutory rate in Argentina was carried out by the

---

[18] It is not clear that there was much discretion during the preceding years until the last years of Perón's tenure with the creation of the new states. It is clear, however, that the municipality of Buenos Aires increased its importance in revenue-sharing in the 1950s.

administration of Arturo Frondizi, which came into office through elections. Frondizi apparently enjoyed a unified control of the legislature and had come into office with the support of the *Peronistas*, but he had a fundamentally weak position vis-à-vis the provinces. The most popular party among the electorate was the proscribed *Partido Justicialista*. This administration constitutes an ambiguous moment in terms of the history of Argentine democracy because the president was democratically elected but contestation was severely limited (see O'Donnell's [1973] "impossible game").

A new conference of finance ministers was called by the Frondizi administration to discuss redrawing the fiscal pact. Negotiations led to the increase of the statutory rate to 42 percent (including 6 percent for Buenos Aires). This was a compromise between the position voiced by some provinces (Corrientes, Santiago del Estero, and Entre Rios) that demanded a 50–50 split in the primary distribution through a gradual transition over the next 10 years and the presidential proposal of an increase in the rate to 26 percent.[19] The increase was phased in gradually over five years and also incorporated important changes in the secondary distribution.[20]

It is clear in Figure 7.1 that although the statutory rate would dramatically increase after 1956, in practice, the federal government kept on transferring a share of its total revenue that was similar to what it had done in the preceding decade (around 20 percent). Hence, as in Venezuela, increases in the statutory rate were not always reflected in increases in the funds available to the provinces. This outcome was made possible by a 1954 provision that allowed earmarked federal revenues to be removed from the shareable pool. Perón's legacy for fiscal federalism in Argentina was hence that he left a door wide open for federal discretion. These developments marked the beginning of the end of federal fiscal commitment. In Venezuela, an increase in the statutory rate in the presence of federal discretion allowed the federal government to transfer even fewer funds. Something similar happened in Argentina, although the mechanism was the withholding of funds from the shareable pool.

---

[19] It is important to note that the provinces did not agree to this compromise, but rather it was the consequence of Frondizi trying to sidestep regional politicians by taking the proposal directly to Congress. It turned out that, although his administration had struck a deal with the Senate, the lower chamber ended up adding two additional points to the statutory rate (Consejo Federal de Inversiones, 1965).

[20] The secondary distribution was radically shifted by the elimination of a fixed share that referred to revenue collection in 1934 and by updating the population criterion to refer to a more recent census.

Porto (2003) points out that the reforms of the 1950s thus upset the credibility of revenue-sharing. One problem was related to the lack of reliable information from the states and the federal government for determining the secondary distribution of funds. Although the existence of a professionalized body to administer internal taxes and the central bank's authority to disburse funds to the provinces went a long way in providing certainty to the provinces as to the funds they would have available, the formulas for the secondary distribution used information on local collections of excises in each province, which the provinces believed was often manipulated by the federal government. Partisan differences in the affiliation of the various provincial governments clearly played a role in reinforcing this belief. This resonates with more contemporary debates in Mexico since the 1990s, in which governors demanded a transparent process through which they could know both the formulas and the specific elements used to calculate the distribution of funds resulting from them.[21] The second, and perhaps most important, issue noted by Porto (2003) was the lack of a guarantee that the statutory rates would be respected and that the federal government would consider most of the federal revenues as "shareable."

The administration of President Arturo Illía increased the statutory rate all the way to 46 percent in 1964, but the authoritarian government emerging from the 1966 coup reduced the statutory rate as part of an effort to shift the cost of macroeconomic adjustment from the federal government to the provinces (Eaton, 2001). Moreover, the creation of the so-called Fund for Territorial Integration, meant to compensate the most backward provinces with federally chosen and administered projects, allowed the federal government (as in Venezuela when the *Situado Coordinado* was created and in Brazil during the military regime, when the use of revenue-sharing funds was conditional) to cheat on its promise to transfer funds under the authority of the provincial governments. This fund was an attempt to transform the revenue-sharing funds into another form of discretionary federal expenditure. Authoritarian rule can undo the promises of a transfer system, destroying federal credibility.[22]

---

[21] This issue was so controversial in Argentina that the current system has gone to the extreme of eliminating formulas altogether, substituting them with fixed coefficients.

[22] The Argentine military governments reversed the trend toward decentralization. But this should not lead to a facile conclusion that democracies increase revenue-sharing, whereas autocracies decrease it. As noted by Eaton (2001, 2004), there is no evidence to suggest that changes that increased the statutory rates in Argentina were more likely to be carried out by democratically elected presidents. In fact, as discussed in the case of Venezuela in

The outgoing military administration of Alejandro Lanusse in 1973 undertook a radical reform of the revenue-sharing system. It increased the statutory rate, creating a 50–50 division between the federal government and the provinces;[23] it created an independent Federal Tax Commission to administer the system and a regional development fund, the *Fondo de Desarrollo Regional*, with 3 percent of the federal revenues. The law also established that any new federal tax would have to be included in the shareable pool. The increased pool of shareable taxes would exclude any earmarked revenue, which meant that in practice, as suggested by Figure 7.1, the increase in the transferred funds relative to total federal revenue was only marginal.

Eaton (2001, 2004) suggests that these measures were a last effort by the military to keep the *Peronistas* at bay, tying their hands by granting more power to the provinces, which tended to be more conservative. In particular, the provision that made any new taxes part of the revenue pool diminished the incentives for the *Peronistas* to increase taxes. In fact, when the last indirect provincial taxes were unified through the establishment of a federal value-added tax in 1973, this new tax became part of the shareable pool. The instability of the 1970s, however, made this arrangement of short duration. In the last months of Isabel Perón's rule, the VAT was removed from the shareable pool and provinces were allowed to collect their own overlapping sales (turnover) taxes. The system had returned to the 1930s.

The Argentine revenue-sharing system collapsed in 1983. As discussed by Cetrángolo and Jiménez (1998), the conflicts that led to the breakdown were related to the impossibility of finding a compromise between the federal government and the provinces on how to deal with the macroeconomic crisis. Shareable revenues dropped after 1982, and the fiscal reform aimed at reactivating the economy backfired, generating ever-increasing pressures on provincial finances. By the end of 1984, the revenue-sharing law was to expire. Because there was no agreement on how to modify it, the three years up to 1987 were characterized by an informal allocation of transfers in

the last chapter and will be clear for Brazil in the next chapter, there is no evidence linking the generosity of statutory rates and regime type in any of the Latin American federations. Democracy probably improves compliance, but it does not determine the statutory rate of the revenue-sharing transfers.

[23] Strictly speaking, the statutory rate was 48.5 percent, plus a regional development fund of 3 percent.

lieu of revenue-sharing through the so-called *Aportaciones del Tesoro Nacional* (ATNs).[24]

There was no law in force to determine the precise allocation of funds. The breakdown of the revenue-sharing system is primarily attributable to the power of the provinces and their adamant opposition to letting the federal government adjust its finances at their expense (Eaton, 2001). It is important to note that the balance of power during the democratically elected administration of Raúl Alfonsín involved a divided Congress and the coexistence of a *Radical* president with a majority of *Peronista* governors in the provinces. Moreover, as discussed by Jones et al. (2001), the incentives in the electoral system after the transition to democracy led to a strong sense of allegiance by local politicians toward their provincial governors.

When the revenue-sharing system collapsed in 1983, ATNs became twice as large as revenue-sharing funds. The ATNs had already been increased dramatically, beyond revenue-sharing funds, during the turmoil of the 1970s. In fact, a striking feature of the Argentine fiscal system is that the federal government made transfers to the provinces through alternatives to revenue-sharing, often undoing whatever distributional effects were being sought in revenue-sharing. The basic distinction between revenue-sharing and ATNs was that the latter "were not automatic in their amounts, distribution among the provinces, and receipt; and were unilaterally determined by the national government" (Porto, 2003:45). Hence, the rising importance of ATNs in Argentina is similar to Federal Public Investment (IPF) in Mexico: Funds to the provinces were allocated to projects determined by the federal government, not local interests.

7.6. Statistical Analysis of the Evolution of Revenue-Sharing

In a fashion similar to the analysis of the *Situado Constitucional* in Venezuela carried out in the last chapter, it is possible to estimate statistically the determinants of the relative size of revenue-sharing as a percentage of "shareable" resources in Argentina (*coparticipación/shareable*) and the relative size of revenue-sharing as a percentage of the total available federal revenue (*coparticipación/total*). The first indicator provides a measure of the compliance with the revenue-sharing agreements in terms of how closely it matches the statutory rate. The second indicator reveals the degree to which

---

[24] Porto (2003) notes that discretionary ATNs had already existed since the late 19th century, but they never represented a significant part of provincial finances until the 1970s.

Table 7.1. *Revenue-Sharing Compliance in Argentina (Standard Errors in Parentheses)*

	Shareable	Total
L1	0.8**	0.77**
	(0.08)	(0.08)
Statutory	0.08	0.08*
	(0.05)	(0.04)
Demo	3.05**	2.02**
	(1.06)	(0.83)
N	65	65
F	79.12	73
Durbin-Watson	1.99	1.96
R-squared	0.891	0.883

Economic controls: Size of federal government
(REV/GDP), federal deficit, GDP per capita.
* Significant at the 95% level.
** Significant at the 99% level.

Argentine federal authorities kept resources out of the revenue-sharing pool in order to cheat on their transfer promises.

The econometric specification in Table 7.1 is the same as in the Venezuelan case, including as independent variables the lag of the dependent variable, the statutory rate, the regime type (where democracy is coded as 1), and economic controls (GDP per capita, the federal deficit, and the size of the federal government, using data from the Oxford Latin American History Database). The first column in the estimation shows the determinants of revenue-sharing as a percentage of shareable funds, and the second assesses it as a percentage of all funds.

The pairwise correlation between the statutory rate and the actual funds disbursed as a percentage of shareable revenue, at 0.79, is higher in Argentina than in Venezuela. However, it is clear from Figure 7.1 that the ebb and flow between democratic and authoritarian regimes was reflected in the fact that the statutory rate for revenue-sharing often was not respected. But the main finding of the econometric estimations is that the evolution of Argentine revenue-sharing shows predominantly a very high degree of inertia: For every percentage point of revenue that was shared to the provinces the previous year, around eight-tenths of a point would be shared the next year.

The second major finding is that the compliance estimation suggests that the Argentine federal governments have not been particularly bound by the statutory rate. The strong temporal inertia suggests that they have been generous, but not scrupulous about obeying the law. The Argentine system of revenue-sharing, in fact, is the one that exhibits the most dynamic behavior of all the Latin American federations, increasing revenue to the subnational levels regardless of the statutory rate. In a way, this means that Argentine federal governments have increased funds to the provinces regardless of the stability or change in the statutory rate. This is most likely attributable to an effort to construct regional coalitions through the use of the revenue-sharing system as an expenditure transfer system rather than a true compensation for the abdication in tax authority.

The third finding in the estimations is that democracy, rather than the establishment of higher rates in the law, seems to be the one factor that can generate larger revenue-sharing funds. The federation with the highest variance in democratic and authoritarian experiences in Latin America has been Argentina, and it is there that a most pronounced effect of democracy is perceived: Three percentage points of additional revenue would be transferred in Argentina under democratic rule as compared with authoritarian rule.[25]

A simulation of the effect of the coefficients in the evolution of revenue-sharing provides a story similar to the one that emerged from Venezuela, although in this case there is little response to the statutory rate per se. Figure 7.2 shows the evolution of revenue-sharing according to the coefficients of the estimation for revenue-sharing as a percentage of total federal revenue, assuming a statutory rate of 10 percent during the first 10 years and 20 percent in the subsequent decade. As before, all the control variables are set at their mean values, and the graph shows alternative simulations under democratic or autocratic regimes. It is clear that democracy makes compliance much more likely, but the general trend in the simulations is produced by the inertia of previous revenue-sharing rather than legal changes in revenue-sharing. Autocratic rule in Argentina is predicted to basically keep revenue-sharing at a rate below 15 percent regardless of the statutory rate. In both cases, however, the trend in Argentine fiscal transfers is predicted to increase over time.

---

[25] It is important to note that this result hinges, however, on considering the Frondizi administration a democratic government.

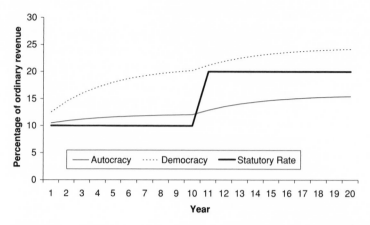

Figure 7.2. Simulation of effect of democracy on revenue-sharing in Argentina.

Hence, the analysis suggests that Argentine democratic governments were not able to withstand pressures to transfer larger resources to the provinces over time. But that did not mean that they were bound by legal statute any more than their authoritarian counterparts. Both authoritarian and democratic governments in Argentina seem to have distributed funds according to the political realities they faced rather than the law. Democracies distributed more, but not because of their respect for legal procedures. A similar story emerges from the secondary distribution, which is discussed in the next section.

7.7. The Distribution of Revenue-Sharing among Provinces in Argentina

The Argentine revenue-sharing system was initially meant to return to the provinces the taxes that they would have collected had they retained fiscal authority. However, from the beginning, an effort was made to gradually move toward a system that would redistribute the additional revenue made possible by the fiscal bargain in relatively equal per capita terms. During the first 20 years of the revenue-sharing system, the population criterion gradually grew in importance in the attempt to create a system that would allocate funds in a way similar to the *Situado* in Venezuela. However, in the turbulent years after the Great Depression, the federal government did not update population figures in the calculation of the revenue shares for each province. In fact, all the way until the 1950s, the population figures

Table 7.2. *Criteria in the Secondary Distribution of Argentine Revenue-Sharing*

Year (Law)	
1934 (12.139)	Revenue collected from shareable tax in each jurisdiction (share decreases over time from 90% to 0%)
	Population (share increases over time from 10% to 100%)
1935 (12.143 and 12.147)	Population (30%)
	Provincial expenditures (30%)
	Provincial total transfers in the previous year (30%)
	Revenue collected from the shareable tax in each jurisdiction (10%)
1947 (12.956)	Population (27.14%)
	Budgeted provincial expenditures (27.14%)
	Provincial revenue (27.14%)
	Revenue collected from the shareable tax in each jurisdiction (9.05%)
	Inverse of population (9.52%)
1951 (14.060)	Revenue collected from the shareable tax in each jurisdiction
1954 (14.390)	Population (78.4% at the end of transition in 1957)
	Production in each province of the taxable products (19.6% at the end of transition in 1957)
	Inverse of the revenue shared per capita (2%)
1959 (14.788)	Population (25%)
	Provincial revenues (25%)
	Provincial expenditures (25%)
	Equal provincial lump sum (25%)
1973 (20.221)	Population (65%)
	Development gap per capita (25%)
	Housing quality
	Education attainment
	Cars
	Inverse population density (10%)
1988 (23.548)	Fixed coefficients

Sources: Based on *Ministerio de Hacienda* (1938), Cetrángolo and Jiménez (1998), and Porto (2003).

used to calculate the shares referred to the 1914 census! This lack of a population update worked against provinces experiencing immigration and faster growth.

Table 7.2 shows the evolution of the criteria driving the secondary distribution of *coparticipación* among the Argentine provinces during the 20th century.[26] There was a clear trend away from derivation-based principles, such as the revenue collected in the provinces or their budgets, toward distributions that reward poorer regions and giving a greater weight to population criteria.

After Perón's ascent to power, a clear redistributive component favoring the provinces of the interior was introduced. As discussed in the previous section, Perón constructed a ruling coalition on the basis of the mobilized workers in the capital city, together with the more rural, backward provinces of the interior, against the relatively modern, outward-oriented Pampas (see Gibson, 1996). This coalition was reflected in the correction of population figures, which benefited primarily the federal capital, and the introduction of inverse factors for population and revenue in the distribution formulas of 1947 and 1954, which benefited the interior provinces. Perón also created new provinces in the interior, which contributed to cementing the coalition and enhancing the malapportioned representation of his party in the legislature.

The redistributive strategy continued after the downfall of Perón when the Frondizi administration, besides increasing the statutory rates, created a formula where one-quarter of the funds would be distributed equally among provinces, regardless of their size. In contrast with Venezuela, which also introduced equal distribution of shares at around that time, half of the formula was still linked to provincial financial indicators, not population. But in 1973 the redistributive elements substituted any derivation principle. The military government of Lanusse, like Frondizi before him, increased the statutory rate while creating a highly redistributive system: Two-thirds of the funds would be distributed on the basis of population, and one-third would be allocated on the basis of development gaps and favoring sparsely populated provinces. The historical inertia of this redistributive allocation remains in place in the fixed coefficients established since 1988 (Cetrángolo and Jiménez, 1998; Porto, 2003).

It is possible to track this history of the shifts in formulas by looking at the shares of some individual provinces through time. Figure 7.3 shows the transformation in the shares that some of the most advanced provinces (Mendoza, Cordoba, and Buenos Aires), the federal capital, and a backward province (Corrientes) experienced in the course of the 20th

---

[26] The table refers to the main funds, ignoring many of the taxes and transfers that comprise the labyrinth.

Argentina

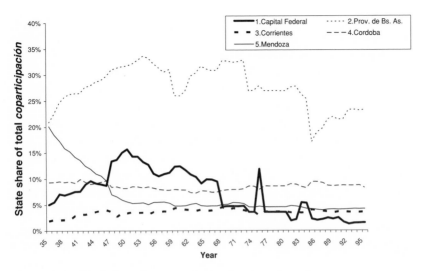

Figure 7.3. Evolution of revenue-sharing in selected provinces.

century.[27] Some of the trends are related to the way in which the federal capital was losing revenue shares, allowing other provinces to make relative gains in resources. Another feature that decreased the share of the larger provinces was related to the creation of new provinces. The evolution of economic activity would also affect relative shares. But the most important factor in the evolution of shares in Figure 7.3 is related to the creation of formulas that increasingly get away from a derivation principle in favor of redistribution.

The state-weighted Gini coefficient of *coparticipación* shares in Argentina, which was reported in Table 6.1, summarized the evolution of the distribution of funds through time. It is important to remember that a value of 0 denotes a condition where all the funds are distributed equally among provinces, regardless of the province's size or economic importance, whereas a value of 1 denotes a condition where one province would hypothetically receive all the funds. Shares in Argentina were less equally distributed across provinces than in Venezuela. The Gini coefficient of around 0.5 observed from the 1930s until the early 1970s suggests that Argentina

[27] I thank Matías Iaryczower for sharing his historical dataset on the Argentine secondary distribution.

was midway between distributing all the funds to one province and giving them out equally to all.

Following the analysis of redistribution provided by Porto (2003), the first period, from 1935 to 1946, was hence characterized by a slight equalization of shares, which reflected shifts in formulas in favor of the consumer provinces as opposed to the producing ones. This is more noticeable in the evolution of Mendoza in Figure 7.3, which loses revenue share throughout the period. A second period of redistribution (which Porto dates from 1947 to 1958) involved a surge in the share of funds for populated provinces, which was mostly attributable to the updating of census figures. During those years, the agricultural production regions lost somewhat, but there was also a gain for some interior provinces that were also engaged in agriculture (although not export oriented).

Porto (2003) suggests that not much redistribution occurred in the 1950s with the Frondizi reforms that increased the statutory rate. However, given that the population distribution in Argentine provinces was very unequal, inequality increased slightly as the distribution followed population criteria more closely. The main point, however, was that the increase in the statutory rate allowed revenue-sharing to become detached from production indicators. This was reinforced particularly after 1973, when the formulas included criteria favoring redistribution toward the interior provinces. Sawers calculates that by 1988 the Argentine federal government was transferring resources, including ATNs, to the interior provinces on the order of 5 percent of GDP (Sawers, 1996:248). The current distribution coefficients, which date from 1988, have implied that some poor provinces, such as La Rioja, Jujuy Tucumán, and Catamarca, which had benefited from the development gap element in the previous formula, have lost resources in favor of the richer regions. However, the overriding trend has been for Argentina to retain a distribution that if weighted by population has become more equal but if weighted by production would reveal a trend toward greater redistribution.

There are excellent analyses of the determinants of the distribution patterns of revenue-sharing in Argentina in recent years (Kraemer, 1997; Porto and Cont, 1998; Jones, Sanguinetti, and Tommasi, 2000; Porto and Sanguinetti, 2001; Gibson, Calvo, and Falleti, 2004). The most important finding in these analyses is confirmation that the Argentine system is redistributive in its allocation of funds in favor of poor, sparsely populated provinces and that malapportionment in the two chambers of the legislature provides a powerful determinant of funding, particularly when looking at the allocation not just of revenue-sharing but also of discretionary transfers through ATNs. Kraemer (1997) finds a "Menem" effect (referring to President Carlos Menem) in terms of a great disproportion of funds sent to Menem's home province, La Rioja, a result that underscores the degree to which the determination of the allocation of funds was political and not simply based on objective criteria of fiscal or socioeconomic indicators.

The malapportionment effect is very strong in quantitative terms. Porto and Sanguinetti have shown that a 1 percent increase in their indicator of malapportionment for the lower chamber is reflected in around a 0.5 percent increase in the per capita allocation of transfers to a province (Porto and Sanguinetti, 2001:252). These results are similar in both scope and magnitude to the patterns in Brazil, which are discussed in the next chapter. Coupled with the discussion of redistribution across Venezuela, this suggests that the construction of peripheral coalitions through the use of fiscal transfers is a generalized phenomenon in the Latin American federations and not just one Argentine idiosyncratic trait.

7.8. Recent Developments

Argentine fiscal federalism in the last decade of the 20th century was marked by the establishment of political agreements negotiated almost every year rather than a permanent institutional solution. After the breakdown of the system in the 1980s, a sequence of fiscal pacts were used to reestablish order in the federal arrangement (Tommasi, 2002). Those fiscal pacts have been political agreements that sought to reconcile differences between provinces together with the pressing macroeconomic stabilization imperatives of the federal government. In a compromise with the provinces, in 1987 a fiscal reform was passed that reestablished the revenue-sharing system with a statutory rate that was increased to 57 percent. This was, however, a Pyrrhic victory for the provinces.

In 1992 and 1993, revenue-sharing was reduced as a consequence of a bargain related to the pension system. A guaranteed floor was established that promised 35 percent of federal revenue, regardless of its type, to the provinces if they in turn accepted that 15 percent of their revenue shares would be kept for a social security bailout and a fund to compensate federal expenditure programs in the provinces (see Tommasi, 2002). The system has remained complex throughout all the fiscal pacts. Figure 7.2 suggests that what some scholars have called a process of "recentralization" (Falleti, 2001; O'Neill, 2001; and Wibbels and Remmer, 2000) during those years has in fact allowed provinces to retain a larger share of the available resources than in the past. That is, although provinces are not enjoying the full statutory rate, the graph in Figure 7.2 suggests that transferred funds have increased. The bargain involving the pension funds was not too bad from the point of view of the provinces. The crucial fact to highlight, however, remains that the Argentine fiscal arrangements have not provided a mechanism that can ensure compliance with a well-established institutional framework.

In 1994, a new constitution was drafted. The new constitution established revenue-sharing explicitly, almost a century later than in the Venezuelan case and six decades after the initial calls for constitutional provisions for revenue-sharing had been made in the 1930s. The pressure to embed revenue-sharing into the constitution, however, was not for the purpose of creating a relatively fixed and stable arrangement. Revenue-sharing since 1995 has included a fund to finance the devolution of formerly federal education functions, which is earmarked for this purpose, and funds for urban renewal, provision of public services, education, and infrastructure, as well as some funds for regional imbalances and shares of specific taxes such as on electricity. The determination of the allocation of funds has not been driven by the institutional rules created by the constitution but by ad hoc fiscal agreements between the provinces and the federal government (Tommasi, 2002). Hence, Argentine fiscal federalism, although now seemingly driven by constitutionally mandated rules and formulas, remains at its core the product of an accumulation of political bargains.

The macroeconomic adjustment efforts of the 1980s and 1990s were shaped by the way in which provincial governments were not responsible in their financial behavior. Wibbels and Remmer (2000) have argued that the maintenance of subnational patronage networks, as reflected by party competition variables, has determined the different capacities of provincial governments to adjust their public finances. Jones, Sanguinetti, and Tommasi (2000) argue that the issue is more one of a common pool resource problem, where all provinces have incentives to increase spending, incur deficits, and pass the bill to the federal government. In their findings, the federal government can improve the fiscal discipline of the provinces only when it has the same partisan affiliation as the provincial governors. Regardless of whether the primary mechanism for fiscal indiscipline in the provinces is induced by the party system configuration or the institutional setup of fiscal institutions, the fact is that Argentine provinces contributed to a large degree to the financial crisis of 2002. This has parallels with the evolution of Brazilian federalism, discussed in the next chapter.

Throughout this process, Argentine provinces have kept more authority to tax in their own jurisdictions than the Venezuelan or Mexican states. In particular, provinces in Argentina still collect more than one-third of their revenue from their own taxes, most importantly from an economically inefficient sales tax. Hence, although Argentine scholars complain about the dependence of provincial finances on federal transfers, the provinces still have more tax authority and more countervailing power, compared with the federal government, than the Mexican or Venezuelan states. Nonetheless, whereas in Mexico and Venezuela the federal pact was being revitalized at the end of the 20th century, in Argentina an anachronistic fiscal arrangement seems to be impossible to reform (Tommasi, 2002). The stalemate has its origins in the partisan makeup of Argentine provinces and the fundamental lack of trust in the credibility of promises from the federal government.

8

Brazil

THE RETENTION OF FISCAL AUTHORITY

8.1. Resilient Federalism

In contrast with Venezuela, Argentina, and Mexico, the fiscal pact in Brazil did not involve a centralized federal commitment. States in Brazil successfully resisted the pressures for centralization from the federal government, retaining a highly peripheralized fiscal arrangement. The precedents of revenue-sharing date back to the 1930s, which would suggest a development parallel to Argentina and Mexico. However, in Brazil the federal bargain did not become centralized. Federal transfers to the states and municipalities did not become firmly established until the 1960s, after the collapse of democracy, and a substantial amount of fiscal authority always remained controlled by the states.

Most discussions of Brazilian federalism suggest that decentralization has varied according to the political regime. Military rulers in Brazil tried to centralize taxation by controlling the most important sources of revenue and granting the federal government the residual power to create new taxes (Varsano, 1996; Abrucio, 1998). This was not unlike efforts by Getulio Vargas, within the authoritarian *Estado Novo*, to centralize revenue after 1937. However, what is striking about Brazil is not the variation in centralization but that state politicians remained – as they did with Vargas – too strong to subdue. The efforts at unitarian imposition of both Vargas and the military in the 20th century largely failed. Vargas had to concede the sales tax to the states, and could not strip from them the power to tax exports. The military had to allow the states to retain control of the value-added tax.

In terms of the theoretical framework of Chapter 1, Argentina and Mexico followed the path of a centralized fiscal bargain, whereas Venezuela represented a unitary imposition. The Brazilian fiscal evolution shows instead that a centralized fiscal bargain can be resisted when regional interests are well organized and capable of threatening to go their own way. This "off the equilibrium path" threat is what allowed states to remain more fiscally autonomous than their counterparts in any of the other Latin American federations. Brazilian regionalism remained strong even throughout military rule (Hagopian, 1996; Abrucio, 1998). The threat of force was an essential ingredient in explaining this outcome: State-level police forces constituted true armies that could effectively challenge the federal government.

Brazil witnessed a succession of democratic and authoritarian regimes. But the authoritarian period of 1964–1988 was a rather peculiar arrangement characterized by a high degree of political openness. In this sense, the authoritarian interlude in Brazil was more similar to Mexico's *apertura* since the 1980s than to the authoritarian regimes in Argentina or Venezuela. Elections at the state and municipal levels were quickly restored, even as the military crafted electoral laws in their favor and would not relinquish control of the national government (Souza, 1997). Lamounier (1985) has characterized the regime as a "perverse poliarchy," meaning that although the opposition could contest elections, electoral processes became a mechanism to legitimize, in a plebiscitary manner, the military's hold on power.

The military governments in Brazil successfully remained in office to a large extent because of their success in channeling regional demands and appeasing local interests, which were articulated by local political forces. The revenue-sharing system that the military created primarily played the role of channeling fiscal resources to further these goals. It was not, as in the other Latin American federations, a system to centralize control over taxation.

This chapter is organized in a fashion parallel to the previous chapters. The next section sketches the overall trends in fiscal authority in Brazil in order to discuss the evolution of the fiscal arrangement more thoroughly in subsequent sections. Section 8.3 discusses the origins of the fiscal arrangement, explaining the reasons why states remained such powerful actors in the Brazilian federation. Section 8.4 analyzes the creation of revenue-sharing by the military, and Section 8.5 provides a statistical analysis of the evolution of revenue-sharing funds and federal compliance. Section 8.6 addresses the distributional consequences of the revenue-sharing system. Finally, Section 8.7 discusses some of the more recent developments in Brazilian federalism and the prospects for its future evolution.

8.2. Strong States and the Retention of Fiscal Authority

Brazilian states are the strongest subnational jurisdictions in Latin America. Figure 1.3 in Chapter 1 clearly showed the high degree of fiscal decentralization that has characterized Brazil throughout the 20th century. It is important to recall that Figure 1.3 reported the degree of revenue centralization, without subtracting federal transfers, of the revenue-sharing system created in the 1960s. Hence, it is clear that subnational governments in Brazil have kept substantial control over taxation independently of any funds they might receive as transfers from the federal government.

In contrast to the other Latin American federations, the general trend in Brazil was for subnational jurisdictions to increase their share of total national revenue. That trend was interrupted, however, by the military interlude, which was marked by a jump in centralization during the 1960s and 1970s. However, after democratization, the Brazilian federal system basically returned to its historically high levels of decentralization.

The two most important taxes in Brazil, apart from social security contributions, are the income tax (Imposto de Renda, IR), created in 1924, which is controlled by the federal government, and the sales taxes, which have been controlled by the state governments. During the first half of the 20th century, tariffs and export taxes were very important sources of revenue both for the federal and the state governments. However, their importance sharply diminished after the 1930s.

Figure 8.1 shows that the state-controlled sales tax (initially a turnover tax but later transformed into a value-added tax) was, for most of the 20th century, the most dynamic and significant source of finance. The income tax, both personal and corporate, grew very quickly during the first two decades after it was implemented but thereafter stagnated as a source of revenue until the 1980s. In most countries around the world, sales taxes, particularly when they are structured as value-added taxes, are controlled by the national government. Brazil is the one major exception. The graph depicts the sales tax as a percentage of federal finances in order to highlight the opportunity cost, from the point of view of the federal government, of not controlling this source of taxation.

The Brazilian revenue-sharing system was established relatively late compared with those of the other Latin American federations. In 1937, municipalities received a share of the federal income tax. The 1946 Constitution explicitly established an intergovernmental revenue-sharing system in which states had to transfer 10 percent of their sales taxes to their

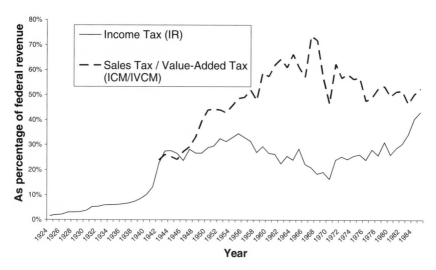

Figure 8.1. Revenue from direct and indirect taxes in Brazil.

municipalities (Varsano, 1996). Municipalities also obtained an increase in their share of the federal income tax from 10 to 15 percent. But these transfers did not involve the states until the 1960s. It was only when the military government implemented a far reaching fiscal reform with the transformation of the state sales tax into a value-added tax in 1966 that a revenue-sharing system comprising both states and municipalities was established (see Mahar, 1971; Eaton, 2004).

The revenue-sharing system was primarily structured around two federal taxes, the income tax (IR) and the tax on industrialized products (Imposto sobre Produtos Industrializados, IPI). In addition, states and municipalities received minor shares from taxes on fuels, electricity, minerals, transportation, cars, and real estate. Figure 8.2 shows the evolution of the statutory rate and the actual revenue shares distributed to the states in Brazil as a share of the total revenue collected from the income tax and the tax on industrialized products.[1]

It is clear that revenue-sharing has increased in importance, constituting a sizable component of the fiscal system. To anticipate some of the

---

[1] The share distributed to the municipalities was at around the same percentage as that allocated to the states, but the graph only shows the state statistics in order to make comparisons with the other Latin American federations somewhat clearer.

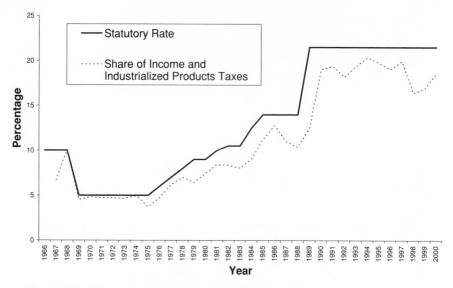

Figure 8.2. State revenue-sharing in Brazil.

discussion of Section 8.4, the military governments realized in the early 1970s that if they wanted to stay in power they needed to abandon their efforts at fiscal centralization and instead use transfers as a strategy to appease regional interests (Ames, 1987). The military used decentralization and federal transfers (both discretionary and a highly redistributive revenue-sharing system they put into place) as part of a broad coalition strategy in which the poor northeastern states were used as a foil to counterbalance the autonomy of the largest, more industrialized states in the south, most crucially Sao Paulo. This strategy was accompanied by an opening in the political system through the peculiar coexistence of authoritarianism and competitive elections after 1974. The strategy worked because it allowed the military to stay in office, in an environment of stability, for a relatively long time. The transition to democracy, which occurred between 1985 and 1989, was accompanied by demands for further decentralization. Overall, the revenue-sharing system in Brazil has since the 1990s distributed resources to states and municipalities at levels comparable to those observed in Mexico and Venezuela. But in contrast to those Latin American federations where virtually the only source of subnational revenue is composed of those transfers, in Brazil states also control resources from their own collection of the value-added tax.

8.3. Origins: The Politics of the States

In order to understand the fiscal evolution of Brazil, one must start by noting that since the establishment of the Brazilian federation in 1889 the key political players have been the governors rather than any national political figure. States, and in particular the elites of Minas Gerais and Sao Paulo, had reached a regional compromise in which presidential power was shared among both states in the "coffee and milk" politics of the period.[2] The export orientation of the economy was underpinned by a stable political arrangement that respected regional autonomy and ensured that a large share of the revenues collected from international trade would remain in the local sphere.

Since 1889, the constitution had established exclusive revenue sources for each level of government. Brazilian constitutions were thus different from those of Mexico and Argentina in that they explicitly provided for the exclusive assignment of taxes among levels of government (Blanco Cossio, 1998:29). The federation had exclusive authority over import duties, excises, and taxes on industrial products, whereas the states had exclusive authority over export taxes, which were levied even on interstate commerce. When income taxation was introduced in Brazil in 1924, it was established under federal jurisdiction, and over time it gradually grew in importance. Income tax revenue came to account for around 25 percent of total federal revenue collection after the 1940s (Varsano, 1996).

Municipalities also started to receive a transfer from the federal government out of income taxes, which is the direct precedent of the revenue-sharing system, in 1937. As in the other Latin American federations, customs duties, not direct or indirect taxes, were the most important source of revenue before the 1930s. Customs duties were even more important in Brazil because the economic structure relied so heavily on international commodity markets, for coffee in particular. However, the dislocations in the international economy after 1929 forced the Brazilian governments to seek to tap into domestic sources of revenue (de Oliveira, 2000:39).

The old Brazilian republic (1889–1930) allowed the state elites of Sao Paulo and Minas Gerais to share power, thereby limiting the authority of

---

[2] Beyond any doubt, the best understanding of this process is provided by the three studies by Love (1980), Wirth (1977), and Robert Levine (1978) of Sao Paulo, Minas Gerais, and Pernambuco, respectively. In addition to these works, it is useful to consult Love's (1971) study of Rio Grande do Sul. For a brief summary of the processes and an annotated bibliography, see Love (1993).

the president and the federal government. Those two states, together with Rio Grande do Sul, represented half of the electorate, they contributed to around half of GDP in the 1920s, and controlled powerful state militias that counterbalanced any temptation by the federal government to intervene (Love, 1993:181).[3] The pacted democracy of this period might suggest a comparison with Venezuela after 1958, but the arrangement in Brazil could not be more different from Venezuela's: It was predicated on the strength of the governors, whereas in Venezuela the arrangement depended on their weakness.

Substantial parliamentary debates had since the 19th century called for the elimination of interstate taxes (see Camara dos Deputados, 1914). Liberal elites, as in Mexico during the 1920s, understood all too well that an integrated domestic market would be conducive to better economic performance. States, however, retained illegal taxes on interstate commerce all the way until 1942 (Love, 1993:187). This was done notwithstanding the explicit prohibition of 1904 establishing that "the exchange of national or foreign goods shall be free of any tax from the federation, the states or the municipalities, when it is the object of trade between states or the Federal District" (my translation, Camara dos Deputados, 1914:576). The federal government was simply not powerful enough to enforce interstate free trade.

The politics of governors of the era was a pact based on regional coalitions but cemented through the threat of force. The south monopolized power because it had the military strength to do so. Not only were the states in the north and the northeast excluded from the spoils of national power, but their state governors were often deposed through federal interventions. Federal military intervention was not an uncommon practice in Argentina or Mexico,[4] but in Brazil the powerful southern states were immune from this threat to the extent that they had their own standing armies. In fact, state governments were the ones that often provoked political change at the federal level through the use of their militias. This happened in 1930 (Love, 1971) and again in the 1964 coup (Abrucio, 1998:60).

The First Republic came to an end with the Vargas "revolution." The regime change was already boiling in the states, with the so-called rebellions

[3] Minas Gerais and Sao Paulo shared a common interest in keeping state control of the taxation of coffee exports, although Minas Gerais was somewhat more dependent than Sao Paulo on taxes on interstate commerce (Wirth, 1977).
[4] See *Ministerio del Interior* (1933) for the debates in Argentina and González Oropeza (1983) for a legal analysis of Mexico's federal interventions.

216

of the *tenentes*, local coups challenging the traditional elites in the states. The *tenentes* provided decisive support for political change. But the ascent of Getulio Vargas was far from assured. The pacification of regional interests was achieved through skillful bargains with different groups. Vargas provided a debt bailout that included the powerful state of Sao Paulo (Love, 1980), introduced more open politics through an electoral reform in 1932 that guaranteed the secret ballot and gave women the right to vote, and also negotiated concessions with the oligarchic groups (Abrucio, 1998). His mobilization strategy sought to incorporate workers as the basis of a developmentalist import substitution industrialization strategy. In 1937, he consolidated his hold on power by staging a military coup.

On the fiscal front, Vargas introduced a turnover sales tax under exclusive state authority in 1934 (Varsano, 1996), in a distinct effort to find a compromise between centralizing revenue in the federal government while at the same time retaining the peripheralized nature of fiscal authority. Although Vargas attempted to concentrate power in the federal sphere, he depended on the consent of the regional power brokers. He did succeed in creating a more integrated internal market, which would lay the base for industrialization and the federal regulation of foreign trade. The reforms on the fiscal front, although centralizing by Brazilian standards, never involved the abdication of fiscal authority witnessed in Argentina, Mexico, or Venezuela.

In exchange for the new source of revenue from the turnover tax, states agreed to limit their taxation of foreign trade (exports) to a maximum 10 percent rate and were not allowed to tax their commerce with other states (which until then they had treated as "foreign" trade). State governments got a very good deal: They secured control of the source of revenue that would become the most dynamic tax in the coming years.

One cannot understand the nature of the Brazilian fiscal pact without acknowledging that states have controlled indirect taxes since 1934. Lieberman (2003) has argued that the formation of what he calls a "race inclusionary National Political Community" in Brazil prevented that country from creating an efficient and redistributive income tax, in contrast with South Africa, where, he claims, taxes were more redistributive.[5] Although

---

[5] Lieberman (2003) argues that the Brazilian tax system historically has been characterized by being incapable of collecting taxes from the richer groups in society. This inference is grounded on an assumption that redistribution occurs through progressive taxation rather than through the use of transfers. I would argue that the reasons that Brazil did not emphasize income taxation are little related to race or to whether the state had an "adversarial" rather than a "cooperative" relationship with the economically privileged groups in society, to use

his account is suggestive, it overlooks the fact that the most important instruments for redistribution in Brazil were not progressive rates on the income tax but social security contributions and revenue-sharing transfers spent in the states.[6]

Lieberman (2003) concentrates his analysis of the Brazilian fiscal structure on the income tax, which was established at the federal level. He argues that, although he is aware of the importance of subnational sources of taxation, "it [is] possible to speak of income tax collections only at the national level because [in Brazil and South Africa], through constitutional mandates, only the national government has been responsible for that tax base." But the problem with this argument is that, notwithstanding the potential of income taxes as a source of revenue at the beginning of the 20th century, it was the regressive sales tax that became the most relevant source of revenue. This is not something specific to Brazil; as noted by Kato (2003), regressive burdens through indirect taxes, and the institutional innovation of the value-added tax in the second half of the 20th century, are key to understanding redistribution and the development of the welfare state in advanced industrial democracies. More specifically, Kato argues that "the divergent funding capacity of the welfare state is path dependent upon the institutionalization of regressive taxes" (Kato, 2003:1).

In seeking to explain the power to tax in the central state, Lieberman's analysis overlooks the fact that the backbone of the Brazilian fiscal system is not in the federal government but in a decentralized system of indirect tax collection, as shown in Figure 8.1. This does not mean that his conclusion – namely, that the Brazilian system is not very redistributive – is wrong. But the mechanisms he identifies are misplaced. The retention of fiscal authority in the hands of the states, as I discuss further, is what has limited redistribution in Brazil, whereas revenue-sharing and other transfers have been highly redistributive in favor of the poorer states.

Vargas set the stage for a developmentalist strategy that allowed the Brazilian economy to grow very rapidly, constituting one of the miracles

Lieberman's terms (Lieberman, 2003:7). For a long time, Brazilians could tax consumers of coffee from around the world rather than their own citizens. When international sources of revenue became less abundant, state governments were the crucial players in the construction of a fiscal system that taxes consumption and redistributes resources through expenditures on the basis of regional criteria, not progressive income tax rates.

[6] Lieberman (2003) does mention that social security contributions reached 8 percent of GDP after the 1970s (Lieberman, 2003:120), but he fails to link this fact with the redistributive features of welfare state transfers because he argues that these contributions were largely regressive.

of economic growth in the 20th century. The federal government made massive interventions not only through its tariff policies but also in its direct involvement in the economy (for a now classic account, see Evans, 1979). Vargas's *Estado Novo* officially came to an end, however, in 1945. His demise was symbolically marked by a declaration of the local elites of Minas Gerais, in defense of a liberal political order, in 1943 (Camargo, 1993:311). In the same way as his ascent to power depended on the regional power brokers, his fall was the product of forces unleashed from the states.

The new democratic regime was marked by the Vargas legacy. According to von Mettenheim, "the fall of Getulio Vargas in 1945 was due more to the democratic climate of the postwar world, than to the organizational weakness or unpopularity of the *Estado Novo* among Brazilians" (Von Mettnheim, 1995:77). In fact, in her analysis of Brazilian federalism, Camargo (1993) does not even consider the Vargas era to finish until his suicide in 1954. And even then, she considers the Goulart presidency a continuation of the first Vargas regime. New processes of representation and interest articulation were set into place through a corporatist structure created by Vargas. But even with the ascent of unions and business confederations, the main locus of political negotiation remained in the governors and their territorial interests. This resonates with the discussion of Mexico in Chapter 3. In Mexico, in spite of the emergence of corporatist organizations, regional dimensions of political intermediation survived even under a hegemonic party regime. In Brazil, corporatism allowed new actors to enter the political arena, but it did not make the old actors disappear. In terms of fiscal evolution, the democratic period between 1945 and 1966 kept the revenue system in place with only marginal changes.

8.4. Authoritarianism and Revenue-Sharing

Although there was a strong sense among many scholars that the military had become a fixed feature of the political landscape in Latin America during the 1970s, it is important to note that the military's hold on the federal government in Brazil was far from assured.[7] The main potential challengers came from the states. In particular, as noted by Abrucio, the state militias of Sao Paulo, Minas Gerais, and Guanabara played a crucial role in supporting the 1964 coup (Abrucio, 1998:60). In the 1965 state elections, however, the

---

[7] See, for example, the essays in Stepan (1973) and the assessments with the benefit of hindsight in Stepan (1989), particularly the essay by Bolivar Lamounier.

victorious governors in Minas Gerais and Guanabara were opponents of the military government. They were allowed to step into office in exchange for the federal government being allowed to nominate the secretaries of public safety in those states (Abrucio, 1998:62). In terms of the model in Chapter 1, it is clear that the threat of a conflict in the "off the path" strategy of a unitary imposition involved a credible response on the part of the powerful state governors. In contrast, by the second half of the 20th century, this military threat was nonexistent in Argentina, Mexico, and Venezuela.

The military governments tried to weaken the fiscal authority of the states through two main measures. On the one hand, the military created a system of transfers that pitted winners against losers. On the other hand, municipalities received substantial funds, which allowed the federal government to use municipalities as a countervailing force against state governors (see Souza, 1997; Abrucio, 1998). The control over export taxes finally became exclusively federal, and any new taxes were residually claimed by the federal government. This last feature shifted the nature of tax authority because the states were no longer able to adjust to revenue shortfalls by enjoying some flexibility in their tax structure. As in the other Latin American federations, centralization in taxation was viewed by the Brazilian military governments as a precondition for a successful process of import substituting industrialization. The process of industrialization initiated by Vargas was "deepened" by the military (O'Donnell, 1973).

In contrast with Argentina and Mexico, the revenue-sharing system was created on the basis of a highly redistributive formula that would allocate resources disproportionately to the poorer states, away from the powerful and developed states in the south. The establishment of rates for the value-added tax was granted to the Senate, so states would not enjoy authority in this aspect of tax design. And half of the revenue from the value-added tax would be earmarked for projects according to federal developmental priorities. This last provision was similar to the *Situado Coordinado* created in Venezuela at around the same time and discussed in Chapter 6.

As can be seen in Figure 8.2, the percentage of revenue that the Brazilian system shared with the states was relatively high, particularly if one considers that the level is twice as high as depicted in the graph if one includes the municipalities.[8] The Venezuelan and Mexican tax systems

---

[8] I do not discuss the role of municipalities in the Brazilian revenue-sharing system, even though I am well aware that the federal government has used decentralization as a way to empower local governments and reduce the influence of state governors. For a good discussion, see Eaton (2004).

incorporated a broader array of taxes in the shareable pool, but the Brazilian system provided much higher shares, more similar to what was transferred in Argentina.

In terms of the issue of compliance, in contrast with Argentina and Venezuela, in Brazil the statutory rate was closely respected over time. As shown in Figure 8.2, although there were some years in which shortfalls are noticeable, particularly following 1974 and 1986, the military governments did not cheat state and municipal governments out of their promised transfers. When the military government needed to withhold funds from the states and municipalities, it adjusted the statutory rates, as occurred in 1969, but it complied with them.

Figure 8.2 also shows that after 1975 revenue-sharing exhibited an upward trend. Larger revenue shares do not necessarily mean that there is greater overall decentralization because that depends on the exercise of fiscal authority by the states. In principle, the military rulers in Brazil saw the creation of this highly redistributive revenue-sharing system as an alternative to local tax authority. Transfers would make the states more financially dependent on the federal government.

However, the increases in the statutory rate after the 1970s can be understood in the context of the slow democratization that took shape in Brazil from the local to the national level rather than as an effort by the military to substitute state tax authority. In his illuminating book, Abrucio argues that "few analysts perceive the importance of the 1974 elections for the change in the federal structure of the military regime" (Abrucio, 1998:80). The 1974 elections were a political shock to the military, which had expected to do well in them but did not.

Lamounier suggests that this outcome cut short the initial strategy of "Mexicanization" that the military was attempting to create with ARENA (Aliança da Renovação Nacional, Alliance for National Renovation), a hegemonic party like the PRI (Lamounier, 1985:30). Instead, the political system had to be decompressed through the creation of a credible calendar of elections, even if some of them remained indirect. The "endogenous and gradual" democratization (Lamounier, 1985:45) of Brazil meant that although the military were not willing to give up power, some of the traits of democratic checks and balances constrained their behavior.

The increase in the statutory rate reflected the political pressures the military rulers experienced from the states. In particular, although the government retained control of the two federal legislative chambers, it became hostage to the governors. Governors became the main allies of

President Ernesto Geisel, but they also extracted important concessions in exchange for that support. In particular, they sought increases in financial resources, the elimination of earmarking in federal transfers, and the reestablishment of state capacity to access credit markets.

Accordingly, as Figure 8.2 suggests, the constitutional amendments of 1974 and 1980 increased the statutory rate. In 1984 and 1985, rates were further increased as a response to the pressures arising from the democratization process that culminated with the 1988 Constitution, which guaranteed to the states a statutory rate of 21.5 percent plus an additional 3 points for regional development and an additional 10 percent of the IPI for states that did not tax the export of manufactured goods (Rezende and Afonso, 2002).

8.5. Statistical Analysis of the Evolution of Revenue-Sharing

As in the previous chapters, it is possible to provide econometric evidence of the determinants of the evolution of revenue-sharing in Brazil, although the time frame is more limited in this case, which reduces the number of observations available for the analysis. I do not depart from conventional approaches in focusing on revenue-sharing, but the fact that so much tax authority in Brazil remains in the states must qualify any comparison with the other Latin American federations. Thus, although there seems to be some convergence across Latin America in the sense that since the 1980s Brazil, Mexico, and Venezuela have been transferring around 15 percent of their federal revenue to their states, this obscures the fact that Brazilian states have far more resources than states in Venezuela or Mexico because the main source of finance for the richer states is not federal revenue-sharing but the value-added tax. This places Brazilian decentralization closer to what is found in Argentine provinces, where substantial revenue is available to them. The main difference, however, is that in Argentina two-thirds of the funds come from revenue-sharing rather than the provinces' own tax collection.

I estimate the determinants of two dependent variables analogous to those in Argentina: state revenue-sharing as a fraction of the federal income tax and the tax on industrialized products, which are the most important "shareable" sources, FPE/(IR + IPI); and the relative size of revenue-sharing from the FPE as a percentage of total government income, including debt (*participação/total*). The estimation does not include several small funds

Brazil

Table 8.1. *Compliance with Shareable Pool in the Latin American Federations*

	IPI + IR	Total
L1	0.27**	0.33*
	(0.1)	(0.16)
Statutory	0.71**	0.07
	(0.09)	(0.06)
Demo	0.7	−2.16
	(0.96)	(1.62)
N	28	32
F	119	43
Durbin-Watson	2.34	1.89
R-squared	0.972	0.307

Economic controls: size of federal government (REV/GDP), federal deficit, GDP per capita.
* Significant at the 95% level.
** Significant at the 99% level.

that are transferred to the states; nor does it comprise transfers to the municipalities.[9]

As in the previous chapters, the estimations include as independent variables the lag of the dependent variable, the statutory rate, the regime type, and several economic control variables. The pairwise correlation between the statutory rate and the actual funds disbursed in Brazil at 0.97 is very high. But the correlation obscures, rather than sheds light on, the political process that made those statutory rates come about. Table 8.1 reports the estimations. Although there is some inertia in the revenue-sharing system, as reflected in the lag of the dependent variable, that inertia is much lower than for Argentina and Venezuela.

The overriding feature that explains the evolution of revenue-sharing as a percentage of the shareable taxes, as shown in the first estimation, is the statutory rate. For every additional percentage point of the statutory rate, one can expect the revenue of the states to increase by 0.71. The statutory rate fails to show a significant effect as a percentage of all the revenue collected by the federal government, but this is attributable to some extent to the very small number of observations and the fact that during the 1980s and 1990s Brazilian federal finances relied very heavily on public debt.

[9] For an analysis of pre-1964 patterns, see Mahar (1971).

The fact that the regime type variable does not seem to have an effect might be an artifact of the peculiarity of the democratic arrangement during the years of the military governments. That is, except for the initial period, military rule in Brazil was rather "soft," and regional politicians could use representative institutions and other channels to advance their policy agendas and force some degree of accountability from the federal government. Hence, at least on the fiscal federalism front, one could argue that the authoritarian interlude was in fact much shorter than what is normally assumed.

Hence, the econometric estimations suggest that compliance with revenue-sharing was very high in Brazil. When there was an increase in the funds available to the states, this was usually the consequence of an explicit, openly visible change in the statutory rate. The military regime does not seem to have behaved differently in its compliance from the democratic governments that came into office after 1988. In terms of revenue-sharing as a percentage of total federal inflows, the Brazilian federal government behaved like the Argentine one in that many of the funds during the decades of macroeconomic imbalance came from sources outside the shareable revenue (in Brazil this was mostly debt), so the statutory rate had no effect, statistically speaking, on the overall share of funds states received.

8.6. Redistribution in the Brazilian Federation

The Brazilian fiscal federal arrangement is usually discussed in the literature as being characterized by massive redistribution. The bargaining strength of the north and northeastern states, and their disproportionate representation in both the Chamber of Deputies and the Senate, allowed the creation of a transfer system that takes resources away from the strongest states in the southeast. The degree of redistribution embodied by the fiscal arrangement, however, is not captured correctly by a partial analysis that concentrates only on the transfer system. Brazilian states did not give up on their tax authority, as in other Latin American federations, when they created a revenue-sharing system, so the scope of redistribution through the federal government was reduced accordingly.

Several studies have analyzed the distribution of resources across Brazilian states. Kraemer (1997) studied per capita transfers to states in 1991, including both revenue-sharing and discretionary transfers through the so-called *convenios* (which often represented more funds than revenue-sharing), finding that overall spending is not very redistributive, notwithstanding that

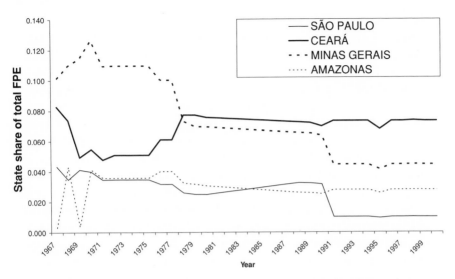

Figure 8.3. Evolution of revenue-sharing for selected states in Brazil.

revenue-sharing is designed for redistribution. The main conclusion of his analysis of Brazilian transfers is that "the intensity of representation in the Senate is *the* driving force determining the distribution of transfers in the states" (Kraemer, 1997:43). This is the same type of finding that underlies the analysis by Gibson, Calvo, and Falleti (2004), although they pool the Brazilian data with state-level data from other federations in the Americas, including the United States. Diaz-Cayeros (2004) finds that the effect of malapportionment in Brazilian transfers is very strong, even when controlling for the size of states (which is technically indistinguishable from the malapportionment in the Senate). That is, Brazilian transfers are disproportionately delivered to states that have a greater representation in the lower chamber.

Figure 8.3 shows the evolution of the distribution of funds in a selection of Brazilian states through time. In a fashion similar to what was done in the previous two chapters, the graph shows the share of revenue-sharing funds that were allocated to Sao Paulo and Minas Gerais, contrasting those states with the more backward, smaller states of Ceará and Amazonas. Both Sao Paulo and Minas Gerais lost resources over time, although the relative economic stagnation of Minas Gerais worked to its advantage, allowing that state to retain much more resources than the more developed Sao Paulo. But even though Minas Gerais seemed to do relatively well in comparative terms, the shares do not reflect the relative population or its trends. Ceará, with just 4.4 percent of the population of the country, received larger transfers than Minas Gerais, which represent 10.5 percent of the population. This trend is even more striking when comparing the evolution of Sao Paulo, with 21.8 percent of the population, with Amazonas, a small state in the north with a meager 1.6 percent of the population. The system has been highly redistributive from the south towards the north and northeast, becoming even more so after the transition to democracy in 1988.

The distribution of funds across states in the FPE was, from the outset, meant to be redistributive. The 1965 law established that 5 percent of the funds would be allocated according to the land surface of each state and 95 percent would be allocated through a formula combining population and the inverse of the per capita income of each state. The formula was not meant to return tax revenue to the region where it was generated. Although the Brazilian formula was not as complex as the formulas used in Mexico and Argentina, it was not a simple combination of population and income criteria. Instead of establishing a weighted sum that would allocate resources according to the inverse of per capita income, weighted by population shares, the formula established factors that were capped at the bottom and the top. This meant that the smallest states (less than 2 percent of the population) would get the same weight and that any state with more than 10 percent of the population would be weighted only five times more than a small state but not more. This was obviously aimed at reducing the share of Sao Paulo. The revenue-sharing system also had a provision that would reserve one-fifth of the funds to be allocated only to the north and northeastern states. This was in addition to the so-called special fund (*Fundo Especial*), composed of 2 percent of the IPI and IR, which would be allocated to those same poorer states.

The 1988 constitutional process established that revenue-sharing formulas would be revised in order to correct the imbalances in the distribution to some of the larger states. However, as noted by Rezende and Afonso (2002), this revision never came about because conflicts of interest among the states were too intense. After 1992, revenue-sharing allocations ended up being determined through negotiations that fixed shares according to historical patterns. This bears a rather striking resemblance to the outcome in Argentina, where the Constitutional Convention also resulted in fixed revenue coefficients once it became impossible for agreements to be reached.

The distribution rules for revenue-sharing funds in Brazil responded to a political imperative similar to the Argentine strategy, initiated by Perón, of using the poorer, more backward provinces to foil the power of the larger states.[10] Since 1942, the southeastern states (Minas Gerais, Sao Paulo, Rio Grande do Sul, and Espiritu Santo) had collected on average 66 percent of the sales tax, whereas the northeastern states collected only 11 percent. This meant that the assignment of the most important taxes to the states reinforced the derivation principle, allowing the richer states to retain the largest share of those resources. The revenue-sharing system was designed in an explicit effort to undo the distributional effects of state tax authority.

In a strategy that is also reminiscent of Perón's, the military governments increased the number of states, ensuring that the rules of representation in the Senate would give the northeast an edge in commanding majorities. As discussed by Stepan (1999), the military regime created Mato Grosso do Sul in 1978 and Rodonia in 1982, and it fused Guanabara and Rio de Janeiro in the south. This coalitional strategy was continued by the constitutional assembly of 1986–1988, which admitted three more states: Tocantins, Roraima, and Amapa. Therefore, by 1990, the block of states from the north, northeast, and center-west, with 43 percent of the population, controlled 74 percent of the seats in the Senate (Stepan, 2000:157).

Federalism constitutes an institutional design in which states should be protected from majorities that might seek to harm individual members. That is the reason that upper chambers, for instance, are usually apportioned according to the principle of equal representation per political unit. As Stepan (2004) has discussed, this feature of federalism is "demos constraining" because it makes a federal regime less likely to meet the "one person, one vote" criterion. However, there is little doubt that in Brazil the malapportionment has worked in the direction of ensuring that the rich states of the south cannot decide national distribution policies.[11] But the fact that states have retained fiscal authority means that there is less room for federal redistribution in Brazil than in the other Latin American federations.

The state-weighted Gini coefficient of revenue-sharing funds in Brazil oscillated between 0.6 and 0.65 during the first 15 years of revenue-sharing, only to become a steady 0.61 since the late 1980s. This means that the

[10] As in Argentina, the military government used the central bank to channel the revenue-sharing funds to states and municipalities created by the 1967 reform (Longo, 1984:66), which suggests that similar credibility problems were also present there.

[11] In spite of the clear imbalance in the rules of territorial representation, Brazil is not the most malapportioned of the Latin American federations: That honor goes to Argentina, in both its lower and upper chambers (see Snyder and Samuels, 2004).

Brazilian distribution was further away from distributing funds to each state in equal lump sums, regardless of their population, than any of the other Latin American federations. The relatively unchanging distribution of revenue-sharing does not measure, of course, the distributional consequences of discretionary federal transfers, the bailouts of state banks, particularly in 1997, and the preservation of indirect taxation controlled by the states.

8.7. Federalism, Fragmentation, and the "Fiscal War"

As noted by Samuels (2003) and Hagopian (1996), the success of local interests in achieving greater decentralization in the constitutional process in 1987–1988 in Brazil can be explained by the fact that even under military rule, Brazilian politics remained highly localist. The constitution, drafted as part of the democratization process, eliminated a set of state excises on communications, fuels, electric power, minerals, and transportation, to be incorporated into a broad-based value-added tax, the ICSM (*Imposto sobre Circulacao de Mercadorias e Servicos*), with rates freely determined by the states (Souza, 1997:39), and eliminated federal exemptions and restrictions on the use of funds by the states (Varsano, 1996:14). The constitution, as discussed previously, also reaffirmed the revenue-sharing system in place.

Souza has argued that the constitutional provisions related to decentralization were meant to legitimize the return to democracy based on mechanisms of popular participation and weakening the old political coalitions supporting the federal government (Souza, 1997:73). In fact, Camargo (1993) argues that the coalitions that were created by the Vargas regime have survived, even without Vargas, until today. In the economic realm, she argues, the Vargas legacy was only abandoned once the modernizing, privatizing, and liberalizing project of Collor de Mello led to a reduction in the size of the state and a model of development based on the internationalization of the Brazilian economy.

The constitutional reforms reflected a compromise in the realm of fiscal authority. The advanced industrialized states won the autonomy to define their tax policies, and the poor states benefited from the increase in revenue-sharing transfers and the elimination of their conditionality (Cazeiro Lopreato, 2002:111). The constitution reversed the provision of the military regime that had given residual tax authority to the federation. Explicit limits were established on the interference of the federal government in the revenue collection of the states. States rather than the Senate would determine the rates of the VAT.[12] Conditionality on federal transfers was eliminated, and restrictions were placed on federal credit. Finally, the federal government would not be able to grant tax exemptions, but the states would be able to use fiscal instruments to provide incentives for economic activity (Cazeiro Lopreato, 2002).

The direct impact of these changes, beyond the greater authority of the states, was that a "fiscal war" emerged in which states tried to use fiscal benefits to attract private investment. As discussed by Rezende and Afonso (2002), the main weapon in this fiscal war was the complexity of the VAT, which allowed states to shift the burden of tax incentives granted to investors toward other states. In the end, the fiscal war backfired in that it ceased to be an instrument for attracting investments, as all the states engaged in it (see Varsano, 1997, and de Oliveira, 2000). Much of the contemporary Brazilian discussion, in a debate that echoes debates in Mexico during the 1920s and 1930s, stresses that state tax authority is inefficient, dangerous, and potentially destabilizing.

Indeed, the last decade of the 20th century in Brazil was characterized by a stark difficulty in forming national political coalitions to support various policy changes because of the peripheralizing tendencies of the political system. Moreover, the financial crisis of 1997 was attributed to a large extent to the imprudent fiscal behavior of the states. As discussed by Bevilaqua (2002), the bailouts to the states in Brazil have not only been the consequence of weak institutional controls to induce subnational fiscal discipline but also of the creation of a reputation on the part of the federal government that it would step in to save states if they went into financial problems (as it did in 1989, 1993, and 1997).

A final issue that democracy brings about is whether the forms of representation will make regional cleavages more or less salient in Brazil in the years to come. Brazilian deputies cultivate the "personal vote," notwithstanding the incentives in the electoral system. A well-established result in the literature on electoral systems, as discussed by Ames (2001), is that in open-list proportional representation, legislators should target their appeals to small slices of the electorate rather than a median voter in territorial jurisdictions. If the Brazilian electoral system was based on single-member districts, as in the United States, there would be great incentives to cultivate the personal vote and appeal to territorial constituencies. Hence, from

---

[12] The Senate would retain authority in establishing rates for interstate sales, minimum rates, and maximum rates in the case of controversies among states.

the point of view of electoral design, Brazilian deputies should not cater to territorially concentrated regional interests.

However, Brazilian legislators remain locally oriented in their appeals because their ambition is channeled through careers in the state level ladder of elective and administrative posts, often controlled by the governors, not in the reelection for a particular single-member district (Samuels, 2003). Municipalities have become aligned with the state rather than the federal interests because they gain resources for patronage from "their" governors, which they can use to further their political ambitions. This is similar to the short-term localist perspectives that characterize Argentine representatives.

Ames has argued that the fragmentation and "excess of veto players" (Ames, 2001:18) in Brazil reinforced the pervasiveness of patronage and pork barrel politics, or what is generally referred to in Latin America as political clientelism. He provides evidence that legislative amendments, which in Brazil signal catering to individual territorial constituencies, improve the chances of electoral success. Although Samuels (2003) dissents from the importance Ames attaches to the use of pork barrel legislation to further individual reelection prospects, he nevertheless provides rather compelling evidence that subnational governments are favored with resources.

The motivation in Samuels's work is not so much credit claiming by individual politicians toward constituents, because he argues that legislators have little control over the execution of federal expenditures, but rather cementing a coalition with governors and other local politicians by bringing more resources to their states. Hence, federal spending patterns, as reflected in legislative amendments, appear to follow the incentives created by a peripheralizing federalism: When legislators seek statewide offices, they target their amendments to increase funding for the states; when they seek municipal ones (i.e., to become mayors), they target pork in a narrow way, toward specific jurisdictions, in the year of the municipal election (Samuels, 2003:154).

In a way, one could argue that this is nothing new in terms of Brazilian historical developments because patronage and clientelism have been prevalent in Brazil at least since the 19th century (Graham, 1990). National priorities in Brazil had to be articulated through a peripheralized system of clientelistic exchanges brokered by regional political elites (Hagopian, 1996; Geddes, 1994). This is not to say that Venezuela, Mexico, or Argentina were not characterized also by clientelism. But the most significant feature of the Brazilian fiscal pact is that throughout the 20th century states retained control over the most important and dynamic sources of revenue: first export duties and later indirect taxation through the sales and value-added taxes. This provided them with the necessary autonomy to deliver patronage financed with their own funds and demand that federal expenditures respond to their local interests (Ames, 2001; Samuels, 2003) to a degree none of the local elites in the other Latin American federations achieved.

The revenue-sharing system was an effort by the military governments to weaken the states and increase centralization. However, this effort largely failed. The federal governments, even under military rule, soon realized that they needed the support of the state elites in order to hold onto power. As the authoritarian regime opened up political spaces in subnational elections, it increasingly devolved resources toward the state and municipal levels. The legacy of the revenue-sharing system in Brazil was therefore not an abdication of tax authority by the states but rather the creation of an additional redistributive system of allocation of funds to states and municipalities besides federal discretionary spending. The allocations within revenue-sharing would not undo the distributional consequences of the fiscal bargain as embodied in state control of the most important source of revenue, the value-added tax. Brazilian federalism is still characterized by the rejection of a centralized fiscal compromise. States have not given up their capacity to tax, nor are they likely to do so in the near future.

9

Conclusion

STATE-BUILDING, POLITICAL
INSTITUTIONS, AND FISCAL
AUTHORITY

This book has studied fiscal centralization and regional bargaining in the context of a century of political development in the Latin American federations. The general argument concerning the dilemma of fiscal centralization is relevant for many developing countries around the world. In this concluding chapter, I discuss the relevance of several insights drawn from the discussion of the Mexican and Latin American cases to substantive discussions in comparative politics. I sometimes make explicit comparisons between the Latin American federations and other developing countries. At other times, I discuss the research design that would be necessary in order to carry out an empirical validation of hypotheses. Finally, some of the issues I deal with belong to the realm of speculation.

I primarily address questions related to state-building and the construction of fiscal authority. This chapter is organized around the significance of the findings to the literature on nation-building, turning then to the political organization of fiscal structures and then to the political economy of federalism and the problems of regional compensation and redistribution.

9.1. Nation-Building

Perhaps the most fundamental issue this book has addressed, through the lens of the construction of national fiscal authority, is the problem of state-building. This topic has received renewed attention in the context of the "failed states" literature (Heldman and Ratner, 1993) and in the reconstruction of political authority in turbulent places such as Iraq and Afghanistan. The literature leans toward emphasizing the international aspects of state-building.[1] In the case of Iraq and Afghanistan, it is somewhat paradoxical that the removal by force of relatively stable, although obviously repressive, political regimes gave way to a process in which the occupying forces have suffered great pains to establish political order. This book provides insights into the domestic determinants of state-building in fragmented polities.

The process of state-building in Latin America during the 19th century was anything but easy. Civil wars, coups, and regional rebellions punctuated the century as the countries' borders stabilized. Only dictators, as personified by various *caudillos*, seemed to be able to bring about stability. But by the 20th century a stable formula had emerged to keep the countries together while retaining some degree of regional independence. The formula involved a large degree of centralization. In this sense, it is not obvious that Latin America is a model of successful federalism. But on the grounds of stability, the Latin American solution for state-building was very successful.

My findings suggest that in Latin America both democratic and authoritarian regimes constructed ruling coalitions by using similar devices to appease regional interests, an insight originally formulated by Ames (1987). Both the Mexican *dictablanda* emerging from the Revolution and the Brazilian *democradura* of the military governments between 1964 and 1988 were remarkably stable political regimes. (The terms *dictablanda* and *democradura* come from a soft (*blanda*) dictatorship or a harsh (*dura*) democracy.) Their stability was based not on force but on the distribution of funds to the regions. Neither of those regimes was as repressive as, for example, the military *juntas* in Argentina or the Venezuelan dictatorships before 1958. Venezuelan democracy after 1958, in spite of its failings at accountability, was also remarkably stable. The Latin American federations suggest that in order to hold power at the center, national governments construct alliances and coalitions cooperating with regional powerholders. This logic also holds in Argentina, although more as an aspiration than a reality: The regimes in that country have been much less successful than the other Latin American federations in bringing about political stability, but the governance strategies they pursued were similar. In all cases, regional political

---

[1] For example, the Rand report on state-building concentrates on the role of an external military presence and the effects of financial assistance in the process of creating a stable political authority (Dobbins et al., 2003).

forces were not repressed but channeled into institutional forms of political contestation.

Elections at the local and state levels can therefore play a crucial role in federal systems by providing a mechanism through which competition for local office can be structured without threatening national leaders. Neither the military in Brazil nor the PRI in Mexico eliminated elections at that local level because those contests conveyed important information about citizens' dissatisfaction with the regime, allowed local elites to compete within clearly established institutional channels, and selected out the leaders with whom the center would bargain to construct a national coalition.[2] Venezuela was different in that gubernatorial elections were suspended after 1958. The return to local representation was not associated with a better articulation of political agreements but led instead to the breakdown of a hitherto stable political arrangement.

The effectiveness of federal mechanisms for coalition formation exhibited in Latin America did not necessarily involve democracy at the national level, as the Brazilian authoritarian interlude and the Mexican hegemonic party rule suggest. But it did involve the articulation of regional interests through political organizations, namely political parties, which structured political ambition. This allowed a regional structure parallel to the federal one, making local politicians queue for their turn in political terms rather than use the threat of force against the center. The key role political parties play in bringing about what Huntington (1968) calls "institutionalization," and therefore political stability, applies to the Latin American fiscal bargains.

National levels of government in Latin America have been more powerful than any individual constituent region (perhaps with the exception of Sao Paulo in the early half of the 20th century), but it would have been impossible for any of the federal presidents in Latin America, even charismatic leaders such as Cárdenas, Perón, or Vargas, to govern without the support (sometimes tacit but often explicit) of the regional leaders. This is true even of Venezuela, the most centralized of the Latin American federations, where regional leaders of the competing parties were selected to lead the state governments according to their regional strength, even though

---

[2] This does not mean all Latin American regimes followed the same path in this respect. In Argentina, the articulation between national and provincial interests was more complex, and elections were often interrupted by authoritarian interludes, but it involved, as in Brazil and Mexico, the creation of provincial-level links between politicians and voters as an essential feature in the political system.

a president from a given party could theoretically have chosen to appoint only members of his party to head the regional governments.

The Latin American formula for regional coalition formation involved appeasing the most important regional powers but also using the more backward regions as a means of counterbalancing the strength of the richer states and provinces. That "redistributive" coalition was only possible once national governments could create stable systems that guaranteed the flow of financial and fiscal resources. To the extent that transfer systems involved a credible commitment from the federal government, local elites were willing to cooperate with the federal government rather than compete against it: Their political survival was enhanced, rather than threatened, by the stability brought about by the federal government. They could use the funds provided by the transfer systems to finance their extensive patronage networks, and in the case of Brazil they retained the authority to tax in order to pursue their political ambitions locally.

Hence, the fiscal evolution of the Latin American federations suggests that the creation of a system of financial flows between the center and the periphery is an important condition for the consolidation of political authority. Politicians must solve what I have called "the fundamental dilemma of fiscal centralization": There will always be temptations for the center to behave opportunistically and renege on its transfer promises. A democratic state is the greatest guarantee for commitment to a system of intergovernmental transfers. But absent democracy, the Latin American federations suggest that political systems characterized by an accountability deficit can create some degree of credibility to the extent that local politicians have links through political parties that allow them to trust the center.[3]

In the fragmented polity of Afghanistan, Rubin (2002) notes that financial reconstruction and the creation of a fiscal system were key aspects of the consolidation of national power by the Taliban. Once the center provided

---

[3] The reason that the Mexican and the Venezuelan political pacts enticed trust from state politicians toward the federal government was because of the existence of national political parties that structured progressive political ambition. In Brazil, national parties were not the prime mechanism through which politicians could enforce federal compliance. Therefore, governors retained decentralized fiscal authority. But the political parties were useful labels that aligned various regional coalitions, with governors playing the key role in them. In Argentina, the succession of regimes and the "impossible game" during the proscription of the *Peronistas* led to the eventual collapse of the revenue-sharing arrangement: Regional politicians could not trust the federal government to abide by its promises.

the valuable public good of a stable currency and a system of payment, it was possible to reestablish trade (to the benefit of opium traders) and taxation (to the benefit of regional and national politicians). In fact, the historical precedent of the creation of Afghanistan as a political entity under British control in 1880 was founded on putting in place a centralized system of tax collection (Malikyar and Rubin, 2002: 6). Malikyar and Rubin (2002) suggest that the contemporary challenges in the construction of political authority in Afghanistan are not unlike these precedents: Arguably, the connection between political authority and the control of financial flows is the most prominent problem for center–periphery relationships in that country.

An insightful observation on the critical nature of this relationship is provided by a deputy governor of Qandahar: "Financial dependence attaches offices in the periphery to the center. Because financial needs of provincial offices are not met by the center, orders are naturally taken from the source that provides resources, i.e. the governor" (quoted in Malikyar and Rubin, 2002:43). This resonates with the historical debates on centralization in Argentina and Mexico and with contemporary debates on decentralization throughout Latin America.

The problems of state-building in Afghanistan and the creation of centralized fiscal authority in Latin America – the product of specific conditions and circumstances – can be linked to the historical process of consolidation of power by the European nation-states. Charles Tilly, with his famous dictum "wars make states," has clarified the profound link between territorial control, revenue extraction, and military might (Tilly, 1990). To the extent that an organization is able to collect revenue in order to exert force within a given territory, one can say that a "state" is in place. Moreover, Tilly suggests a crucial link between the centralization of authority and political representation:

As rulers bargained directly with their subject populations for massive taxes, military service, and cooperation in state programs, most states took further steps of profound importance: a movement towards direct rule that reduced the role of local or regional patrons and places representatives of the national state in every community, and expansion of popular consultation in the form of elections, plebiscites, and legislatures. (Tilly, 1990:63)

This is consonant with Bates's (2004) account of how militarized lineages allied with the cities in order to achieve a "taming of violence" and the emergence of the modern state. Tilly's and Bates's formulations of

236

Conclusion

state-building depart in an important way from the early formulations in the nation-building literature associated with Karl Deutsch, T. N. Eisenstadt, and most prominently Stein Rokkan.[4] In Tilly's account and Bates's discussion of state-building in Africa, outcomes are contingent and not driven by a linear modernization process. The old vintage nation-building literature assumed all too often that modernization processes were meant to bring about the establishment of rationalized bureaucracies, the reduction of ethnic divisions, and the attenuation of peripheral tensions as part of a "development syndrome" (Coleman, 1971). This literature was probably too influenced by a postwar optimism that suggested that developing countries would easily follow the path laid out by European nations.

The study of Latin American federations through the lens of fiscal authority suggests the degree to which the emergence of strong centralized states is actually rather contingent and is related not just to the external threats of war, as Tilly and Bates suggest, but also the internal military threats of units within the political unit. It is all too easy to assume that the process of centralization was simply an accompanying characteristic of the development strategy of import substitution industrialization (ISI) or a cultural feature attributable to colonial heritage.

The long Latin American experience suggests that the articulation of political interests between center and periphery in the process of state-building can experience reversals in which regions on the periphery can reassert control over their tax authority, placing limits on the holders of national power. Peripheral regions do benefit from transfer systems to the extent that they are established as tools for redistribution, but the centralized fiscal bargain is contingent on specific political conditions and not a "natural" result of the modernization process. The Latin American development process suggests that although events such as the Great Depression of 1929 affect all countries, the responses to international forces varied according to the political conditions prevailing in each country.[5]

More generally, my study of fiscal centralization suggests that, in principle, there is no direct link between modernization and fiscal centralization; nor is there a necessary link between the external conditions and the

---

[4] The literature is quite extensive. See, in particular, Rokkan et al. (1999), the Festschrift for Rokkan edited by Torsvik (1981), the essays in Eisenstadt and Rokkan (1973), and the seminal work by Deutsch (1961).

[5] Dependency theory saw in those international events a developmental dead end that would doom countries to centralization, poverty, authoritarianism, and social exclusion (Evans, 1979).

path taken by the process of fiscal centralization. Some countries become richer and more democratic, and their populations become more literate, healthier, and better nourished – in a word, more developed – while fiscal authority may remain decentralized.[6] External conditions can provide common shocks, but centralization is primarily driven by domestic processes that vary in each country, and those domestic processes, not international forces, determine the degree of redistribution, democratic accountability, or social inclusion in the polity.[7]

It is clear that fiscal institutions were crafted to further political goals, and in that sense, they are endogenous. In the context of state formation in West Africa, Catherine Boone (2003) has noted that national institutions are endogenous products of the interaction between local elites, whose strength and bargaining possibilities are determined by agrarian structures, and national leaders seeking a developmentalist national project. In Boone's framework, variations of state centralization, or what she more appropriately calls the "political topographies" of the state, are the consequence of power-sharing compromises between various political actors. Boone provides a description of potential outcomes in the construction of political authority, and my commitment model highlights the strategic choices and off-the-equilibrium-path threats that sustain those outcomes.

My framework suggests more precisely the nature of the problem between local and national politicians: Commitment problems cannot be solved unless the fates of politicians are articulated through political organizations, most notably parties. The commitment model developed in this book and analyzed in the Latin American federations is consistent with Boone's (2003) mapping of political outcomes in West Africa. What Boone (2003) calls the "power sharing" strategy is equivalent to a successful transfer system in the fiscal centralization game, whereas "non-incorporation" corresponds to the situation where local elites reject a transfer, keeping control of their tax authority. Her "usurpation" and "administrative occupation"

---

[6] In the best study of the process of Mexican state-building in the 20th century, Wayne Cornelius (1973) noted that the construction of political authority during the Cárdenas years was related to the skill with which he brokered political deals with regional elites and created new political resources through the establishment of corporatist organizations. The modernization process was a consequence of the stable political pact rather than the reverse.

[7] In Diaz-Cayeros (2004), I provide some tentative evidence suggesting that centralization around the world is primarily driven by a convergence effect. Institutional features such as democracy and federalism can slow down that convergence, however, allowing local political actors to retain fiscal authority.

outcomes are related to the strategies where the center attempts to impose unitarism.

The main difference between my game of fiscal centralization and Boone's theory, however, is that her theoretical framework implicitly *assumes* that local politicians cannot resist the center and hence her notion of usurpation. In my account, the threat of local politicians resisting unitarian solutions is precisely what forces the center to seek a centralized federal compromise. In the context of West African villages, Boone is clearly right in assuming that deconcentrated village institutions cannot successfully fight the center. But in the Latin American federal context, states did have the possibility of resisting usurpation, which in my account is the threat that sustains the federal compromise equilibrium.

Boone's theory of endogenous institutional creation provides a solution to the general problem of "broadcasting power," which Jeffrey Herbst (2000) has pointed out as a critical failure of the African states. Herbst has proposed that African states developed very differently from Tilly's (1990) account of European state formation because of the low population density, the nature of the political boundaries between states, and the international environment faced by African state-builders.[8] In Herbst's account, geographical factors cannot easily change, which makes the task of state-building rather daunting.

Comparisons between Africa and Latin America would be very useful for understanding the nature of centralized political authority. Although in Latin America population densities are more similar to those of Europe than of Africa, national leaders in the vast federal countries did find "African" problems of how to extend their power beyond the limits of the capital city and its surrounding area. On the other hand, although Latin America's international conditions were more similar to those of Africa than of Europe, the "European" problem of facing challengers to national power from within was a central aspect of state-building.

It turns out that the Latin American solution for centralizing authority was different from the European account by Tilly (1990) or the African failures documented by Herbst (2000). It hinged on articulating bargains with the local powerholders, respecting their autonomy, while at the same time redistributing resources toward the sparsely populated and backward

---

[8] Boone's (2003) work provides grounds for more optimism than that of Herbst (2000), suggesting that when village-level organizations can be articulated into the national arena, it is possible for central states to successfully bring about political stability.

regions. That is, Latin American federal governments governed by centralizing tax authority, allowing already rich regions to become richer while transferring resources to the periphery in order to buy off the support of local elites. This coalition was made possible through the creation of national party systems that would structure political ambitions.

9.2. Fiscal Politics and Tax Structure

State formation is intrinsically linked to the capacity of the state to collect taxes. Tilly (1990) and Bates (2004) have argued that the survival of nations in the interstate system provoked their fiscal imperatives. Those imperatives, the argument goes, led to the creation of more competent states and bargains in which rulers gave up discretion and the arbitrary use of power, giving way to representation. The goal of rulers was to be more powerful and survive in the international arena. If this argument is correct, then the central challenge in the state-building literature is to understand what allows a country to collect taxes effectively. Whereas in Bates (2004) and Tilly (1990) tax collection is primarily geared toward paying for wars against external enemies, in my account the problem of tax collection is related primarily to the struggle over tax bases that are originally controlled by constituent jurisdictions that can mount challenges to the powerholders at the central level.

The simple hypothesis stating that tax collection is related to state strength becomes a complex issue once the intricacies of multitiered government are taken into account. Tax collection (or expenditures) by the central government divided by the value of production, as reflected by GDP, is the most common approach to measuring the size of the state. Presumably, larger states also reflect more competent states. Although all authors who use central government expenditures or revenues to assess the size of the state acknowledge that this is an imperfect measure, it becomes clear from the study of the evolution of the Latin American federations that looking at central government taxation is seriously misconceived if one seeks to understand politics through the fiscal lens.[9]

[9] Persson and Tabellini (2003) find that government is larger in countries with a greater share of the population over 65, when the economy is more open to international trade, and when the government exports oil. They also report that central governments in federal countries as a percentage of their GDP account for around 5 percentage points less than unitary ones.

240

Conclusion

Venezuelan fiscal evolution can be understood well by looking only at the finances of the central government (and, of course, the oil sector), but the same cannot be said about the Brazilian, Argentine, or Mexican fiscal histories. There is no direct correlation between centralization and the size of the central government; there is no relationship between tax collection, the generosity of intergovernmental transfers, and the assignment of expenditures to each level of government; and the historical study of the cases suggests that the ratio of federal to state fiscal burdens can vary widely over time. At the very least, a problem with the generalized use of national data for cross-sectional analysis of state size without considering the subnational sphere is that one might wrongly conclude that small governments have some virtues when this might be the consequence of smaller central governments in federal countries so that causes would in fact be related to decentralization, not government size.

A related issue is that too much attention in the scholarly literature is devoted to the question of the size of government.[10] Fukuyama (2004) has noted that competence in collecting taxes should be kept distinct from discussions concerning the size of the state. Whereas the former relates to the capacity of bureaucracies and central governments to mobilize resources for national goals, the latter refers to the scope of state activity. This book has implicitly considered the effects of the size of the state, but from a vantage point of federal arrangements and the centralized structure of tax systems, which are at the core of the question of state competence. In federal countries, state activity involves several tiers of government, and the mobilization of fiscal resources is made in the pursuit of state or provincial goals, which might be quite distinct from the federal ones. Hence, in federal systems the question of the size of the state becomes multidimensional because the conclusions one might draw about the effects of federal government size might be different from those related to state or municipal governments.

An important research agenda that the discussion of Latin American federal tax authority opens up is related to the choice of tax structures. The institutional innovation of the income tax at the end of the 19th century and its progressive adoption in the 20th century increasingly allowed central governments to rely less on customs and other sources of taxation related to international trade and the taxation of commodities. But the story of fiscal centralization also suggests that a parallel phenomenon was related

---

[10] See Boix (2003), Mueller (2003), and Persson and Tabellini (2003).

to the control by national governments of indirect taxation, which had previously been mostly controlled by local fiscal authorities.[11] In particular, the emergence of value-added taxes in OECD countries during the second half of the 20th century is as important as the income tax in providing an explanation for the growth of government and the generosity of the welfare state (see Kato, 2003).[12]

To the extent that national governments were able to control the most important sources of revenue, this enabled them to engage in regional redistribution and seek to industrialize through a growing participation in the economy by the federal government. If national governments had windfall rents available, as in the case of oil revenue in Mexico after the 1970s and Venezuela throughout most of the 20th century, it was even easier to achieve fiscal centralization because regions wanted to have a share of those resources, which were extracted directly by the federal government.

Since the work of Sven Steinmo (1993), there has been an increasing interest in comparative politics in understanding the "path dependent" processes through which tax structures are established.[13] Most of the recent work on the politics of taxation attempts to understand political interests and preferences as endogenous variables jointly determined with the formation of fiscal institutions. The analysis in this book suggests that fiscal outcomes do not become established simply by fixing a statutory rate in revenue-sharing institutions. The central problem is the endogenous compliance with fiscal institutions. Fiscal institutions are a locus of contention for national and local politicians in which abiding with the agreements is the central problem of fiscal centralization. To paraphrase Weingast (1995), if the center is powerful enough to concentrate tax authority and transfer resources to the states, it can use that power to *not* transfer those resources. Although my evidence does not suggest that state or provincial governments undergo a change in their preferences in the acceptance of centralized fiscal bargains (because they still prefer to control as much of the financial

---

[11] It is conceivable that the same variables that explain the degree of centralization in the fiscal arrangement can also account for variations in the structure of tax systems.

[12] Tariff policies in Latin America are usually seen as purposeful strategies aimed at building an import substitution industrialization development project, but it is also possible that they were an unintended consequence of the process of fiscal centralization.

[13] Schumpeter's original insight that the study of the state can be most effective when looking into its finances and tax structure is no longer a neglected possibility of research but has spurred a vibrant research agenda; see, for example, Swank and Steinmo (2002); Timmons (2004); and Lieberman (2003).

Conclusion

resources as possible), they do engage in a cooperative interaction with the federal government when the party system effectively articulates their interests and federal promises of transfers are complied with.

9.3. Federalism, Decentralization, and Redistribution

A great deal of interest has concentrated in the last few years on understanding the processes that have led to fiscal decentralization around the world (Manor, 2000). The wave of decentralization has been associated with a process of democratization to the extent that, particularly in Latin America, local-level government officials have become more important (Nickson, 1995). This prominence of local political actors has been expressed not only in their capacity to muster more resources to provide public goods but also in their representation qualities: In contrast to just a few years ago, most local officials in Latin America are now directly elected.[14]

However, before witnessing decentralization, Latin American federations went through a process of political centralization, as this book has shown. Garman, Haggard, and Willis (2001) believe that decentralization in Latin America is primarily a response to democratization pressures in which the control of nominations in political parties plays a central role: The extent of decentralization depends on the extent to which nominations are controlled locally. This argument would imply that the process of centralization that preceded decentralization would also be driven by changes in the party system. That is, centralization should have proceeded more fully to the extent that control over party nominations, induced either by electoral rules or changes in the nationalization of the party systems, was centralized in party leaderships.

But the relationship could have the opposite cause. Chhibber and Kollman (2004) have analyzed the formation of party systems in three federations – India, Canada, and the Unites States – and the relatively decentralized unitary system of the United Kingdom. Fiscal centralization is established as a crucial variable that determines party system nationalization, although the authors are careful to say that it is possible that some endogeneity problem exists. In this book, I have argued that tax centralization and the subsequent creation of transfer systems from the federal to the state level are contingent on whether politicians can establish some

[14] For a nuanced view of the conditions under which democratization might be connected to decentralization in Latin America, see Eaton (2004).

insulation for local elites from local electoral threats. The nationalization of party systems provides precisely that kind of insulation because local politicians can attenuate local risks through a hedging effect generated by national electoral processes. In my view, this process precedes the concentration of tax authority in federal hands and lends credibility to the transfer bargain through which local elites are assured resources.

This idea is directly linked to the original insight by Riker (1964) suggesting that the degree of centralization in a federal regime, and in general the workings of federalism, depend on the configuration of the party system. This insight has been recast in a more contemporary light by Filippov, Ordeshook, and Shvetsova (2004). In their view, the stability of federal arrangements depends on three levels of institutions. The first level is made up of the constitutional provisions that limit the scope of action of the partners in the federation. The second level involves institutions that structure the state, such as presidentialism and bicameralism. The third level belongs to the realm of party integration. In the view of Filippov, Ordeshook, and Shvetsova (2004), given that federalism is an $N + 1$ bargaining game, where outcomes are not predetermined because any institutional setup can produce any potential outcome, enforcement of the federal bargain works by making mechanisms of the lower levels produce self-enforcing political equilibria that allow political actors to respect the rules of levels one and two (see their schematic summary; Filippov, Ordeshook, and Shvetsova, 2004:294).

My own account of federalism in Latin America is concentrated on their level-two institutions, but my emphasis is on fiscal institutions, not political ones. I do not devote much attention to the role of the Senate, presidentialism, or electoral rules because I take them as given. The agenda of endogenizing the choice of those institutions far exceeds the scope of this book. But another reason to focus on fiscal institutions is that I am not so concerned with the stability of the federal pact per se but rather with the nature of centralized fiscal agreements and the problem of compliance. In that sense, my work is mostly concerned with the possibility that the central government subverts federalism by behaving opportunistically in the transfer systems than with whether the parts of the federal arrangement make efforts to bring down the federal pact.

This difference in emphasis explains why in Filippov, Ordeshook, and Shvetsova (2004) practically all the references to developing-country federations are related to India and Russia, whereas my own work is about the Latin American federations. In the Russian case in particular, Solnick (2002) has persuasively argued that the central problem of fiscal federalism is that republics and other regions have been able to obtain bilateral agreements with the federal government instead of there being a uniform federal policy. This bilateralism has resulted in a greater capacity for regions to blackmail the federal government into transferring increasing funds on the threat of making the federal arrangement as a whole unravel (Treisman, 1999). The central concern with the dissolution of the political entity in Russia is not the core risk that political actors perceive in Latin America.

However, the Latin American experience might shed some light on when it might be possible for fiscal federalism to "buy" the support of would-be secessionist regions. All the Latin American federalisms are characterized by a high degree of asymmetry, so the sheer fact that some regions are more powerful than others is not what explains the instability of federalisms in other developing countries as compared with those of Latin America. Latin American countries always had regions that were expensive to buy off. What seems to be crucial in the federal experience of Latin America is the construction of the redistributive coalition in which both powerful states have been appeased while poorer regions have become allies of the center in supporting its hold on power.

An important result in the formal models of federalism that have been developed in the last few years is that compliance with a transfer system cannot simply be bought with money. As discussed by Alesina and Spolaore, a transfer system cannot induce compliance of the constituent units of a political entity simply by increasing the resources available so long as borders are flexible and the possibility of secession is present (Alesina and Spolaore, 2003:67). This same kind of result emerges from a simple prisoner's dilemma game presented by Filippov, Ordeshook, and Shvetsova (2004), in which cooperation does not emerge from increasing the size of transfers. In short, the technological advantages of centralized taxation or any other efficiency advantages that federalism might have over unitarism or completely fragmented forms of governance cannot explain why federal systems can stay in place.

The analysis of the Latin American experiences suggests that cooperation came from the articulation of political careers and other structures of political mediation in which governors and other local political actors found it to their advantage to comply with the federal arrangement. In none of the countries were regional grievances strong enough to motivate the type of secessionist efforts observed, for example, in Chechnya. It is possible, however, that 19th-century Latin America did have some parallel with the types of problems of most concern to Filippov, Ordeshook, and Shvetsova (2004) and that among the developing countries are most pertinent in countries such as Nigeria, Russia, or India. Hence, an integration of two research agendas, the one concerned with federal stability and the other with centralization, could fruitfully explore the 19th century in Latin America in order to understand processes that are in urgent need of illumination in our contemporary world.

This takes me back to the question of state-building. A core concern of the nation-building literature has been to understand the way in which different countries have dealt with their peripheries.[15] The study of Latin America might suggest some hypotheses linking the centralization of fiscal authority and democracy with regional redistribution.

Regional politicians in Argentina, Brazil, and Mexico sought to devise a credible commitment in their transfer systems and to agree on a distribution of the gains from cooperation, but the specific solutions provided by each country differed. Venezuela all but eliminated federalism by making governors bureaucrats appointed by the center and established a simple and very stable proportional rule for the distribution of funds; Argentina tinkered with its transfer system every time there was political upheaval, and outcomes were dictated more by political compromises than institutional agreements in which redistribution toward the interior cemented the ruling coalition; Brazilian state elites never trusted the center and were powerful enough to resist the centralization attempted by the military rulers, limiting the scope for redistribution; and Mexico shifted from a system where no commitment could be established, to one where the fiscal compromise involved little redistribution, and then to a highly centralized arrangement in which greater redistribution is foreseeable in the future.

But in all the systems a central question that politicians confronted, and that I have not dealt with directly, is the relationship among federalism, inequality, and redistribution. Beramendi (2003) has clarified that the relationship between inequality and redistribution in federal arrangements is an endogenous one. It is not possible simply to posit that inequality is related to more or less decentralization because in Beramendi's view this depends on the interaction with regional risks and the way in which politicians bargain to construct political institutions. In principle, he has shown that it is possible for institutions to be devised in such a way that any distributive outcome can be generated by varying the degree of decentralization.

[15] See Rokkan and Urwin (1983).

246

Conclusion

Beramendi's (2003) analysis of Germany after the unification suggests, for example, that by allowing the Länder to control nine additional percentage points of the value-added tax, the ranking of inequality among the German regions was preserved instead of achieving a greater redistribution. This same type of mechanism operates in Brazil in the sense that, as I have shown, redistribution is far less pervasive than the sole focus on transfers would suggest. Because states control the most important source of revenue, they are also able to keep inequality in place by reducing the scope of redistribution.

Beramendi (2003) also suggests that this type of mechanism, in which local elites use federalism as a way to ensure that higher decentralization prevents redistribution, is the mechanism that explains the responses of the United States to the Great Depression and its failure to create a universal system of unemployment insurance. The South used federalism to protect its labor market structure and hence did not allow the federal government to play a greater role in the redistribution of incomes and risks among wage earners. In this respect, it is worth quoting Riker's discussion of the link between freedom and federalism in the context of the U.S. South:

> To one who believes in the majoritarian notion of freedom, it is impossible to interpret federalism as other than a device for minority tyranny. At the present time in the United States (i.e. from roughly 1954 to that future time, if it ever comes, when most Negroes have full citizen rights) the chief question of public morals is whether or not the national decision [of civil rights] will be enforced. To those who wish to enforce it, the plea for states' rights or for maintaining the guarantees of federalism is simply a hypocritical plea for the special privilege to disregard the national majority, and of course, to permit one minority, segregationist Southern whites, to tyrannize another minority, the Southern Negroes. (Riker, 1964:142)

If one connects this insight with the fact that Latin American countries are some of the most unequal societies in the world, and that in spite of social revolutions, land reform, the construction of partial welfare states, redistributive transfers to the poor regions, and (sometimes) economic growth the differences between rich and poor in the Latin American federations remain abysmal, one cannot help but consider the possibility that the solutions each country has found to the dilemma of centralized fiscal federal bargains have played a key role in the reproduction of this inequality.

The hope in Latin America, as in other places in the world, is that democratization and the strengthening of governments that are closer to citizens, and hence more likely to provide for their needs, will produce a new era of economic growth, accountability, and social progress. Our understanding of the political economy of regionalism is still relatively limited. But in spite of our great ignorance, it is my firm conviction that we can learn from the study of fiscal authority to produce better governments and thus more acceptable outcomes for the vast majority of poor citizens who populate the developing world.

References

Abrucio, Fernando Luiz. 1998. *Os baroes da federacao*. Sao Paulo: Editora Hucitec.

Acemoglu, Daron, and James A. Robinson. 2001. "A Theory of Political Transitions." *American Economic Review* 91:938–963.

Acevedo Monroy, José Alberto. 1997. "Economía política de la asignación territorial del gasto público en México, 1990–1995." Tesis de licenciatura de Economía y Ciencia Política, México: ITAM.

Administratión Federal de Ingresos Públicos (AFIP). 1999. *Estadísticas tributarias año 1999*. Buenos Aires: AFIP.

Aguilar Villanueva, Luis F. 1996. "El federalismo Mexicano: Funcionamiento y tareas pendientes." In *¿Hacia un nuevo federalismo?*, edited by A. Hernández Chavez, pp. 109–152. México: Fondo de Cultura Económica.

Aldrich, John. 1995. *Why Parties? The Origin and Transformation of Party Politics in America*. Chicago: University of Chicago Press.

Alesina, Alberto, Enrico Spolaore, and Romain Wacziarg. 2001. "Economic Integration and Political Disintegration." *American Economic Review* 90:1276–1296.

Alesina, Alberto, and Enrico Spolaore. 2003. *The Size of Nations*. Cambridge, MA: MIT Press.

Alvarado Mendoza, Arturo. 1992. *El portesgilismo en Tamaulipas: Estudio sobre la constitución de la autoridad pública en el México postrevolucionario*. México: El Colegio de México.

Ames, Barry. 1987. *Political Survival: Politicians and Public Policy in Latin America*. Berkeley: University of California Press.

Ames, Barry. 2001. *The Deadlock of Democracy in Brazil*. Ann Arbor: University of Michigan Press.

Anderson, Roger Charles. 1971. "The Functional Role of Governors and Their States in the Political Development of México, 1940–1964." Unpublished Ph.D. Dissertation, University of Wisconsin-Madison.

Anuario estadístico de la República Argentina (various years). Buenos Aires: Instituto Nacional de Estadística y Censos.

Arellano Cadena, Rogelio. 1996. "Nuevas alternativas a la descentralización fiscal en México." In ¿Hacia un nuevo federalismo?, edited by A. Hernández Chavez, pp. 203–224. México: Fondo de Cultura Económica.

Baloyra, Enrique, and John D. Martz. 1979. *Political Attitudes in Venezuela*. Austin: University of Texas Press.

Banco Central de Venezuela. 1942. *Memoria correspondiente al ejercicio anual*. Caracas: Litografia del Comercio.

Banco Central de Venezuela. 1978. *La economia Venezolana en los ultimos treinta y cinco anos*. Caracas: BCV.

Barrios Ross, Armando. 1998. "Las finanzas públicas de los estados en Venezuela." In *Descentralizacion en perspectiva*, edited by R. de la Cruz. Caracas: Ediciones IESA.

Bates, Robert. 1981. *Markets and States in Tropical Africa*. Berkeley: University of California Press.

Bates, Robert, Avner Greif, Margaret Levi, and Jean-Laurent Rosenthal. 1998. *Analytic Narratives*. Princeton, NJ: Princeton University Press.

Bates, Robert H. 2004. *Prosperity and Violence*. London: W.W. Norton.

Bates, Robert H., and Da-Hsiang Donald Lien. 1985. "A Note on Taxation, Development and Representative Government." *Politics and Society* 14(1):53–70.

Bednar. 2000. "Formal Theory and Federalism." *APSA Comparative Politics Newsletter* (Winter) 11(1):19–22.

Benjamin, Thomas. 1990. "Laboratories of the New State, 1920–1929: Regional Social Reform and Experiments in Mass Politics." In *Provinces of the Revolution: Essays on Mexican Regional History, 1910–1929*, edited by T. Benjamin and M. Wasserman, pp. 71–92. Albuquerque: University of New México Press.

Benson, Nettie Lee. 1954. *La diputación provincial y el federalismo Mexicano*. México: El Colegio de México.

Beramendi, Pablo. 2003. *Decentralization and Income Inequality*. Madrid: Centro de Estudios Avanzados en Ciencias Sociales, Instituto Juan March.

Betancourt, Rómulo. 1940. *Venezuela: Política y petróleo*. Bogotá: Editorial Senderos.

Beteta, Ramón. 1935. *Economic and Social Program of México (a Controversy)*. México. (Papers presented at the Latin American round table at the Institute of Public Affairs at the University of Virginia, July 1935).

Beteta, Ramón. 1951. *Tres años de política hacendaria, 1947–1948–1949: Perspectiva y acción*. México: Secretaría de Hacienda y Crédito Público.

Bevilaqua, Afonso Sant'anna. 2002. "State Government Bailouts in Brazil." *Research Network Working Paper* R-441. Washington: Interamerican Development Bank.

Blanco, Eugenio A. 1956. *La politica presupuestaria, la deuda publica y la economia nacional*. Buenos Aires: Ministerio de Hacienda de la Nacion.

Blanco Cossio, Fernando Andres. 1998. *Disparidades economicas inter-regionais, capacidade de obtencao de recursos tributarios, esforco fiscal e gasto publico no federalismo Brasileiro*. Rio de Janeiro: BNDES.

Blankart, Charles. 2001. "Popitz's Law, Bryce's Law and Government Centralization in Prussia and in Germany." *Journal of Public Finance and Public Choice* 19:71–94.

References

Boix, Carles. 2003. *Democracy and Redistribution*. Cambridge: Cambridge University Press.

Bolton, Patrick, and Gérard Roland. 1997. "The Breakup of Nations: A political economy analysis." *Quarterly Journal of Economics* 112:1057–1090.

Boone, Catherine. 2003. *Political Topographies of the African State*. Cambridge: Cambridge University Press.

Brams, Steven, and A. Taylor. 1996. *Fair Division: Procedures for Allocating Divisible and Indivisible Goods*. Cambridge: Cambridge University Press.

Brandenburg, Frank. 1955. "México: An Experiment in One-Party Democracy." Dissertation, University of Pennsylvania.

Brandenburg, Frank. 1964. *The Making of Modern México*. Englewood Cliffs, NJ: Prentice-Hall.

Burgess, Robin, and Nicholas Stern. 1993. "Taxation and Development." *Journal of Economic Literature* 31:762–830.

Buve, Raymond Th. J. 1990. "Tlaxcala: Consolidating a Cacicazgo." In *Provinces of the Revolution: Essays on Mexican Regional History, 1910–1929*, edited by T. Benjamin and M. Wasserman, pp. 237–272. Albuquerque: University of New México Press.

Calvo, Ernesto, and Juan Manuel Abal Medina. 2001. *El federalismo electoral Argentino*. Buenos Aires: INAP.

Camara dos Deputados, Brasil. 1914. *Impostos interestaduales, 1900–11*. Paris: Typographia Aillaud, Alves & Cia.

Camargo, Aspasia. 1993. "La federación sometida: Nacionalismo desarrollista e inestabilidad democrática." In *Federalismos Latinoamericanos: México/Brasil/Argentina*, edited by M. Carmagnani, pp. 300–362. México: Fondo de Cultura Economica.

Camp, Roderic A. 1974. "Mexican Governors since Cárdenas: Education and Career Contacts." *Journal of Inter-American Studies and World Affairs* 16 (November): 454–481.

Camp, Roderic A. 1977. "Losers in Mexican Politics: A Comparative Study of Official Party Precandidates for Gubernatorial elections, 1970–75." In *Quantitative Latin American Studies: Methods and Findings*, edited by James Wilkie and Kenneth Fuddle. *Statistical Abstract of Latin America Supplement Series*, Vol. 6:23–33, Los Angeles: UCLA Latin American Center.

Camp, Roderic A. 1984. *The Making of a Government: Political Leaders in Modern México*. Tucson: University of Arizona Press.

Camp, Roderic A. 1990. "México." In *Handbook of Political Science Research on Latin America: Trends from the 1960s to the 1990s*, edited by D. Dent. New York: Greenwood Press.

Camp, Roderic A. 1995. *Political Recruitment across Two Centuries: México, 1884–1991*. Austin: University of Texas Press.

Camp, Roderic A. 1996. *Mexican Political Biographies, 1935–1991*. Tucson: The University of Arizona Press.

Campuzano Montoya, Irma. 1995. *Baja California en tiempos del PAN*. México: La Jornada.

Caravaglia, Juan Carlos, and Juan Carlos Grosso. 1987. *Las alcabalas novohispanas (1776–1821)*. México: Archivo General de la Nación.

Careaga, Maite, and Barry Weingast. 2003. "Fiscal Federalism, Good Governance, and Economic Growth in México." In *In Search of Prosperity*, edited by D. Rodrik, pp. 399–435. Princeton, NJ: Princeton University Press.

Carmagnani, Marcello. 1993. *Federalismos Latinoamericanos: México/Brasil/Argentina*. México: El Colegio de México.

Carrillo Batalla, Tomas Enrique. 1968. *Political fiscal*. Caracas: Ediciones del Concejo Municipal del Distrito Federal.

Carrillo Batalla, Tomas Enrique. 1987. *La reforma del sistema fiscal Venezolano*. Caracas: República de Venezuela, Comisión de Estudio y Reforma Fiscal.

Cazeiro Lopreato, Francisco Luiz. 2002. *O colapso das finanças estaduais e a crise da federacao*. Sao Paulo: UNESP.

Cerruti, Mario. 1993. *México en los años 20: Procesos políticos y reconstrucción económica*. San Nicolás de los Garza: Universidad Autónoma de Nuevo León.

Cetrángolo, Oscar, and Juan Pablo Jiménez. 1998. "Reflexiones sobre el federalismo fiscal en Argentina." *Desarrollo Económico, Revista de Ciencias Sociales* 38:293–327.

Chapoy Bonifaz, Beatriz Dolores. 1992. *Finanzas nacionales y finanzas estatales*. México: UNAM.

Cheibub, Jose Antonio. 1988. "Political Regimes and the Extractive Capacity of Governments: Taxation in Democracies and Dictatorships." *World Politics* 50:349–376.

Chhibber, Pradeep, and Ken Kollman. 2004. *The Formation of National Party Systems*. Princeton, NJ: Princeton University Press.

Clinton, Joshua, Simon Jackman, and Doug Rivers. 2004. "The Statistical Analysis of Roll Call Data." *American Political Science Review* 98:355–370.

Coleman, James S. 1971. "The Development Syndrome: Differentiation–Equality–Capacity." In *Crises and Sequences in Political Development*, edited by L. Binder, J. S. Coleman, J. La Palombara, L. W. Pye, S. Verba, and M. Weiner, pp. 75–100. Princeton, NJ: Princeton University Press.

Collier, Ruth Berins, and David Collier. 1991. *Shaping the Political Arena: Critical Junctures, the Labor Movement, and Regime Dynamics in Latin America*. Princeton, NJ: Princeton University Press.

Comisión de Inversiones. 1954. "El sistema fiscal Mexicano y la necesidad de su revisión." In *Consideraciones para un programa nacional de inversiones 1953–58 in Secretaría de Programación y Presupuesto (SPP) Antología de la planeación en México*. México: FCE.

Consejo Federal de Inversiones. 1965. "Coparticipacion provincial en impuestos nacionales." Buenos Aires: Edicion del CFI.

Consejo Federal de Inversiones. 1991. *Gastos e ingresos públicos provinciales, 1970–85*. Buenos Aires: El Consejo.

Contreras, Ariel José. 1977. *México 1940: Industrialización y crisis política México*. México: Siglo XXI Editores.

Contreras Quintero, Florencio. 1966. *La ley de inversion del situado y de coordinacion con el presupuesto nacional*. Caracas.

References

Convención Nacional Fiscal (CNF1). 1926. *"Memoria de la Primera Convención Nacional Fiscal."* México: Secretaria de Hacienda y Crédito Público.

Convención Nacional Fiscal (CNF2). 1947 [1933]. *Memoria de la Segunda Convención Nacional Fiscal.* México: Secretaria de Hacienda y Crédito Público.

Convención Nacional Fiscal (CNF3). 1947. *Memoria de la Tercera Convención Nacional Fiscal.* vol. 1. México: Secretaria de Hacienda y Crédito Público.

Coppedge, Michael. 1993. *Strong Parties and Lame Ducks: Presidential Partyarchy and Presidentialism in Venezuela.* Stanford, CA: Stanford University Press.

Cornelius, Wayne. 1973. "Nation Building, Participation, and Distribution: The Politics of Social Reform under Cárdenas." In *Crisis, Choice and Change*, edited by G. Almond, S. Flanagan, and R. Mundt, pp. 379–498. Boston: Little Brown.

Cornelius, Wayne, Todd Eisenstadt, and Jane Hindley. 1999. *Subnational Politics and Democratization in México.* La Jolla: Center for U.S.-Mexican Studies, University of California-San Diego.

Cumberland, W. W. 1935. "Agrarian Background of the Six Year Plan." In *Economic and Social Program of México (a Controversy)*, edited by R. Beteta. México.

De Figuereido, Rui, and Barry Weingast. 2005. "Self-Enforcing Federalism." *Journal of Law, Economics, and Organization* 21(1):103–135.

de la Cruz, Rafael. 1998. *Descentralizacion en perspectiva.* Caracas: Ediciones IESA.

de la Fuente, Iturriaga. 1976. *La revolución Hacendaria: La hacienda pública con el Presidente Calles.* México: Secretaría de Educación Pública Foro 2000.

De Remes, Alain. 1998. "The Causes of Juxtaposition: A Theoretical Framework for the Study of Municipal and State Elections in México." *Serie Documentos de Trabajo de Estudios Políticos*, 96. México: Centro de Investigación y Docencia Económica.

de Oliveira, Luiz Guilheime. 2000. *Federalismo e guerra fiscal.* Sao Paulo: Ediciones Pulsar.

Departamento de la Estadística Nacional. 1926. *La riqueza de México y el poder constructor del gobierno.* México: Departmento de Estadística Nacional.

Deutsch, Karl. 1961. "Social Mobilization and Political Development." *American Political Science Review* 55(3):493–511.

Diaz-Cayeros, Alberto. 1995. *Desarrollo económico e inequidad regional: Hacia un nuevo pacto federal en México.* México: CIDAC/Miguel Angel Porrúa/Fundación Naumann.

Diaz-Cayeros, Alberto. 1997b. "Political Responses to Regional Inequality: Taxation and Distribution in México." Ph.D. thesis, Duke University.

Diaz Cayeros, Alberto. 2004. "Coaliciones legislativas y reforma fiscal en México." *Política y Gobierno* 11(2):231–262.

Diaz-Cayeros, Alberto, Federico Estevez, and Beatriz Magaloni. Forthcoming. "The Erosion of Party Hegemony, Clientelism and Portfolio Diversification: The Programa Nacional de Solidaridad (Pronasol) in México." In *Patrons or Policies? Patterns of Democratic Accountability and Political Competition*, edited by H. Kitschelt and S. Wilkinson. Cambridge: Cambridge University Press.

Diaz-Cayeros, Alberto, and Joy Langston. 2004. "The Consequences of Competition: Gubernatorial Nominations and Candidate Quality in México, 1994–2000" (typescript).

Dirección de Pensiones Civiles de Retiro. 1932. *Segundo censo de empleados sujetos a la ley general de pensiones civiles de retiro*. México: Imprenta Franco Elizondo Hnos.

Dirección Nacional de Análisis e Investigación Fiscal. 2002. *Recaudación Tributaria Anual*. Buenos Aires: Ministerio de Economía y Producción.

Dirección Nacional de Coordinación Fiscal con las Provincias. 2002. *Distribución de recursos de origen nacional a provincias*. Buenos Aires: Ministerio de Economía y Producción.

Dirección Nacional de Programación Presupuestaria República Argentina. 1970. *Presupuestos provinciales, 1965–1970*, edited by Secretaria de Estado de Hacieuda, Ministerio de Economia Hacienda y Finanzas, Dirección Nacional de Programación Presupuestaria. Buenos Aires: Secretaria de Estado de Hacienda.

Dobbins, James, John G. McGinn, Keith Crane, Seth G. Jones, Rollie Lal, Andrew Rathmell, Rachel Swanger, and Anga Timilsina. 2003. "America's Role in Nation-Building: From Germany to Iraq." Santa Monica, CA: Rand Corporation.

Domínguez, Jorge, and Chapell Lawson. 2004. *México's Pivotal Democratic Election*. Stanford, CA: Stanford University Press.

Domínguez, Jorge, and James McCann. 1996. *Democratizing México*. Baltimore: Johns Hopkins University Press.

Domínguez, Jorge, and Alejandro Poiré. 1999. *Toward México's Democratization*. New York: Routledge.

dos Santos, Wanderly Guilherme. 2003. *O calculo do conflito: Estabilidade e crise na politica Brasileira*. Belo Horizonte: Editora UFMG.

Douglas, Mary. 1986. *How Institutions Think*. Syracuse, NY: Syracuse University Press.

Dresser, Denise. 1991. *Neopopulist Solutions to Neoliberal Problems: México's National Solidarity Program*. Current Issues Brief, vol. 4. La Jolla: Center for U.S.-México Studies, University of California-San Diego.

Duchacek, Ivo. 1970. *Comparative Federalism: The Territorial Dimension of Politics*. New York: Holt, Rinehart and Winston.

Eaton, Kent. 2001. "Decentralisation, Democratisation, and Liberalisation: The History of Revenue Sharing in Argentina, 1934–1999." *Journal of Latin American Studies* 33:1–28.

Eaton, Kent. 2004. *Politics beyond the Capital: The Design of Subnational Institutions in South America*. Stanford, CA: Stanford University Press.

Eisenstadt, S. N., and Stein Rokkan. 1973. *Building States and Nations*. Beverly Hills, CA: Sage.

Elazar, Daniel. 1984. *American Federalism: A View from the States*, 3rd edition. New York: Harper and Row.

Elster, Jon. 1989a. *The Cement of Society: A Study of Social Order*. Cambridge: Cambridge University Press.

Elster, Jon. 1989b. *Nuts and Bolts for the Social Sciences*. Cambridge: Cambridge University Press.

Evans, Peter B. 1979. *Dependent Development: The Alliance of Multinational, State, and Local Capital in Brazil*. Princeton, NJ: Princeton University Press.

References

Falcón, Romana. 1977. *El agrarismo en Veracruz: La etapa Radical (1928–1935)*. México: El Colegio de México.

Falcón, Romana. 1984. *Revolución y Caciquismo en San Luis Potosí, 1910–1938*. México: El Colegio de México.

Falleti, Tulia. 2001. "Federalismo y descentralización educativa en la Argentina. Consecuencias (no queridas) de la descentralización del gasto en un país federal." In *El federalismo electoral Argentino: Sobrerrepresentación, reforma política y gobierno dividido en la Argentina*, edited by E. Calvo and J. M. Abal Medina, pp. 205–230 at p. 278. Buenos Aires: Instituto Nacional de la Administración Pública: Editorial Universitaria de Buenos Aires.

Filippov, Mikhail, Peter C. Ordeshook, and Olga Shvetsova. 2004. *Designing Federalism*. Cambridge: Cambridge University Press.

Floyd, Mary B. 1992. "Política y economía en tiempos de Guzmán Blanco: Centralización y desarrollo, 1870–1888." In *Política y economía en Venezuela: 1810–1991*, edited by Fundación John Boulton. Caracas: Fundacion John Boulton.

Fukuyama, Frances. 2004a. *State-Building: Governance and World Order in the 21st Century*. Ithaca, NY: Cornell University Press.

Gadsden, Carlos. (ed.) 1995. *Memoria del Encuento Hacia un nuevo federalismo*, pp. 35–72. Guanajuato: Gobierno del Estado de Guanajuato.

Garciadiego, Javier. 1996. "Manuel Gómez Morín en los años 'Veintes': Del abanico del oportunidades al fin de las alternativas." In *El Banco de México en la reconstrucción económica nacional*. México: Editorial Jus/Centro Cultural Manuel Gómez Morín.

Garman, Christopher, Stephan Haggard, and Eliza Willis. 2001. "Fiscal Decentralization: A Political Theory with Latin American Cases." *World Politics* 53: 205–236.

Garrido, Luis Javier. 1982. *El partido de la revolución institucionalizada: La formación del nuevo estado en México (1928–1945)*. México: Siglo XXI Editores.

Geddes, Barbara. 1994. *Politician's Dilemma: Building State Capacity in Latin America*. Berkeley: University of California Press.

Gibson, Edward L. 1996. *Class and Conservative Parties: Argentina in Comparative Perspective*. Baltimore: Johns Hopkins University Press.

Gibson, Edward L., Ernesto F. Calvo, and Tulia G. Falleti. 2004. "Reallocative Federalism: Legislative Overrepresentation and Public Spending in the Western Hemisphere." In *Federalism and Democracy in Latin America*, edited by Edward. L. Gibson, pp. 173–196. Baltimore: Johns Hopkins University Press.

Gibson, Edward L., and Tulia G. Falleti. 2004. "Unity by the Stick: Regional Conflict and the Origins of Argentine Federalism." In *Federalism and Democracy in Latin America*, edited by Edward. L. Gibson, pp. 226–254. Baltimore: Johns Hopkins University Press.

González Casanova, Pablo. 1965. *La democracia en México*. México: ERA.

González Casanova, Pablo, and Cadena Roa. 1995. *La república Mexicana de Aguascalientes a Zacatecas*. México: La Jornada Ediciones.

González Oropeza, Manuel. 1983. *La intervención federal en la desaparición de Poderes*. México: UNAM.

González Oropeza, Manuel. 1995. *El federalismo*. México: UNAM-IIJ.

Goodman, Louis W. 1995. *Lessons of the Venezuelan Experience*. Baltimore: Johns Hopkins University Press.

Graham, Richard. 1990. *Patronage and Politics in Nineteenth-Century Brazil*. Stanford, CA: Stanford University Press.

Grindle, Merilee. 1977. *Bureaucrats, Politicians and Peasants in México*. Berkeley, CA: University of California Press.

Gutierrez, Irma Eugenia. 1990 *Hidalgo*. (Biblioteca de las entidades federativas). México: CIIH-UNAM.

Haber, Stephen, Armando Razo, and Noel Maurer. 2003. *The Politics of Property Rights: Political Instability, Credible Commitments, and Economic Growth in México, 1876–1929*. Cambridge: Cambridge University Press.

Hagopian, Frances. 1996. *Traditional Politics and Regime Change in Brazil*. Cambridge: Cambridge University Press.

Hansen, Roger D. 1971. *The Politics of Mexican Development*. Baltimore: Johns Hopkins University Press.

Heldman, Gerald B., and Steven R. Ratner. 1993. "Saving Failed States." *Foreign Policy* 89:3–20.

Herbst, Jeffrey. 2000. *States and Power in Africa*. Princeton, NJ: Princeton University Press.

Hernández Chávez, Alicia. 1979. *La mecánica Cardenista*. México: E1 Colegio de México.

Hernández Chávez, Alicia. 1993. "Federalismo y gobernabilidad en México, 1917–1992." In *Federalismos Latinoaméricanos: México/Brasil/Argentina*, edited by M. Carmagnani, pp. 263–299. México: Fondo de Cultura Económica.

Hernández Chávez, Alicia. 1994. *La tradición republicana del buen gobierno*. México: Fondo de Cultura Económica.

Hernández Chávez, Alicia. 1996. *¿Hacia un nuevo federalismo?* México: Fondo de Cultura Económica.

Hernández Rodriguez, Rogelio. 1992. "La división de la élite política Méxicana." In *México: Auge, Crisis y Ajuste*, edited by Carlos Bazdresch et al., pp. 239–266. México: Fondo de Cultura Económica.

Heston, Alan, Robert Summers, and Bettina Aten. 2002. *Penn World Table Version 6.1*. Philadelphia: Center for International Comparisons, University of Pennsylvania.

Hettich, Walter, and Stanley L. Winer. 1997. "Political Economy of Taxation." In *Perspectives on Public Choice: A Handbook*, edited by D. C. Mueller. Cambridge: Cambridge University Press.

Hirschman, Albert O. 1958. *The Strategy of Economic Development*. New Haven, CT: Yale University Press.

Huntington, Samuel. 1968. *Political Order in Changing Societies*. New Haven, CT: Yale University Press.

Inman, Robert P., and Daniel L. Rubinfeld. 1997. "The Political Economy of Federalism." In *Perspectives on Public Choice: A Handbook*, edited by D. C. Mueller, pp. 73–105. New York: Cambridge University Press.

International Monetary Fund (IMF). various years. *Government Finance Statistics*. Washington, DC: IMF.

References

Izquierdo, Rafael. 1995. *Política hacendaria del desarrollo estabilizador, 1958–1970*. México: Fondo de Cultura Económica.

Jackman, Simon. 2004. "IDEAL Point Estimation and Roll Call Analysis via Bayesian Simulation, Version 0.4." Department of Political Science, Stanford University (March 20).

Jannetti Díaz, Maria Emilia. 1989. "La coordinación fiscal y los ingresos estatales." *Comercio Exterior* 39(9).

Jarach, Dino. 1966. *Coparticipación provincial en impuestos federales*, vol. 2. Buenos Aires: Consejo Federal de Inversiones.

Jillson, Calvin, and Rick K. Wilson. 1994. *Congressional Dynamics Structure Coordination and Choice in the First American Congress, 1774–1789*. Stanford, CA: Stanford University Press.

Jones, Mark P., Sebastian Saiegh, Pablo Spiller, and Mariano Tommasi. 2001. "Amateur Legislators – Professional Politicians: The Consequences of Party-Centered Electoral Rules in a Federal System." *American Political Science Review* 46(3): 656–669.

Jones, Mark P., Pablo Sanguinetti, and Mariano Tommasi. 2000. "Politics, Institutions, and Fiscal Performance in a Federal System: An Analysis of the Argentine Provinces." *Journal of Development Economics* 61:305–333.

Karl, Terry Lynn. 1997. *The Paradox of Plenty*. Berkeley: University of California Press.

Kato, Junko. 2003. *Regressive Taxation and the Welfare State: Path Dependence and Political Diffusion*. Cambridge: Cambridge University Press.

Kaufman, Robert R. 1977. "México and Latin American Authoritarianism." In *Authoritarianism in México*, edited by J. L. Reyna and R. S. Weinert, pp. 193–232. Philadelphia: Institute for the Study of Human Issues.

Kaufman, Susan Purcell. 1977. "The Future of the Mexican System." In *Authoritarianism in México*, edited by J. L. Reyna and R. S. Weinert, pp. 173–192. Philadelphia: Institute for the Study of Human Issues.

Kelley, R. Lynn. 1977. "Venezuela Constitutional Forms and Realities." In *Venezuela: The Democratic Experience*, edited by J. Martz and D. J. Myers, pp. 32–53. New York: Praeger.

Kennedy, Peter. 1996. *A Guide to Econometrics*. Cambridge, MA: MIT Press.

King, Gary. 1998. *Unifying Political Methodology: The Likelihood Theory of Statistical Inference*. Ann Arbor: University of Michigan Press.

Kornblith, Miriam, and Luken Quintana. 1981. "Gestión fiscal y centralización del poder en los gobiernos de Cipriano Casto y de Juan Vicente Gómez." *Politeia* 10:143–219.

Kornblith, Miriam, and Thais Maingón. 1985. *Estado y gasto público en Venezuela, 1936–1980*. Caracas: Universidad Central de Venezuela.

Kraemer, Moritz. 1997. "Intergovernmental Transfers and Political Representation: Empirical Evidence from Argentina, Brazil and México." IDB Working Paper 345. Washington, DC: IDB.

Lajous, Alejandra. 1992. "La primera campaña del PNR y la oposición vasconcelista." In *La sucesión presidencial en México, 1928–1988*, edited by C. Martínez Assad. México: Editorial Patria.

Lamounier, Bolivar. 1985. "Authoritarian Brazil – Revisitado." No. 11 in *IDESP Textos* São Paulo: Instituto de Estudos Econômicos, Sociais e Políticos de São Paulo.

Langston, Joy, and Alberto Diaz-Cayeros. 2002. "What Does it Take to Be a Governor?" (Unpublished manuscript, México).

Levi, Margaret. 1988. *Of Rule and Revenue*. Berkeley: University of California Press.

Levine, Daniel. 1973. *Conflict and Political Change in Venezuela*. Princeton, NJ: Princeton University Press.

Levine, Daniel. 1978. "Venezuela since 1958: The Consolidation of Democratic Politics." In *The Breakdown of Democratic Regimes*, edited by J. Linz and A. Stepan, pp. 82–109. Baltimore: Johns Hopkins University Press.

Levine, Robert M. 1978. *Pernambuco in the Brazilian Federation, 1889–1937*. Stanford, CA: Stanford University Press.

Lieberman, Evan. 2003. *Race and Regionalism in the Politics of Taxation in Brazil and South Africa*. Cambridge: Cambridge University Press.

Lieuwen, Edwin. 1968. *Mexican Militarism: The Political Rise and Fall of the Revolutionary Army, 1910-1940*. Albuquerque: University of New México Press.

Londregan, John Benedict. 2000a. *Legislative Institutions and Ideology in Chile*. Cambridge: Cambridge University Press.

Londregan, John Benedict. 2000b. "Estimating Legislators' Preferred Points." *Political Analysis* 8:35–56.

Longo, Carlos Alberto. 1984. *A disputa pela receita tributária no Brasil*. Vol. 34 in Série Ensaios econômicos. São Paulo: IPE/USP.

Love, Joseph. 1971. *Rio Grande do Sul and Brazilian Regionalism, 1882–1930*. Stanford CA: Stanford University Press.

Love, Joseph. 1980. *Sao Paulo in the Brazilian Federation, 1889–1937*. Stanford: Stanford University Press.

Love, Joseph. 1993. "Federalismo y regionalismo en Brasil, 1889–1937." In *Federalismos Latinoamericanos: México/Brasil/Argentina*, edited by M. Carmagnani, pp. 180–223. México: Fondo de Cultura Economica.

Lujambio, Alonso. 1995. *Federalismo y congreso en el cambio politico de México*. México: UNAM.

Mahar, Dennis. 1971. "The Failures of Revenue Sharing in Brazil and Some Recent Developments." *Bulletin for International Fiscal Documentation* 25:71–80.

Malikyar, Helena, and Barnett R. Rubin. 2002. *Center–Periphery Relations in the Afghan State: Current Practices, Future Prospects*. New York: New York University. Center on International Cooperation.

Manor, James. 2000. *The Political Economy of Democratic Decentralization*. Washington, DC: The World Bank.

Mariñas Otero, Luis. 1965. *Las constituciones de Venezuela*. Madrid: Ediciones Cultura Hispánica.

Martínez Almazán, Raúl. 1980. *Las relaciones fiscales y financieras intergubernamentales en México*. México: Instituto Nacional de Administración Pública.

Martínez Assad, Carlos. 1990a. *Balance y perspectiva de los estudios regionales en México*. México: UNAM/M. A. Porrúa.

References

Martínez Assad, Carlos. 1990b. *Los rebeldes vencidos: Cedillo contra el estado Cardenista*. México: Fondo de Cultura Económica.

Martínez Cabañas, Gustavo. 1985. *La administración estatal y municipal en México*. México: Instituto Nacional de Administración Pública.

Martz, John. 1966. *Acción Democrática*. Princeton, NJ: Princeton University Press.

Martz, John, and Enrique Baloyra. 1978. *Political Attitudes in Venezuela: Societal Cleavages and Public Opinion*. Austin: University of Texas Press.

Martz, John D., and David J. Myers. 1977. *Venezuela: The Democratic Experience*. New York: Praeger.

Mascareño, Carlos. 2000. *Balance de la descentralización en Venezuela: Logros, limitaciones y perspectivas*. Caracas: PNUD.

McCubbins, Mathew D., and Gregory W. Noble. 1995. "Perceptions and Realities of Japanese Budgeting." In *Structure and Policy in Japan and the United States*, edited by M. D. McCubbins and P. F. Cowhey, pp. 81–118. Cambridge: Cambridge University Press.

McDonald, Ian M., and Robert E. Solow. 1981. "Wage Bargaining and Employment." *American Economic Review* 71:896–908.

McKelvey, Richard D. 1986. "Covering, Dominance and Institution-Free Properties of Social Choice." *American Journal of Political Science* 30:283–314.

Memoria de Hacienda. 1948. "Memoria de Hacienda de 1948." In *Ministerio de Hacienda* (1982) *150 años del Ministerio de Hacienda: exposiciones de motivos de las memorias del despacho durante el período 1830–1980*. 5 Vols. Caracas: Ediciones de la Presidencia de la República, Ministerio de Hacienda.

Merino Huerta, Mauricio. 1991. *Fuera del centro*. Veracruz: Universidad Veracruzana.

Meyer, Jean. 1996. "Los mejores años del Presidente Calles." In *El Banco de México en la reconstrucción económica nacional*, edited by Miguel Mancera and Jean A. Meyer, pp. 19–26. México: Editorial Jus/Centro Cultural Manuel Gómez Morín.

Meyer, Lorenzo. 1977. "Historical Roots of the Authoritarian State in México." In *Authoritarianism in México*, edited by J. L. Reyna and R. S. Weinert. Philadelphia: Institute for the Study of Human Issues.

Meyer, Lorenzo. 1986. "Un tema añejo siempre actual: El centro y las regiones en la historia Mexicana." In *Descentralización y democracia en México*, edited by B. Torres. México: El Colegio de México.

Ministerio da Fazenda. Various years. *Anuario Economico Fiscal*. Brasilia: Secretaria da Receita Federal, Centro de Informacoes.

Ministerio de la Economía. 1986. *Informe de la Secretaria de Hacienda sobre el comportamiento de las finanzas públicas provinciales*. Buenos Aires: Ministerio de la Economía.

Ministerio de la Economía. 1987. *Relaciones fiscales nación – Provincias: Bases para un nuevo pacto federal*. Buenos Aires: Secretaria de Hacienda.

Ministerio de Hacienda. 1938. La obra financiera del Poder Ejecutivo nacional de 1932 a 1937. Buenos Aires: [G. Kraft].

259

Ministerio de Hacienda. 1946. Conferencia de Ministros de Hacienda: [actas] / Republica Argentina, Ministerio de Hacienda de la Nación. Buenos Aires: El Ministerio.

Ministerio de Hacienda Republica de Venezuela. 1955. *Estadistica fiscal: Anos 1944–45 a 1953–54.* Caracas: Editorial Sucre.

Ministerio de Hacienda. 1982. 150 *años del Ministerio de Hacienda: exposiciones de motivos de las memorias del despacho durante el período 1830–1980.* 5 Vols. Caracas: Ediciones de la Presidencia de la República, Ministerio de Hacienda.

Ministerio del Interior. 1933. *Intervención federal en las provincias.* Buenos Aires: Talleres Gráficos de Correos y Telégrafos.

Ministerio do Interior. 1985. *Financas publicas dos estados de Goias, Maranhao, Mato Grosso e Para.* Brasilia: PRODIAT.

Mitchell, Brian. 2003. *International Historical Statistics – The Americas.* New York: Palgrave.

Mogollón, Olivia. 1996. "Pobreza y distribución de recursos descentralizados del fondo de desarrollo social municipal." Paper delivered at the Congreso Nacional de Ciencia Política, México.

Molinar Horcasitas, Juan. 1991. *El tiempo de la legitimidad: Elecciones, autoritarismo y democracia en México.* México: Cal y Arena.

Molinar Horcasitas, Juan, and Weldon, Jeffrey. 1994. "Electoral Determinants of National Solidarity." In *Transforming State–Society Relations in México: The National Solidarity Strategy,* edited by W. Cornelius, A. Craig, and J. Fox, pp. 123–142. San Diego, CA: Center for U.S.–Mexican Studies.

Montinola, Gabriella, Yingyi Qian, and Barry R. Weingast. 1995. "Federalism, Chinese Style: The Political Basis for Economic Success in China." *World Politics* 48:50–81.

Morton, Rebecca. 1999. *Methods and Models: A Guide to the Empirical Analysis of Formal Models in Political Science.* Cambridge: Cambridge University Press.

Moulin, Hervé. 2003. *Fair Division and Collective Welfare.* Cambridge, MA: MIT Press.

Mueller, Dennis C. 2003. *Public Choice III.* Cambridge: Cambridge University Press.

Murilo de Carvalho, Jose. 1993. "Federalismo y centralización en el imperio Brasileño: Historia y argumento." In *Federalismos Latinoamericanos: México/Brasil/Argentina,* edited by M. Carmagnani, pp. 51–80. México: Fondo de Cultura Economica.

Nacif, Benito. 1996. *Political Careers, Political Ambitions and Career Goals.* Documentos de Trabajo del CIDE, División de Estudios Políticos, vol. 51. México: CIDE.

New York Tax Foundation. 1935. *Tax Systems of the World,* sixth, seventh, eighth, and ninth Editions. New York: New York Tax Foundation.

Nickson, Andrew R. 1995. *Local Government in Latin America.* Boulder, CO: Lynne Rienner.

North, Douglass C. 1981. *Structure and Change in Economic History.* Cambridge: Cambridge University Press.

References

North, Douglass C., and Barry R. Weingast. 1989. "Constitutions and Credible Commitments: The Evolution of the Institutions of Public Choice in 17th Century England." *Journal of Economic History* 49:803–832.

Nuñez Miñana, Horacio, and Alberto Porto. 1983. *Distribución de la coparticipación federal de impuestos: análisis y alternativas.* Buenos Aires: Comisión Nacional de Inversiones.

Oates, Wallace. 1972. *Fiscal Federalism.* London: Harcourt Brace.

O'Donnell, Guillermo. 1973. *Modernization and Bureaucratic-Authoritarianism: Studies in South American Politics.* Berkeley: Institute of International Studies, University of California.

Olavarría, Jorge. 1988. *Dios y federación.* Caracas: Editorial Arte.

O'Neill, Katherine. 2001. "Return to Center? Fiscal Decentralization and Recentralization in Comparative Perspective." Paper Presented at the Annual Meeting of the American Political Science Association, Washington, DC.

Ordeshook, Peter. 1986. *Game Theory and Political Theory: An Introduction.* Cambridge: Cambridge University Press.

Ortiz Mena, Antonio. 1966. "Contenido y alcances de la política fiscal." *Actividad Económica en Latinoamérica* 75:6–18.

Ortiz Mena, Antonio. 1998. *El desarrollo estabilizador: Reflexiones sobre una epoca.* México: Fondo de Cultura Económica.

Osborne, Martin J., and Ariel Rubinstein. 1990. *Bargaining and Markets.* San Diego: Academic Press.

Ostrom, Elinor. 1991. "Rational Choice Theory and Institutional Analysis: Towards Complementarity." *American Political Science Review* 85:237–243.

Pacheco Ladrón de Guevara, Lourdes C. 1990. *Nayarit,* México: CIIH-UNAM.

Pansters, Wil. 1992. *política y poder en México: Formación y ocaso del cacicazgo avilacamachista en puebla, 1937–1987.* Puebla: Centro de Estudios Universitarios Universidad Autónoma de Puebla.

Partido Nacional Revolucionario (PNR). 1931. *Un año de gestión del CEN.* México: PNR.

Partido Nacional Revolucionario (PNR). 1934a. *La cuestión agraria.* México: PNR.

Partido Nacional Revolucionario (PNR). 1934b. "Plan Sexenal," reprinted in Partido Revolucionario Institucional 1981, *Historia Documental del Partido de la Revolución,* vol. 2, 1932–1933, edited by P. Partido. Revolucionario Institucional, pp. 335–374. México: PRI.

Partido Revolucionario Institucional (PRI). 1981. "Historia documental del Partido de la Revolución." In *PNR 1929–1932,* vol. 2. México: PRI.

Penfold-Becerra, Michael. 2004. "Federalism and Institutional Change in Venezuela." In *Federalism and Democracy in Latin America,* edited by Edward L. Gibson, pp. 197–225. Baltimore: Johns Hopkins University Press.

Persson, Torsten, and Guido Tabellini. 2003. *The Economic Effects of Constitutions.* Cambridge, MA: MIT Press.

Pirez, Pedro. 1986. *Coparticipación federal y descentralización del estado.* Buenos Aires: Centro Editor de América Latina.

Poiré, Alejandro. 2002. "Bounded Ambitions: Party Nominations, Discipline, and Defection: México's PRI in Comparative Perspective." Unpublished Ph.D. dissertation, Harvard University, Department of Government.

Poole, Keith, and Howard Rosenthal. 1987. "Analysis of Congressional Coalition Patterns: A Unidimensional Spatial Model." *Legislative Studies Quarterly* 12:55–75.

Porto, Alberto. 1990. *Federalismo fiscal: El caso Argentino*. Buenos Aires: Editorial Tesis.

Porto, Alberto. 2003. "Etapas de la coparticipacion federal de impuestos." Documento de Federalismo Fiscal, Universidad Nacional de la Plata.

Porto, Alberto, and Walter Cont. 1998. "Presupuestos provinciales, transferencias intergubernamentales y equidad." *Desarrollo Económico, Revista de Ciencias Sociales* 38:267–291.

Porto, Alberto, and Pablo Sanguinetti. 2001. "Political Determinants of Intergovernmental Grants: Evidence from Argentina." *Economics and Politics* 13(3): 237–256.

Powell, John Duncan. 1971. *Political Mobilization of the Venezuelan Peasant*. Cambridge, MA: Harvard University Press.

Przeworski, Adam. 1985. *Capitalism and Social Democracy*. Cambridge: Cambridge University Press.

Przeworski, Adam. 1990. *The State and the Economy under Capitalism*. Fundamentals of Pure and Applied Economics, vol. 40. Chur: Harwood Academic Press.

Przeworski, Adam. 1991. *Democracy and the Market: Political and Economic Reforms in Eastern Europe and Latin America*. Cambridge: Cambridge University Press.

Putnam, Robert D., Robert Leonardi, and Raffaella Y. Nanetti. 1993. *Making Democracy Work: Civic Traditions in Modern Italy*. Princeton, NJ: Princeton University Press.

Razo, Armando. 2003. "Social Networks of Limited Dictatorship: Theory and Evidence from México's Early Industrialization (1876–1911)." Ph.D. dissertation, Stanford University, Political Science Department.

República Argentina, Ministerio de Hacienda de la Nación. 1938. *La obra financiera del poder ejecutivo nacional de 1932 a 1937*. Buenos Aires: Ministerio de Hacienda de la Nacion.

República Argentina, Ministerio de Hacienda de la Nación. 1946. *Primera Conferencia de Ministros de Hacienda*. Buenos Aires: Ministerio de Hacienda de la Nación.

Republica do Brasil. various years. *Anuário econômico-fiscal*. Brasilia: Secretaria da Receita Federal, Centro de Informações Econômico-Fiscais.

Retchkiman, Benjamín, and Gerardo Gil Valvidia. 1981. *El federalismo y la coordinación fiscal*. México: UNAM.

Rey, Juan Carlos. 1989. *El futuro de la democracia en Venezuela*. Caracas: Universidad Central de Venezuela.

Reyna, José Luis, and Richard S. Weinert. 1977. *Authoritarianism in México*. Philadelphia: Institute for the Study of Human Issues.

Rezende, Fernando. 1996. "El federalismo fiscal en Brasil." In *¿Hacia un nuevo federalismo?*, edited by A. Hernández Chávez, pp. 225–241. México: Fondo de Cultura Económica.

References

Rezende, Fernando, and Jose Alberto Afonso. 2002. "The Brazilian Federation: Facts, Challenges and Perspectives." Paper presented at the Conference "Federalism in a Global Environment," Stanford, CA.

Riker, William H. 1964. *Federalism: Origin, Operation, Significance*. Boston: Little Brown.

Rock, David. 1987. *Argentina, 1516–1987: From Spanish Colonization to Alfonsín*. Berkeley: University of California Press.

Rodden, Jonathan. 2003. "Reviving Leviathan: Fiscal Federalism and Growth of Government." *International Organization* 57:695–729.

Rodríguez, Linda Alexander. 1985. *The Search for Public Policy: Regional Politics and Government Finances in Ecuador, 1830–1940*. Berkeley: University of California Press.

Rodríguez, Victoria. 1997. *Decentralization in México: From Reforma Municipal to Solidaridad to Nuevo Federalismo*. New York: Westview Press.

Rodriguez, Victoria, and Peter Ward. 1995. *Opposition Government in México*. Albuquerque: University of New México.

Rohde, David W. 1979. "Risk Bearing and Progressive Ambition: The Case of the United States House of Representatives." *American Journal of Political Science* 23:1–26.

Rokkan, Stein, Peter Flora, Stein Kuhnle, and Derek W. Urwin. 1999. *State Formation, Nation-Building, and Mass Politics in Europe: The Theory of Stein Rokkan Based on His Collected Works*. Oxford: Oxford University Press.

Rokkan, Stein, and Derek W. Urwin. 1983. *Economy, Territory, Identity: Politics of West European Peripheries*, edited by European Consortium for Political Research (ECPR). London: Sage Publications.

Romero Kolbeck, Gustavo, and Victor Urquidi. 1952. *La exención fiscal en el Distrito Federal como instrumento de atracción de industrias*. México: Departamento del Distrito Federal.

Rubin, Barnett R. 2002. *The Fragmentation of Afghanistan: State Formation and Collapse in the International System*. New Haven, CT: Yale University Press.

Rubinstein, Ariel. 1982. "Perfect Equilibrium in a Bargaining Model." *Econometrica* 50(1):97–110.

Saenz, Josué. 1941. "Las areas en las finanzas públicas." *El Trimestre Económico* 8: 20–48.

Saiegh, Sebastian, and Mariano Tommasi. 1999. "Why Is Argentina's Fiscal Federalism so Inefficient? Entering the Labyrinth." *Journal of Applied Economics* 2(1):169–209.

Samuels, David. 2003. *Ambition, Federalism, and Legislative Politics in Brazil*. Cambridge: Cambridge University Press.

Samuels, David, and Scott Mainwaring. 2004. "Strong Federalism, Constraints on the Central Government, and Economic Reform in Brazil." In *Federalism and Democracy in Latin America*, edited by Edward L. Gibson, pp. 85–130. Baltimore: Johns Hopkins University Press.

Sawers, Larry. 1996. *The Other Argentina: The Interior and National Development*. Boulder, CO: Westview Press.

Scharpf, Fritz. 1988. "The Joint Decision Trap: Lessons from German Federalism and European Integration." *Public Administration* 66:239–278.

Schlesinger, Joseph A. 1966. *Ambition and Politics: Political Careers in the United States.* Chicago: Rand-McNally.

Schlesinger, Joseph A. 1991. *Political Parties and the Winning of Office.* Ann Arbor: University of Michigan Press.

Schmitter, Philippe C. 1971. *Interest Conflict and Political Change in Brazil.* Stanford, CA: Stanford University Press.

Schofield, Norman, Bernard Grofman, and Scott L. Feld. 1988. "The Core and the Stability of Group Choice in Spatial Voting Games." *American Political Science Review* 82:195–211.

Schumpeter, Joseph A. 1991. "The Crisis of the Tax State." In *The Economics and Sociology of Capitalism,* edited by R. Swedberg, pp. 99–140. Princeton, NJ: Princeton University Press.

Scott, Robert E. 1959. *Mexican Government in Transition.* Urbana: University of Illinois Press.

Secretaría de Hacienda y Crédito Público (SHCP). 1973. *Primer informe sobre las relaciones fiscales entre la federación y los estados.* Mazatlán: SHCP.

Secretaría de Programación y Presupuesto. 1985. "Inversión pública y planeación regional por cuencas hidrológicas." In *Antología de la planeación en México,* vol. 2. México: Fondo de Cultura Económica.

Sempere, Jaime, and Horacio Sobarzo. 1996. "La Descentralización fiscal en México: Algunas propuestas." In *México hacia un nuevo federalismo fiscal: Lecturas del trimestre económico,* vol. 83, edited by R. Arellano Cadena, pp. 165–196. México: Fondo de Cultura Económica.

Sentíes, Octavio. 1942. *Federalismo constitucional y centralismo económico.* México: Facultad de Derecho y Ciencias Sociales, UNAM.

Servín, Armando. 1956. *Las finanzas públicas locales durante los ultimos cincuenta años.* Serie de Trabajos Monográficos de la Dirección General de Estudios Hacendarios, vol. 1. México: Secretaría de Hacienda y Crédito Público.

Shepsle, Kenneth A. 1979. "Institutional Arrangements and Equilibrium in Multidimensional Voting Models." *American Journal of Political Science* 57:27–59.

Shepsle, Kenneth A., and Mark S. Bonchek. 1997. *Analyzing Politics: Rationality, Behavior and Institutions.* New York: W. W. Norton.

Sikkink, Kathryn. 1991. *Ideas and Institutions: Developmentalism in Brazil and Argentina.* Ithaca, NY: Cornell University Press.

Silva, José. 1941. "Las jurisdicciones fiscales concurrentes." *El Trimestre Económico* 8:466–486.

Simpson, Eyler N. 1937. *The Ejido: México's Way Out.* Chapel Hill: University of North Carolina Press.

Smith, Peter. 1979. *Labyrinths of Power: Political Recruitment in Twentieth-Century México.* Princeton, NJ: Princeton University Press.

Smith, Peter H. 1974. *Argentina and the Failure of Democracy: Conflict among Political Elites, 1904-1955.* Madison: The University of Wisconsin Press.

References

Snyder, Richard, and David Samuels. 2004. "Legislative Malapportionment in Latin America: Historical and Comparative Perspectives." In *Federalism and Democracy in Latin America*, edited by Edward L. Gibson, pp. 131–172. Baltimore: Johns Hopkins University Press.

Socolik, Helio. 1986. "Transferencias de impostos aos estados e aos municipios." *Revista de Financas Publicas* 367:70–110.

Solís, Leopoldo. 1973. *La economía mexicana*. México: Fondo de Cultura Económica.

Solnick, Steve. 1998. "Hanging Separately? Cooperation, Cooptation and Cheating in Developing Federations." Paper presented at the *Annual Meeting of the American Political Science Association*, Boston.

Solnick, Steve. 2002. *Big Deals: Territorial Politics and the Fate of the Russian Federation*. (book manuscript).

Souza, Celina. 1997. *Constitutional Engineering in Brazil: The Politics of Federalism and Decentralization*. New York: St. Martin's Press.

Steinmo, Sven. 1993. *Taxation and Democracy: Swedish, British and American Approaches to Financing the Modern State*. New Haven, CT: Yale University Press.

Stepan, Alfred C. 1973. *Authoritarian Brazil: Origins, Policies, and Future*. New Haven, CT: Yale University Press.

Stepan, Alfred C. 1989. *Democratizing Brazil: Problems of Transition and Consolidation*. New York: Oxford University Press.

Stepan, Alfred C. 1999. "Federalism and Democracy: Beyond the U.S. Model." *Journal of Democracy* 10:19–34.

Stepan, Alfred. 2000. "Brazil's Decentralized Federalism: Bringing Government Closer to the Citizens?" *Daedalus* 129:145–169.

Stepan, Alfred C. 2004. "Electorally Generated Veto Players in Unitary and Federal Systems." In *Federalism and Democracy in Latin America*, edited by E. Gibson, pp. 323–362. Baltimore: John Hopkins University Press.

Sterrett, Joseph Edmund, and Joseph Stancliffe Davis. 1928. "The Fiscal and Economic Condition of México." Report Submitted to the International Committee of Bankers on México, México.

Stiglitz, Joseph. 1994. *Whither Socialism?* Cambridge, MA: MIT Press.

Suárez, Santiago Gerardo. 1965. *Evolución histórica del situado constitucional*. Caracas.

Sullivan, William M. 1992. "Situación económica y política durante el período de Juan Vicente Gómez, 1908–1935." In *Política y economía en Venezuela: 1810–1991*, edited by Fundación John Boulton, pp. 247–271. Caracas: Fundacion John Boulton.

Swank, Duane, and Sven Steinmo. 2002. "The New Political Economy of Taxation in Advanced Capitalist Democracies." *American Journal of Political Science* 46:642–655.

Thorp, Rosemary. 1998. *Progress, Poverty and Exclusion: An Economic History of Latin America in the Twentieth Century*. Washington, DC: Inter-American Development Bank.

Tiebout, Charles M. 1956. "A Pure Theory of Local Expenditures." *Journal of Political Economy* 64:412–424.

Tilly, Charles. 1990. *Coercion, Capital and European States, AD 990–1992*. Cambridge, MA: Blackwell.

Timmons, Jeff. 2004. "The Fiscal Contract: States, Taxes and Public Services." Paper presented at the American Political Science Association Meeting, Chicago, September.

Tobler, Hans Werner. 1988. "Peasants and the Shaping of the Revolutionary State, 1910-40." In *Riot, Rebellion and Revolution: Rural Social Conflict in México*, edited by F. Katz, pp. 487–520. Princeton, NJ: Princeton University Press.

Tommasi, Mariano. 2002. "Federalism in Argentina and the Reforms of the 1990s." Paper presented at the conference "Federalism in a Global Environment," Stanford, CA.

Tomassi, Mariano, and Pablo Spiller. 2003. "The Institutional Foundations of Public Policy: A Transactions Approach with Applications to Argentina." *Journal of Law, Economics and Organization* 19(2):281–306.

Tomz, Michael, Jason Wittenberg, and Gary King. 2001. "CLARIFY: Software for Presenting and Interpreting Statistical Results." Cambridge, MA: Harvard University.

Torsvik, Per. 1981. "Mobilization, Center–Periphery Structures and Nation Building." Bergen: Universitetsforlaget.

Treisman, Daniel. 1999. *After the Deluge: Regional Crises and Political Consolidation in Russia*. Ann Arbor: University of Michigan Press.

Trevisán, Egidio C. 1941. "Unificación de los impuestos internos en Argentina." *El Trimestre Económico* 13:322–328.

Tsebelis, George. 1995. "Decision Making in Political Systems: Veto Players in Presidentialism, Parliamentarism, Multicameralism and Multipartyism." *British Journal of Political Science* 25:289–325.

Tsebelis, George, and Geoffrey Garrett. 1996. "An Institutional Critique of Intergovernmentalism." *International Organization* 50:269–299.

Urdaneta, Alberto, Leopoldo Martinez Olavarria, and Margarita Lopez Maya. 1990. *Venezuela: Centralizacion y descentralizacion del Estado*. Caracas: CENDES.

Urquidi L., Víctor. 1956. "El impuesto sobre la renta en el desarrollo económico de México." *El Trimestre Económico* 23(92):421–437.

Valenzuela, Georgette José. 1988. "Angel Flores, ¿Candidato de la Reacción?" In *Estadistas, caciques y caudillos*, edited by C. Martínez Assad. México: UNAM–IIS.

Varsano, Ricardo. 1996. "A evolucao do sistema tributario Brasileiro ao longo do seculo: Anotacoes e reflexoes para futuras reformas." Texto para discussao, IPEA. Brasilia: IPEA.

Varsano, Ricardo. 1997. "A guerra fiscal do ICMS: Quem ganha e quem perde." Texto para Discussao, IPEA. Brasilia: IPEA.

Vázquez-Presedo, Vicente. 1976. *Estadísticas históricas Argentinas: Segunda parte, 1914-1939*. Buenos Aires: Ediciones Macchi.

Vázquez-Presedo, Vicente. 1988. *Estadísticas históricas Argentinas: Compendio, 1873–1973*. Buenos Aires: Academia Nacional de Ciencias Economicas.

Vázquez Santaella, José. 1938. "Hacia la federalización fiscal." *El Trimestre Económico* 5:183–205.

References

Veliz, Claudio. 1980. *The Centralist Tradition in Latin America*. Princeton, NJ: Princeton University Press.

Villa Patiño, María del Carmen. 1945. "La contribución federal y la concurrencia fiscal." Thesis, UNAM.

von Mettenheim, Kurt. 1995. *The Brazilian Voter: Mass Politics in Democratic Transition, 1974–1986*. Pittsburgh, PA: University of Pittsburgh Press.

Wasserman, Mark. 1993. "Chihuahua Politics in an Era of Transition." In *Provinces of the Revolution: Essays on Mexican Regional History, 1910–1929*, edited by T. Benjamin and M. Wasserman, pp. 219–236. Albuquerque: University of New México Press.

Weingast, Barry R. 1995. "The Economic Role of Political Institutions: Market Preserving Federalism and Economic Growth." *Journal of Law, Economics and Organization* 11:1–31.

Weldon, Jeffrey. 1996. "The Mexican Congress and the Presidency, 1917–1940." Paper delivered at the annual meeting of the American Political Science Association, San Francisco.

Wibbels, Erik. 2000. "Federalism and the Politics of Macroeconomic Policy and Performance." *American Journal of Political Science* 44:687–702.

Wibbels, Erik, and Karen Remmer. 2000. "The Subnational Politics of Economic Adjustment: Provincial Politics and Fiscal Performance in Argentina." *Comparative Political Studies* 33:419–451.

Wilkie, James. 1978. *La Revolución Mexicana: Gasto federal y cambio social*, 2nd edition. México: Fondo de Cultura Económica.

Wirth, John D. 1977. *Minas Gerais in the Brazilian Federation, 1889–1937*. Stanford, CA: Stanford University Press.

Womack, John. 1984. *Zapata and the Mexican Revolution*. New York: Knopf.

Yates, Paul Lamartine. 1961. *El desarrollo regional de México*. México: Banco de México, Departamento de Investigaciones Industriales.

Zebadúa, Emilio. 1994. *Banqueros y revolucionarios: La soberanía financiera de México, 1914–1929*. México: Fondo de Cultura Económica/El Colegio de México.

Index

269

Index

Cont, Walter, 206
Contreras, Ariel, 84
Contreras Quintero, Florencio, 169
contribución federal, 48, 65, 66, 73, 95, 127, 128
COPEI (Comité de Organización Política Electoral Independiente), 29, 167, 179
Coppedge, Michael, 168, 169
Cornelius, Wayne, 83, 238
Corona del Rosal, Alfonso, 91
corporatism
  Brazil, 219
  and Calles, 83
  and governors, 84, 91, 101, 102
  and hegemonic party, 74, 84
  and nominations, 87, 89
  and PNR, 75, 78, 83
  and presidential power, 99
  and PRM, 86
  and the Senate, 90
  and veto players, 75
credibility, 14, 60, 244
  Argentina, 197
  and democracy, 167, 235
  and institutions, 21, 190
  model, 57
  over time, 19, 190
  of threats, 149
  of transfers, 8, 14, 56, 57, 197
Crisp, Brian, 168
Cumberland, W. W., 94

de Figuereido, Rui, 11
de la Huerta, Adolfo, 54, 55, 59
de la Madrid, Miguel, 112, 114, 116, 118
de Remes, Alan, 90
decentralization, 236, 243
  Argentina, 182
  Brazil, 5, 210, 212, 214, 221, 222, 228
  and inequality, 246
  and parties, 11

and redistribution, 247
  revenue, 4
  and revenue sharing, 4
  and size of government, 241
  Venezuela, 8, 157, 178, 179
democracy, 172
  and accountability, 149, 153
  Argentina, 9, 29, 181, 186, 191, 196, 199, 201, 202
  Brazil, 210, 211, 214, 219, 224, 226, 228
  and checks and balances, 172, 221
  and decentralization, 165
  effect on compliance, 169, 182, 201, 235
  Mexico, 35, 74, 96, 147
  pacted, 167, 216
  and tax rates, 14
  Venezuela, 29, 157, 167, 168, 169, 174, 178
Deutsch, Karl, 237
Diaz, Porfirio, 56
Diaz-Cayeros, Alberto, 4, 23, 51, 62, 68, 90, 92, 105, 111, 113, 122, 133, 143, 145, 225, 238
Díaz Ordaz, Gustavo, 116, 118
Dobbins, James, 233
Douglas, Mary, 51
Dresser, Denise, 143, 145
Duchacek, Ivo, 10

Eaton, Kent, 8, 154, 172, 182, 183, 185, 186, 195, 197, 198, 199, 213, 220, 243
Echeverría, Luis, 112, 118, 131
Eisenstadt, T. N., 237
ejidos, 42, 65, 72
Elazar, Daniel, 10
elections: staggered timing, 98, 99, 132
Elster, Jon, 51
Escobar, Juan, 78
Estévez, Federico, xvi, 143
Evans, Peter, 219, 237

Index

Robert O. Keohane and Helen B. Milner, eds., *Internationalization and Domestic Politics*

Herbert Kitschelt, *The Transformation of European Social Democracy*

Herbert Kitschelt, Peter Lange, Gary Marks, and John D. Stephens, eds., *Continuity and Change in Contemporary Capitalism*

Herbert Kitschelt, Zdenka Mansfeldova, Radek Markowski, and Gabor Toka, *Post-Communist Party Systems*

David Knoke, Franz Urban Pappi, Jeffrey Broadbent, and Yutaka Tsujinaka, eds., *Comparing Policy Networks*

Allan Kornberg and Harold D. Clarke, *Citizens and Community: Political Support in a Representative Democracy*

Amie Kreppel, *The European Parliament and the Supranational Party System*

David D. Laitin, *Language Repertoires and State Construction in Africa*

Fabrice E. Lehoucq and Ivan Molina, *Stuffing the Ballot Box: Fraud, Electoral Reform, and Democratization in Costa Rica*

Mark Irving Lichbach and Alan S. Zuckerman, eds., *Comparative Politics: Rationality, Culture, and Structure*

Evan Lieberman, *Race and Regionalism in the Politics of Taxation in Brazil and South Africa*

Julia Lynch, *Age in the Welfare State: The Origins of Social Spending on Pensioners, Workers, and Children*

Pauline Jones Luong, *Institutional Change and Political Continuity in Post-Soviet Central Asia*

Doug McAdam, John McCarthy, and Mayer Zald, eds., *Comparative Perspectives on Social Movements*

James Mahoney and Dietrich Rueschemeyer, eds., *Historical Analysis and the Social Sciences*

Scott Mainwaring and Matthew Soberg Shugart, eds., *Presidentialism and Democracy in Latin America*

Isabela Mares, *The Politics of Social Risk: Business and Welfare State Development*

Isabela Mares, *Taxation, Wage Bargaining, and Unemployment*

Anthony W. Marx, *Making Race, Making Nations: A Comparison of South Africa, the United States, and Brazil*

Joel S. Migdal, *State in Society: Studying How States and Societies Constitute One Another*

Joel S. Migdal, Atul Kohli, and Vivienne Shue, eds., *State Power and Social Forces: Domination and Transformation in the Third World*

Scott Morgenstern and Benito Nacif, eds., *Legislative Politics in Latin America*

Layna Mosley, *Global Capital and National Governments*

Wolfgang C. Müller and Kaare Strøm, *Policy, Office, or Votes?*

Maria Victoria Murillo, *Labor Unions, Partisan Coalitions, and Market Reforms in Latin America*

Ton Notermans, *Money, Markets, and the State: Social Democratic Economic Policies since 1918*

Roger D. Petersen, *Understanding Ethnic Violence: Fear, Hatred, and Resentment in Twentieth-Century Eastern Europe*

Simona Piattoni, ed., *Clientelism, Interests, and Democratic Representation*

Paul Pierson, *Dismantling the Welfare State? Reagan, Thatcher, and the Politics of Retrenchment*

Marino Regini, *Uncertain Boundaries: The Social and Political Construction of European Economies*

Lyle Scruggs, *Sustaining Abundance: Environmental Performance in Industrial Democracies*

Jefferey M. Sellers, *Governing from Below: Urban Regions and the Global Economy*

Yossi Shain and Juan Linz, eds., *Interim Government and Democratic Transitions*

Beverly Silver, *Forces of Labor: Workers' Movements and Globalization since 1870*

Theda Skocpol, *Social Revolutions in the Modern World*

Regina Smyth, *Candidate Strategies and Electoral Competition in the Russian Federation: Democracy without Foundation*

Richard Snyder, *Politics after Neoliberalism: Reregulation in Mexico*

David Stark and László Bruszt, *Postsocialist Pathways: Transforming Politics and Property in East Central Europe*

Sven Steinmo, Kathleen Thelen, and Frank Longstreth, eds., *Structuring Politics: Historical Institutionalism in Comparative Analysis*

Susan C. Stokes, *Mandates and Democracy: Neoliberalism by Surprise in Latin America*

Susan C. Stokes, ed., *Public Support for Market Reforms in New Democracies*

Duane Swank, *Global Capital, Political Institutions, and Policy Change in Developed Welfare States*

Sidney Tarrow, *Power in Movement: Social Movement and Contentious Politics*

Kathleen Thelen, *How Institutions Evolve: The Political Economy of Skills in Germany, Britain, the United States, and Japan*

Charles Tilly, *Trust and Rule*

Joshua Tucker, *Regional Economic Voting: Russia, Poland, Hungary, Slovakia, and the Czech Republic, 1990–1999*

Ashutosh Varshney, *Democracy, Development, and the Countryside*

Stephen I. Wilkinson, *Votes and Violence: Electoral Competition and Ethnic Riots in India*